Ecology, community and lifestyle

Ecology, community and lifestyle

OUTLINE OF AN ECOSOPHY

ARNE NAESS
Council for Environmental Studies
University of Oslo

Translated and revised by

DAVID ROTHENBERG
Department of Philosophy
Boston University

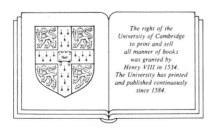

The right of the
University of Cambridge
to print and sell
all manner of books
was granted by
Henry VIII in 1534.
The University has printed
and published continuously
since 1584.

CAMBRIDGE UNIVERSITY PRESS
Cambridge
New York   New Rochelle   Melbourne   Sydney

Published by the Press Syndicate of the University of Cambridge
The Pitt Building, Trumpington Street, Cambridge CB2 1RP
32 East 57th Street, New York, NY 10022, USA
10 Stamford Road, Oakleigh, Melbourne 3166, Australia

First published 1989

This work contains translations of some parts of the fifth edition
of *Økologi, samfunn og livsstil* (© Universitetsforlaget 1976)

Printed in Great Britain at the University Press, Cambridge

British Library cataloguing in publication data
Naess, Arne, 1912–
  Ecology, community and lifestyle: outline of an ecosophy.
  1. Man. Ecology, Philosophical perspectives.
  I. Title   II. Rothenberg, David
  III. Naess, Arne, 1912–   *Økologi, samfunn og livsstil.*
  304.2'01

Library of Congress cataloguing in publication data
  Naess, Arne.
  Ecology, community, and lifestyle.
  Translation of some parts of: *Økologi, samfunn, og livsstil.*
  Bibliography: p.
  Includes Index.
  1. Human Ecology – Philosophy.   I. Rothenberg, David, 1962–
  II. Title.
  GF21.N342513   1989   304.2'01   88-5068
  ISBN 0 521 34406 9

to Peter Reed
1961-1987

*'and you, my mountain, will you
never walk towards me?'*

Kevork Emin

Contents

Translator's Preface

The book before you is entitled *Ecology, community, and lifestyle*. It is not a direct translation of Arne Naess' 1976 work, *Økologi, samfunn, og livsstil*, but rather a new work in English, based on the Norwegian, with many sections revised and rewritten by Professor Naess and myself, in an attempt to clarify the original work as well as bring it up to date.

But this is not as straightforward as it might sound. The project involved cornering Professor Naess in between his numerous intercontinental travels, then escaping the problems of busy Oslo to various mountain retreats scattered throughout the country. As the student, I then questioned the professor on the original manuscript, he responded, and together we reworked the manuscript to make it flow smoothly in English and in the 1980s. After being thwarted by blizzards, breaking a ski or two, locking ourselves out of the wood supply by mistake, we finally emerged with the manuscript in its final form.

But even now there is much more we would like to add! In a developing field like ecophilosophy, there can only be an introduction, not a conclusive summary. So we apologise to those who feel key issues may have been left out, and we also apologise to our editors for trying to work too much in. At Cambridge University Press, Dr Robin Pellew, Susan Sternberg, Alan Crowden, and Peter Jackson have all been especially understanding. Daniel Rothenberg provided insightful criticism of the introduction.

Thanks to Cecilie Schou-Sørensen and Barbro Bakken for typing portions of the manuscript, and to the Council for Environmental Studies at the University of Oslo, without whose support the book would never have become available in English. Under the direction of Paul Hofseth and Ola Glesne, their encouragement testifies to a belief that philosophy has relevance to practical work on problems in the breach between man and nature.

The Ecophilosophy Group, composed of Esben Leifsen, Peter Reed, and myself, provided a forum for the exchange of ideas at the aforementioned institution. It is a tragedy that our work had to be broken up: Peter Reed died under an avalanche in the Jotunheimen mountains last April. His critical, sharp thinking in ecophilosophy crystallised many of our intuitions, and thus added structure to many of the topics discussed in this book. It is dedicated to his memory.

David Rothenberg

Department of Philosophy
Boston University
September 1987

Introduction

Ecosophy T: from intuition to system

The system begins with the immediate . . . The beginning of the system is the absolute beginning . . . How does the system begin with the immediate? Does it begin with it immediately? The answer to this question must be an unqualified no.

Søren Kierkegaard
Concluding
Unscientific Postscript

We feel our world in crisis. We walk around and sense an emptiness in our way of living and the course which we follow. Immediate, spontaneous experience tells us this: intuition. And not only intuition, but information, speaking of the dangers, comes to us daily in staggering quantities.

How can we respond? Has civilisation simply broken away hopelessly from a perfection of nature? All points to a bleak and negative resignation.

But this is only one kind of intuition – there is also the intuition of joy.

Arne Naess gives a lecture somewhere in Oslo. After an hour he suddenly stops, glances quickly around the stage, and suddenly leaves the podium and approaches a potted plant to his left. He quickly pulls off a leaf, scurries back to the microphone, and gazes sincerely at the audience as he holds the leaf in the light so all can see. 'You can spend a lifetime contemplating this', he comments. 'It is enough. Thank you.'

In 1969, Naess resigned his professorship in philosophy after over thirty years of work in semantics, philosophy of science, and the systematic exposition of the philosophies of Spinoza and Gandhi. The threat of ecocatastrophe had become too apparent – there was much public outcry and protest. Naess believed philosophy could help chart a way out of the chaos. Because for him it had always been not just a 'love of wisdom', but a love of wisdom related to action. And action without this underlying wisdom is useless.

Information leads to pessimism. Yet it is still possible to find joy and wonder in immediate experience. The problem is how to make it easier for people to 'begin immediately'. 'I began writing *Ecology, Community, and Lifestyle* because I was pessimistic', he reflects. 'And I wanted to stress the continued possibility for joy in a world faced by disaster.'

Naess offers in this book the basis of a new ontology which posits humanity as inseparable from nature. If this ontology is fully understood, it will no longer be possible for us to injure nature wantonly, as this would mean injuring an integral part of ourselves. From this ontological beginning, ethics and practical action are to fall into place.

So Naess's system begins with an immediate reconsideration of 'what there is', how we perceive things around us. There can be no more spontaneous beginning than this. But the problem, which Kierkegaard points out above (in reference to philosophical systems in general), appears at once – just how does it begin? It cannot begin at once because it must be studied, considered, and perhaps internalised. Only then can we use it in a spontaneous manner.

In this introduction I try to review the background of Naess' system, some of its particulars, and an overview of its position among other philosophies of environmentalism, in order to soften its beginning.

1   Beginning with intuitions

Naess' result is not a work of philosophical or logical argumentation – 'It is primarily intuitions', he says. These are intuitions developed over a long life spent in nature. Arne recalls their beginnings:

> From when I was about four years old until puberty, I could stand or sit for hours, days, weeks in shallow water on the coast, inspecting and marvelling at the overwhelming diversity and richness of life in the sea. The tiny beautiful forms which 'nobody' cared for, or were even unable to see, were part of a seemingly infinite world, but nevertheless *my* world. Feeling apart in many human relations, I identified with 'nature'.[1]

Much later in life Naess will write that the young child's world is that which is close and easily apprehendable around him.[2] It is an easy time to feel that one's identity is tied to immediate nature. But it was in his teens that Naess's awareness expanded to include a bond with people who lived their lives near to nature:

> When fifteen years old I managed through sheer persistency of appeals to travel alone in early June to the highest mountain region of Norway – Jotunheimen. At the foot of the mountain I was stopped by deep rotten snow and I could find nowhere to sleep. Eventually I came across a very old man who was engaged in digging away the snow surrounding and in part covering a closed cottage belonging to an association for mountaineering and tourism. We stayed together for a week in a nearby hut. So far as I can remember, we ate only one dish: oatmeal porridge with dry bread. The porridge had been stored in the snow from the

previous autumn – that is what I thought the old man said. Later I came to doubt it. A misunderstanding on my part. The porridge was served cold, and if any tiny piece was left over on my plate he would eat it. In the evenings he would talk incidentally about mountains, about reindeer, hunting, and other occupations in the highest regions. But mostly he would play the violin. It was part of the local culture to mark the rhythm with the feet, and he would not give up trying to make me capable of joining him in this. But how difficult! The old man's rhythms seemed more complex than anything I had ever heard!

Enough details! The effect of this week established my conviction of an inner relation between mountains and mountain people, a certain greatness, cleanness, a concentration upon what is essential, a self-sufficiency; and consequently a disregard of luxury, of complicated means of all kinds. From the outside the mountain way of life would seem Spartan, rough, and rigid, but the playing of the violin and the obvious fondness for all things above the timberline, living or 'dead', certainly witnessed a rich, sensual attachment to life, a deep pleasure in what can be experienced with wide open eyes and mind.

These reflections instilled within me the idea of modesty – modesty in man's relationships with mountains in particular and the natural world in general. As I see it, modesty is of little value if it is not a natural consequence of much deeper feelings, a consequence of a way of understanding ourselves as part of nature in a wide sense of the term. This way is such that the smaller we come to feel ourselves compared to the mountain, the nearer we come to participating in its greatness. I do not know why this is so.[3]

We need to compare ourselves with the mountain – this is not meant to be a grand metaphor for a possible humanity, like Nietzsche's *Ubermensch* ('six thousand feet above men and time!'), but an actual, living mountain: a model of a nature in which we can fully exist only with fabulous awe. The possibility of modesty is the most human of characteristics. But why is the link between people and nature so central?

Naess would, in time, try to discover 'why this is so' by elaborating a philosophy that leads from the immediate self into the vast world of nature. It is this which is presented in this book. The intention is to encourage readers to find ways to develop and articulate basic, common intuitions of the absolute value of nature which resonate with their own backgrounds and approaches.

The recognition of the problem and its subsequent study using philosophical methods is called *ecophilosophy*. More precisely, it is the utilisation of basic concepts from the science of ecology – such as complexity, diversity, and symbiosis – to clarify the place of our species within nature through the process of working out a total view.

Ecophilosophy leads in two directions. It can be used to develop a deep ecological philosophy, as philosophers continue to elaborate these basic notions and their connections. And it can lend support to a growing international deep ecology movement, which includes scientists, activists, scholars, artists, and all those who are actively working towards a change in anti-ecological political and social structures.

In an attempt to categorise what it is that binds supporters of this movement together, a platform of deep ecology has been developed, which appears in chapter 1. It consists of eight common points to guide those who believe that ecological problems cannot be solved only by technical 'quick-fix' solutions. In practice this can mean simply trying to see a particular problem from the point of view of other interests than our own (i.e. other species, or ecosystems themselves) or it can be an opening to a full scale critique of our civilisation, seeking out false conceptions of reality at the core.

But in any case this platform is meant as a kind of resting point for agreement; a place where those who desire the type of change argued for in this book can look upon to realise where they stand, what it is they share in common in their beliefs.

And such deep matters should not be oversimplified. A recurring theme in this book will be to introduce two basic ecological principles into a philosophical review of our society: unity and diversity. And as the poet A. R. Ammons warns: 'oneness is not useful when easily derived, manyness is not truthful when thinly selective.'[4]

Some kind of agreement is essential if people are to act together towards change in a group, but their differences in perspectives and means for reaching agreement should not be lost in the oneness. The environmental movement will be strongest if it can be shown that its concise set of principles can be derived from a variety of world-views and backgrounds. The more philosophical, religious, and scientific evidence can be found to support the normative values of environmentalism, the more important and universal the movement will be.

The philosophical side of ecophilosophy investigates the particular methods of viewing the world that lead different individuals to something like the platform of deep ecology. Naess calls this reasoning process *ecosophy*, if it becomes articulated in a philosophical manner.

A good portion of this book is devoted to the presentation of Naess's own system of reasoning that leads to the platform, an Ecosophy T. The name T is said to represent his mountain hut Tvergastein ('cross the stones) but it is its personal nature that is most important. It suggests that there might be many other ecosophies (A, B, C, . . .) that each of us could develop for ourselves. Though we are meant to nod in agreement more or less with its conclusions, it is not essential to accept its particular chains of reasoning. It is most important that we are able to reach the system's conclusions using ways of feeling and reason familiar to us, rather than accepting all of Naess's particular steps and defences of his reasoning. For it is important to realise that Naess is less interested in building a system to explain all than he is in teaching us to develop our own systems in our own ways; incomplete, perhaps, but so necessary for us to reach real and grounded similar conclusions – not the least of which is realising that change must begin at once.

2 Interpretation and precisation in Naess's philosophy

An ecosophy is a personal system, a personal philosophy, and for another's to reach us something in it must resound with us immediately. It need not be entirely original.

This is not every philosopher's view on how to use their systems. Some have believed they have solved all the important problems of existence, and others think they have proved that these problems are unsolvable. But Naess would rather have every person take some time to interpret what he presents in their own ways, recognising that many different, distinct, yet mutually acceptable interpretations are possible and compatible.

This notion has its roots in his work in semantics in the 1950s. Naess's view (in *Interpretation and Preciseness*) is that those who communicate do not do so on the basis of sharing a common language, but by mutually interpreting what the other has said based on prior understanding of what the words and expressions mean.[5] A particular word's associations for an individual can be so vast or so specialised that another's use of this same word could be miles away from what the speaker intends. And this is not mere quibbling, but a real block towards the possibility of others' ideas really getting through to us.

But communication is possible. By admitting the use of vague and general terms, which Naess calls the T_0 level, and accepting many parallel interpretations, or precisations, at higher levels. As he explains it:

> Let me give an example of what I mean by precisation, since the concept so often causes misunderstandings. At the vaguest level, T_0, we have the sentence 'I was born in the twentieth century.' The next more precise level, T_1, would have to clarify this information, and clear up possible misunderstanding. For instance, T_1 might be 'I was born in the twentieth century after the death of Christ.' On the other hand, to say 'I was born

in 1912' is not a precisation. It is an elaboration: more information is given on the situation, not the utterance itself . . .. For example, Pascal jumped up from his sleep and shouted 'feu!'. Then 'Dieu!' Then 'Dieu d'Abraham et Isaac!' . . . narrowing successively. Precisising? At the beginning we share in the inspiration. Pascal, though, becomes a bad example in the sense that he got *caught in a specialism*, moving from the fire to a very particular notion of a God, excluding all others.[6]

The type of clarification Pascal offers for his utterance limits the possible effect of his original intuitive inspiration. We want to know just what the 'fire' is, not by narrowing its range but by understanding what was meant. We should approach Naess's normative system Ecosophy T in the same way.[7]

When Arne begins his system with the norm 'Self-realisation!' many associations will be raised. In the text one learns that we are not meant to narrow this realisation to our own limited egos, but to seek an understanding of the widest 'Self', one with a capital S that expands from each of us to include all.

Before too much confusion is engendered, we must reflect upon a second, rather ecological notion of communication: that it does not happen alone. We come up with ideas, we release them to the world, but only if they can be grasped by others can they come to exist collectively and have weight. This is the essence of Naess's 'relational thinking' – nothing exists apart. Neither a person, nor a species, nor an environmental problem. A word only takes life through its meanings and compatible interpretations. This is the practical effect of realising an ecosophical ontology.

We can only etch out the meaning of a concept through its moving place in the field of other concepts and the ways they are perceived. In this process we identify wholes that are perceived to have an organic identifiable unity in themselves, as a network of relations that can move as one. The term chosen for this kind of understandable shape is *gestalt*, borrowed from work in the psychology of perception in the early part of this century.[8] The world provides us with a flood of information, but that which presents itself as living entities is characterised by a certain natural life, which comes to us as a conviction that identity is inherent only in the relationships which make up the entity. As Naess remarked while skiing at night in minus twenty celsius under crystal clear blue darkness and a wide moon: 'the extreme cold is so much a part of the gestalt that if it were any warmer we would really feel uncomfortable.'

The gestalt of ecosophy T as a whole is something that the reader will not be able to perceive step by step, or stride after stride. The exposition of the book is not strictly logical in a syllogistic sense (from A and B follows C), as it is impossible to formulate an ecosophy completely in this way. Arne hints at the meanings. As one forges the connections both his view and ours take shape. Remember two of his underlying beliefs. (1) As persons we cannot escape pretending to act and decide on the basis of a total view. But verbal articulation of this view in its entirety is impossible.[9] (2) The system begins with the immediate. Its own rules should never mask the immediate. Or: If we wish to identify a starting point for a system, spontaneous experience offers itself. But any system used carries with it social contexts that cannot capture or replace the uniqueness of the original experience.

3   Clarification of terms in translation

With these notions in mind, some of the key terms used within ecosophy T can now be introduced. The translation of these terms from Norwegian to English is somewhat problematic. Many of the substantives used (realisation, identification, precisation) convey a more active sense in their Norwegian usage. They are never states to be reached, but processes. The words for 'environment' and 'intrinsic value' are both more familiar terms in the Norwegian. For the translation to succeed, these should be treated not as awkward concepts, but as words to be used in daily speech.

(a)   Milieu/environment

These two terms are used interchangeably for the single Norwegian word *miljø*. Why both? Because, as in French, the Norwegian term has wider and more familiar connotations than the somewhat cumbersome 'environment'. But we have no simple English word to use here. If an easier word existed, the notion of environmental conservation might be more widely accepted in our culture.

What are 'environmental problems'? What is 'degradation of the environment'? Simple: destruction of what surrounds us, the immediate which we are within. Not merely the physical *nature*, but all that we live in, all the gestalts we can identify ourselves within. According to Naess, this harmonises our very identity as it is necessary to reveal our greater selves.

Within these concepts are the related gestalts of *nature* and *life*. The word nature has very many associations in English and Scandinavian languages[10] and we should not forgo any of these associations in a term whose very richness of meanings demonstrates its significance. The particularly scientific interpretations of wild, untouched nature[11] which find their way into ethical categories are complexity, diversity, and symbiosis. These concepts underlie the reasoning toward values throughout the entire work, and are given relational definitions in chapter 7.

I don't want to say too much about how Naess derives a notion of rightness from these terms, but let it suffice to say that he does not uphold a norm of 'life', as this smacks of the danger of 'cult of life' that is a root to certain fascistic philosophies. Perhaps it is too little connected to the individual, or to the fact that one should be prepared, through an ecosophy, to make one's own decisions about the world, and this is then built upon norms with a more dynamic and directional quality than what we get by simply upholding 'life!'

How do we make the link from ethical principles to decisions? With the notion of gestalt understanding comes the possibility of gestalt switch. At first one sees the world one way, but with an increasing awareness of formerly hidden relations, another understanding suddenly comes to light and we make an instantaneous shift. All of a sudden things become clear – a kind of a-ha! experience, the moment of insight. Another way of describing the purpose of *Ecology, Community, and Lifestyle* is as an effort to bring about this moment of ecological gestalt switch – conversion, if you will. Many methods are useful.

Many people who had read the book in its five successive Norwegian editions through the 1970s were consulted to find out what parts were important to them, how they found it useful. There was a tremendous diversity of responses, as there are many motivations for the particular gestalt switch needed to reach an understanding of the abyss between our species and the Earth. One of Naess's aims is to reveal as many possible motivations as possible.

(b)   Self-realisation

One thing common to all these motivations (ways of reaching the switching point) is that they all connect the individual to the principles of interconnectedness in nature. Naess's key concept in this is 'Self-realisation', used throughout the book in various guises. Keeping with his belief in the power of T_0 formulations, Arne stubbornly refuses to pin down this term to a rigid definition:

> People are frustrated that I can write an entire book upon an intuition that is 'nowhere defined or explained'. It is tantalising for our culture, this seeming lack of explanation . . . But if you hear a phrase like 'all life is fundamentally one!' you must be open to *tasting* this, before asking immediately 'what does this mean?' Being more precise does not necessarily create something that is more inspiring.[12]

But, in fact, Naess's use of Self-realisation is a bold attempt to connect the general statement that 'all life is fundamentally one' with our individual needs and desires. Without cleaving away at its potential, I here only mention several points to alleviate misunderstanding.

(1) Self-realisation is not self-centred. Remember the capital S, but at the same time do not think the individual self or ego is dissolved in the larger Self. The diversity of different individuals and approaches remains, as we share and shape our connections to the larger. Still, Dostoyevsky realised what was necessary for Self-realisation when he outlined a prime danger of modern times:

> . . . the isolation that prevails everywhere . . . has not fully developed, not reached its limit yet. For every one strives to keep his individuality as apart as possible, wishes to secure the greatest possible fullness of life for himself; but meantime all his efforts result not in attaining fullness of life but self-destruction, for instead of self-realisation he ends by arriving at complete solitude.[13]

We cannot simply split into units, pursuing our own goals. This is why Naess requires the concept of a greater Self.

(2) If one really expands oneself to include other people and species and nature itself, altruism becomes unnecessary. The larger world becomes part of our own interests. It is seen as a world of *potentials* to increase our own Self-realisation, as we are part of the increase of others'.

(3) The word in Norwegian is *Selv-realisering*: Self-realising. It is an active condition, not a place one can reach. No one ever reaches Self-realisation, for complete Self-realisation would require the realisation of all. Just as no one in certain Buddhist traditions ever reaches nirvana, as the rest of the world must be pulled along to get there. It is only a process, a way to live one's life.

We use the concept as a guideline. It gives us a direction to proceed in; a way to see our actions as part of a larger gestalt. Naess comments on why he has chosen to begin his system in this way:

> Now Self-realisation, like nonviolence, is a vague, and T_0 term . . ..
> There is at the outset something essential: for life, by life. But there must be an arrow. A direction, starting from the self, moving towards the Self. It is a direction I can say *yes* to ethically. We may call it a vector – in tremendous but determinate dimensions.[14]

These metaphors ought to be kept in mind: arrow, direction, vector. They can help clarify the bounds in which Self-realisation can be expanded, if not defined directly. And what precisely are the dimensions? This can perhaps be clarified if we discuss how one moves along the path from one intuition to another.

(c)   Derivation

The process of motion in thought is for Arne synonymous with derivation. And here he precisises in the direction of logical derivation, i.e. from 'Self-realisation!' and 'Self-realisation for all beings!' we can trace a system of syllogisms to derive ecological norms for 'Diversity!' and 'Complexity!' This does not refer to historical derivation, i.e. 'Where have these concepts come from in time?' or derivations of purpose, i.e. 'Why are these concepts useful for me?' (even though both these questions could be addressed within Ecosophy T). It is purely logical derivation which is meant.

Naess wishes to show how we can justify all actions and beliefs by connecting them back to those most fundamental for us, beginning with Self-realisation. It is rigid and pure logic he uses, yet the core statements are still basically intuitive and elusive.

How is the world existent in a gestalt perspective? *Why* do we make use of the relational field? Baruch Spinoza, one of Naess's sources of inspiration, had a response to these questions that might well be echoed today:

> I do not know how the parts are interconnected, and how each part accords with the whole; for to know this it would be necessary to know the whole of nature and all of its parts . . . .. By the connection of the parts, then, I mean nothing else than that the laws, or nature, of one part adapt themselves to the laws, or nature, of another part in such a way as to produce the least possible opposition.[15]

This provides a clue on how to embrace more gestalt relations. Look for things that flow together without opposition. From these can meaningful wholes be discovered. (This involves a breaking down of some of the unnatural oppositions we have come to accept as parts of our culture.)

So we concentrate on finding within each discovered relation a mirror of the larger structure. In this way our total views are hinted at with every single thing we complete. We should not believe that more information will make this clearer. What is needed is a re-orientation in thinking to appreciate what can be learned from specific and simple things through recognising their defining relations with other things. And this accompanies the process of learning to feel as one with them.

(d)   Identification

The process of motion through experience manifests itself through identification, *identifisering* in Norwegian. This is also an active term: it could be thought of as 'identiting'. We discover that parts of nature are parts of ourselves. We cannot exist separate from them. If we try, our Self-realising is blocked. Thus we cannot destroy them if we are to exist fully.

This becomes the root of the most powerful application of ecosophical thinking to specifically environmental conflicts. We must see the vital needs of ecosystems and other species as our own needs: there is thus no conflict of interests. It is a tool for furthering one's own realisation and fullness of life. And this too was realised by a wise old monk in *The Brothers Karamazov*:

> Love all God's creation, the whole and every grain of sand in it. Love every leaf, every ray of God's light. Love the animals, love the plants, love everything. If you love everything, you will perceive the divine mystery in things. Once you perceive it, you will begin to comprehend it better every day . . . for all is like an ocean, all is flowing and blending; a touch in one place sets up movement at the other end of the earth . . ..
> Do not say 'Sin is mighty, wickedness is mighty, evil environment is mighty, and we are lonely and helpless' . . .. Fly away from that dejection, Children![16]

So, if we progress far enough, the very notion of 'environment' becomes unnecessary. Identification in this sense is the widest interpretation of love. In love one loses part of one's identity by gaining a greater identity, something that in its truest sense cannot be spoken of. So at the same time we do not intend to make everything part of ourselves and see ourselves as nonexistent otherwise. We can identify with these parts in nature precisely because they are of an equal status to us; they possess a certain independence from us and our valuing. This is called by Naess *naturens egenverdi*: the intrinsic value of nature.

(e)   *Intrinsic value*

To translate *egenverdi* as 'intrinsic value' makes the term sound somehow unnatural: it is 'own value' that is meant, value in itself. Many ecophilosophers have difficulty with this notion[17], especially in the light of what has been said about our selves and the connections to the Self of nature. What, then, actually exists independent from us? The value is not so much independent from us as independent from our valuation – be it material or aesthetic in nature. Gestalt entities in nature are things to be respected for their own sakes, simply because they are there and near to us. Like friends – we should never use them only as a means to something else. To do so is superficial, seeing only surface interactions. It is intuitively obvious to see the own-ness, intrinsicality, *egenskap* (own-shape, quality) of nature and of friends, but one can easily forget it in daily interaction. We tend to lose friends if we act that way too long. The same could happen with nature.

(f)   Depth
      Wittgenstein noted that ordinary thinking is like swimming on the surface – so much easier than diving into the depths[18]. The framing metaphor is equally applicable to approaches to ecological conflicts.
      It is the work of the philosopher to go deeply into problems and situations which may at first seem simple or obvious, digging out the roots to reveal structures and connections that will then be as visible as the problem first seemed to be easy. This is why a philosophical ecology is a deep ecology. Naess first introduced this term in the early 1970s, and since then, as a T_0 term, it has, not surprisingly, been taken to mean many things (precisised in many different directions): from an ecology with a wider perspective (like 'human ecology') to a form of radical protest that seeks to undermine the deepest roots of 'the system' at once.
      What Naess originally intended was simply stated (in Naess (1973) and chapter 1). Depth only applies to the distance one looks in search of the roots of the problem, refusing to ignore troubling evidence that may reveal untold vastness of the danger. One should never limit the bounds of the problem just to make an easier solution acceptable. This will not touch the core. One should think not only of our species but of the life of the Earth itself. The planet is more than us, more fundamental and basic than our own single species in isolation.
      The word 'shallow' as used to name approaches and solutions which do not take such a wide perspective has an unfortunate defamatory ring. Words like 'narrow' and 'limited' may be no better. Yet some argue that all we can work for in the practical world is for solutions that would be classified under these categories. In one sense the magnitude of any truly deep change would be so vast that perhaps all we can work at is a succession of short-term, limited solutions. But we should not lose sight of the bond between our immediate beliefs and any distant goals. These specific solutions should be linked to our underlying intuition and the understandings derived from this intuition.
      Some examples should clarify how specific situations could be approached with a deep ecological perspective.
      (1) A storm causes a blowdown of trees over a favoured hiking trail in the forests surrounding Oslo. An anthropocentric solution would be to clear away all the trees to make the forest look 'cleaner' and 'neater'. A deeper solution: clear away only what is needed from the trail itself,

recognising that the removal of too many trees might endanger habitats for other species which were *improved* by the blowdown.

(2) A forest fire burns in a popular national park, putting visiting tourists in danger. Should the rangers put it out or let it burn? Fires are a natural part of the healthy existence of a forest. They are thus sometimes necessary. Conditions would have to be carefully considered before the fire is tampered with.

(3) Before building a hydropower project it is customary to estimate the useful life of the dam and lake. How long before it will become filled with silt and be unusable? A suitable lifetime according to the industry might be 30 years. The deeper opinion would be that such a solution to our energy needs is *largely irrelevant*. It may be useful in this limited period, but it is no substitute for longer-term thinking and planning.

(4) In planning an irrigation project in an excessively dry area, one should see it as a process to help the soil and the land itself, not only to improve productivity for man. It is the health of the soil that is at stake; man can only make use of this with due respect for the Earth[19].

(5) Aurlandsdalen is one of the most beautiful river valleys leading from the high plateau of the Hardangervidda to the Sognefjord in western Norway. The watershed has been developed for hydropower as part of a larger scheme, but most of the workings have been built underground, and the cables have not been placed through the valley. So the canyon itself still appears relatively untouched. Satisfying enough for some – but those who remember the rushing falls of earlier days find their gestalt understanding of the valley is disturbed. The amount of water is now merely a trickle, a shadow of its former strength. The dignity of the waterfall is impaired.

It is difficult to come up with convincing examples of deep ecological solutions, because the terms in ecosophy T are so removed from the language planners are accustomed to working with. As Naess might put it (see chapter 3), the middle section of this system pyramid is hollow – no one has taken the time to elaborate the connection between the basic principles of an ecosophy and the specifics of a singular real-world situation. And this is a shame, because, if there is to be any test of the worth of ecophilosophy, this is it. So here is an area where much work can be done!

And in this application of ecosophy it is hoped that some form of optimism can be maintained despite the amount of negative information that bombards us daily. The root of philosophy is in wonder, and this joy in wonder cannot be lost even in a time when conditions appear so grim.

The wonder should be directed, then, at the problems themselves, penetrating them from the essence.

It is this ability to think things through that can be the contribution of the philosopher in our 'desperate time'. When asked on Dutch television if intellectuals had any social responsibility in our present age, Naess responded:

> I think that intellectuals might consider their intellects in a more Spinozistic way, and cultivate . . . a loving attitude towards what (they) have insight into, while considering it in an extremely wide perspective. And intellectuals might do this without making the terrible mistake of becoming sentimental or fanatical.[20]

This is the task of justifying one's views philosophically, even if they are intuitions or emotional views. Naess will argue that such views are an integral component of objective reality, and as such deserve serious consideration in ecological debate. To act responsibly in any conflict or situation where we put forth our views on nature, we should be able to integrate these feelings in the same way as objective, statistical facts:

> . . . as an acting person I take a stand, I implicitly assume very many things, and with my Spinozist leanings towards integrity – being an integrated person as the most important thing – I'm now trying to close down on all these vagaries. I am inviting you to do the same.[21]

As more individuals learn to do this, we are to be left not with a shallow oneness, but with many interpretations of the same core. Upon confronting the system of Ecosophy T, you should take the time to be changed.

On the other hand, one can talk and clarify forever without changing the way one lives and acts. This *is* an age of hypocrisy. Ideals are one thing, actions another. Naess has further comments on such 'integration':

> People could be called 'bags of contradictions'. It is not my job to describe such bags. Actually there is a lot to say about too tightly integrated characters. Not enough room for inconsistencies, spontaneity, play . . . .[22]

4   Where do we place deep ecology?

After showing how Naess makes use of basic words in relation to Ecosophy T, it is useful to consider this ecosophy in comparison with other environmental philosophies, both in what they advise practically and in the way they approach comprehensive points of view. In this process, many interpretations of the original distinction 'deep ecology' come to light, some of which could be called misinterpretations. This is always a danger when speaking at the T_0 level; you may gain many adherents to your ideas, because they are so easily understood in different ways. But some of these understandings will not be what you had in mind! In this section we review the way environmental philosophies have been categorised, and try to clear up some basic misconceptions concerning the interpretation of the concept of deep ecology. A common problem is that the distinction between the *movement* and the *philosophy* is not realised. Philosophising can be an inspiration and a source of support for the movement, but no one is claiming that it can replace practical action of different sorts.

A useful chart which shows a structure analogous to the shallow/deep outline is found in O'Riordan.[23] He contrasts the approaches of ecological and technological environmentalism, or ecocentrism vs. technocentrism. The sub-divisions which O'Riordan employs to elaborate are important as they illustrate the very fluidity of the original terms (see the table).

The basic distinction is accurate, but the separation of deep ecology from self-reliance technologies illustrates a common misreading – narrowing deep ecology away from the practical concerns with people and the community, as if it were merely a discussion of animal or species rights. The points listed under O'Riordan's deep ecology column should be seen as the basis of a conception of the world which is meant to underlie the specific work of developing more appropriate technology and management, not as something more radical or extreme.

The whole designation 'ecocentrism' is closer to an equivalent for what Naess means by 'deep ecology': centring on the ecosphere. Compare O'Riordan's statement 'ecological laws dictate human morality' with Naess' more searching, feeling, and listening way of seeking guidelines in nature:

> There is a kind of deep yes to nature which is central to my philosophy. What do we say yes to? Very difficult to find out – there is a deep unconditionality, but at the same time there is a kind of regret, sorrow, or displeasure . . . Nature is not brutal, but from a human point of view, we do see brutality – as we see yellow in the sun; as we see these fantastically blue mountains outside this window.[24]

And O'Riordan's next sentence says that a part of deep ecology is 'biorights: the rights of unique landscapes to remain untouched'. A response according to Naess might be: not 'unique', not 'rights', but thinking of the landscape first, before human needs, and then devising technologies, and management, that stem from a rootedness in place and nature.

One should be able to see a range of possible optimisms in deep ecology if it is to have any use as a constructive concept – it cannot be considered merely a particularly extreme or pessimistic position along a linear scale.

Ecocentrism and Technocentrism

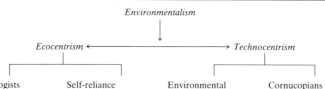

Deep ecologists	Self-reliance Soft technologists	Environmental managers	Cornucopians
Intrinsic importance of nature for the humanity of man	(1) Emphasis on smallness of scale and hence community identity in settlement, work and leisure	(1) Belief that economic growth and resource exploitation can continue assuming: (a) suitable economic adjustments to taxes, fees, etc. (b) improvements in the legal rights to a minimum level of environmental quality (c) compensation arrangements satisfactory to those who experience adverse environmental and/or social effects	(1) Belief that man can always find a way out of any difficulties either political, scientific or technological
Ecological (and other natural) laws dictate human morality			
Biorights – the right of endangered species or unique landscapes to remain unmolested	(2) Integration of concepts of work and leisure through a process of personal and communal improvement		(2) Acceptance that pro-growth goals define the rationality of project appraisal and policy formulation
	(3) Importance of participation in community affairs, and of guarantees of the rights of minority interests. Participation seen both as a continuing education and political function		(3) Optimism about the ability of man to improve the lot of the world's people
		(2) Acceptance of new project appraisal techniques and decision review arrangements to allow for wider discussion or genuine search for consensus among representative groups of interested parties	(4) Faith that scientific and technological expertise provides the basic foundation for advice on matters pertaining to economic growth, public health and safety
(4) Lack of faith in modern large-scale technology and its associated demands on elitist expertise, central state authority and inherently anti-democratic institutions			(5) Suspicion of attempts to widen basis for participation and lengthy discussion in project appraisal and policy review
(5) Implication that materialism for its own sake is wrong and that economic growth can be geared to providing for the basic needs of those below subsistence levels			(6) Belief that all impediments can be overcome given a will, ingenuity and sufficient resources arising out of growth

Source: O'Riordan 1981.

Only such a modification of the classification could make possible O'Riordan's first, and most accurate, summary of deep ecology: 'the intrinsic importance of nature for the humanity of man'.

And yet many have overlooked this core and twisted the term in different directions. A poll of environmental attitudes conducted in the United States in the late 1970s saw it as a particularly long step to take:

> . . . deep ecology is a far more radical position than that taken by most
> supporters of alternative technology involving as it does the *rejection* of
> economic growth and of the assumptions underlying western science,
> the *subordination* of human society to natural processes, and the
> *doctrine* that humans share a profound identity with non-human
> nature.[25] [italics mine]

The use of negative and static imagery presents deep ecology as something quite unrealistic, fixed, and unconstructive through the use of words such as 'subordination' and 'doctrine'. Instead we should see the deep ecology movement as efforts directed towards identity with nature (not non-human, but an extension of humanity). And we are to be not subordinated, but integrated into natural processes. Perhaps economic growth for its own sake is rejected, but not growth or progress if redefined in a more ecological manner.

The unrealism of the above categorisation can be avoided if deep ecology is seen as a root for practical work, not as a code of ethics. But the same idealistic appearance has led Lester Milbrath to describe deep ecologists as a particularly ineffective group:

> The 'deep ecologists' are immersed in nature emotionally and
> philosophically, [though] not very involved in politics and political
> reform. Many of them live in counter-culture communities that are close
> to nature and minimally disturb the biosphere as they interact with
> nature to provide their life needs; in this sense they are *both radical and
> conservative*. Although society may eventually learn important lessons
> from the experiences of these people in their new communities, they do
> not constitute a strong force for near-term social change.[26] [italics mine]

Reflecting upon this categorisation, we should first point out that emotional or philosophical immersion does not preclude political involvement. It should instead be seen as the first step to real long-term change. Breaking away from the system either in thought or in lifestyle should never be seen as an opposition to those working for short-term change; interpreting the deep–shallow division in this way is a mistake. But things that are quickly satisfying have a way of not lasting so long – like shallow ecological solutions.

But Milbrath clearly has an insight into the usefulness of the distinction 'deep ecology' when he calls it both radical and conservative. This hints at the potential strength of a green politics which will be introduced in chapter 6, which should dispel the idea that deep ecology is something wholly non-political.

So much so that some rather conservative lobbies in Washington are quite worried about the movement:

> There is also a trend towards a new revolutionary stream in the environmental movement referred to as 'deep ecology' . . . This *powerful faction* is not merely content with striving for environmental protection, [but] is seeking to cultivate a *liberal*, almost counter-culture view of the world . . . .Today's environmentalist is not merely seeking a clean and safe environment, but is striving for some vague political goal, designed to come about by stopping energy production as we know it.[27] [italics mine]

A far cry from Milbrath's opinion about irrelevance! So some organisations seem afraid of the possibly revolutionary nature of deep ecology. That those who strongly disagree with the tenets of deep ecology are concerned is not a bad thing. But worry and fear are the wrong reactions. Tremendous effort should be spent on communicating with those who disagree – from both sides. Any agenda within deep ecology should not shun the task of communicating with the opponent, in action, writing, or speaking, as Gandhi emphasised over and over again (see chapter 6).

With this in mind there can be a danger of over-rhapsodising the benefits of a new understanding of nature, *especially if you are not prepared to provide this understanding*, but only cry of the need for it:

> Deep ecology is emerging as a way of developing a new balance and harmony between individuals, communities, and all of nature. It can potentially satisfy our deepest yearnings: faith and trust in our most basic intuitions, courage to take direct action, joyous confidence to dance with the sensual harmonies discovered through sport, playful intercourse with the rhythms of our own bodies, the rhythms of flowing water, and the overall processes of life on Earth.[28]

One should be wary of placing too much expectation upon deep ecology. Though the imagery here draws us in, it can be dangerous if no one is taking the time to move beyond these T_0 formulations: many potential supporters might be turned off by them. There can be a danger in flowery rhetorics. This is why Naess avoids a heavily rhetorical style.

But he still encourages those with conflicting opinions and means of communication to continue in their different ways, while he maintains the maxim: 'simple in means, rich in ends'.

We cannot say that any of these interpretations is a false one, but somehow they fail to address the possible significance of deep ecology by limiting it before understanding it. They are also T_0 formulations, and of course only excerpts from much larger works, taken out of context. The easiest step is to put labels on things, but it is so much harder to go beyond such quick epithets as 'shallow' and 'deep'. What all of the above examples of 'readings' indicate is this way that precisation can narrow the meaning of a concept and distort it on the base of limited use of information. The subtitle of this book is '*Outline* of an ecosophy'. It is in many ways only a sketch. But it is our task, as readers, to fill in the space so that misinterpretations will be less frequent.

But to shape deep ecology into a viable area for creative philosophical research, we should provide further guidelines on how to continue. One limits oneself to describe it as some kind of expansion of morality and ethics that covers animals, plants, ecosystems or even the whole natural world. It is a question 'of ontology, not ethics' writes Naess (chapter 2) – a re-examination of how we perceive and construct our world. This has been admirably argued by the Australian philosopher Warwick Fox in a recent paper[29] which defends the ontological approach against a recent (also Australian) critique of deep ecological philosophy[30] which labels all of deep ecology literature 'inconsistent rubbish'.

The interpretation of the whole thing as rubbish comes only if you concentrate too much on the rereading of the sketchy formulations of deep ecology philosophies, rather than using them as suggestions for interpretations based on your own experience. Fox's conclusion, for which he finds support in the writings of many ecophilosophers, is that one should steer clear of 'environmental axiology' – that is, looking for values in nature. Instead, one should seek to change one's whole way of sensing oneself and the world in the direction of identification and Self-realisation that Naess puts forth in this work. Fox summarises:

> The appropriate framework of discourse for describing and presenting deep ecology is not one that is fundamentally to do with the value of the non-human world, but rather one that is fundamentally to do with the nature and possibilities of the self, or, we might say, the question of who we are, can become, and *should* become in the larger scheme of things.[31]

The word 'should' (my emphasis) hints that the question of values still remains. And perhaps it is not value of the Earth, but for the Earth, originating in human choice. But the only way we can come to make this choice is by going deeply into our own experience – yet never with our own interests primarily in mind.

Overviews of ways we choose (or are chosen) to interact and construct the environment are available.[32] There are various trends and poles in such a discussion that are blurred in reality. Is Man a part of nature? Defined by nature? Or are we free to construct nature ourselves, or enter it through various phenomenological approaches which can involve both the observer 'constructing his reality' and 'things presenting themselves'?

Something in this last dual approach is close to what Naess advocates. The sections in the book that suggest this (also perhaps the most difficult) are those in chapter 2 that deal with the gestalt perspective and in particular the concept of *concrete contents* – that all the qualities we sense in things somehow lie in the identity of the things themselves.

The advantage of the concrete contents approach for environmentalism is to demonstrate that the feelings of oneness which we can learn to feel in/with nature actually exist in nature, and are as real as any quantifiable environment that can be subject to cost-benefit analysis.

But as to how we can reorient ourselves, Naess points us toward participatory understanding:

> I'm not much interested in ethics or morals. I'm interested in how we experience the world . . . If deep ecology is deep it must relate to our fundamental beliefs, not just to ethics. Ethics follow from how we experience the world. If you articulate your experience then it can be a philosophy or a religion.[33]

But just how should we experience the world? And then how should we articulate it? Are there examples of the expanded perspective? What would it look, feel, taste, smell, or sound like? How do we know if we are approaching it?

These questions remain. This book suggests a way to proceed. It springs from intuitions, and it will end with them. But they will be yours, no longer only the author's. The system begins and ends with the immediate.

David Rothenberg
Oslo
16.9.86

Notes

1. Arne Naess, 'How my philosophy seemed to develop,' *Philosophers on their Own Work*, Vol. 10 (New York: Peter Lang, 1982), p. 270.
2. See chapter 7 for Naess's views on the process of growing up and the expansion of the self.
3. Arne Naess, 'Modesty and the conquest of mountains', in Michael Tobias, ed., *The Mountain Spirit* (New York: Overlook Press, 1979), pp. 13–16.
4. A.R. Ammons, 'Essay on poetics', *Selected Longer Poems* (New York: W.W. Norton, 1980), p. 50.

5. See I. Gullvåg, 'Depth of intention', *Inquiry* **26**, 1973, p. 33, for a good overview of Naess's work in semantics. Also see Naess's own introduction for the general public, *Communication and Argument* (Oslo: Universitetsforlaget, 1966).
6. From 'Is it painful to think? A discussion with Arne Naess', in Peter Reed and David Rothenberg, ed., *Wisdom and the Open Air* (University of Oslo: Council for Environmental Studies, 1987).
7. In the Norwegian articulation of Naess's notion of normative systems, the verb *presisere* is a central term – the active, verb form of precision, leading to the process of precisation. We have unfortunately had to translate this to the rather awkward English verb 'to precisise.'
8. See the works of Wolgang Kohler (*Gestalt Psychology* and *The Place of Values in a World of Fact*), Kurt Lewin (*Topological Psychology*) for an idea of the theoretical work in gestalt perception study. More recently, Paul Goodman and Frederick Perls (*Gestalt Therapy*) have applied the original ideas in their practical work.
9. See Arne Naess, 'Reflections about total views', *Philosophy and Phenomenological Research*, **25**, 1964, 16–29.
10. See Arthur Lovejoy, 'Nature as aesthetic norm', *Modern Language Notes*, **42**, 1927, 445–51, and Jens Allwood, 'Language, beliefs, and concepts' in *Natural Resources in a Cultural Perspective*, Swedish Research Council, 1979.
11. In Norwegian it is common to use the word 'nature' as an object; a thing to enjoy or experience. We say 'se på den vakre naturen!' – 'look at the beautiful nature!' This usage is not common in English, but it could be.
12. From 'Is it painful to think?'[6]
13. Fyodor Dostoyevsky, *The Brothers Karamazov* (New York: Random House, 1950), p. 363.
14. From 'Is it painful to think?'[6]
15. From letter xxxii, *The Correspondence of Spinoza*, ed. A. Wolf (New York: Russell and Russell, 1966), p. 209.
16. Dostoyevsky[13], pp. 382–3.
17. See, for example J. Baird Caldecott, 'Intrinsic value, quantum theory and environmental ethics', *Environmental Ethics* **7**, No. 3, 1985, 257–76.
18. Attributed.
19. Deeply ecological thinking in practical land use policy planning can be found in the work of Malin Falkemark, a Swedish hydrologist. See, for example, Malin Falkenmark and Gunnar Lind, *Water for a Starving World* (Boulder, Col.: Westview Press, 1976).
20. From a debate between Naess and A.J. Ayer, 'The glass is on the table: an empiricist vs. a total view', in Fons Elders, ed., *Reflexive Water: the Basic Concerns of Mankind* (London: Souvenir Press, 1974), p. 59.
21. Ibid, p. 58.
22. Personal correspondence, August 1986.
23. T. O'Riordan, *Environmentalism* (London: Pion 1981), p. 376.
24. From 'Is it painful to think?'[6]
25. Robert Cameron Mitchell, 'How soft, deep, or left? Present constituencies in the environmental movement for certain world views', *Natural Resources Journal*, **20**, 1980, 348–9.
26. Lester Milbrath, *Environmentalists: Vanguard for a New Society* (Albany: State University of New York Press), 1984, pp. 25–6.
27. T.M. Peckinpaugh, 'The specter of environmentalism: the threat of environmental groups,' (Washington, DC: Republican Study Committee, 1982), p. 3.

28. Bill Devall and George Sessions, *Deep Ecology: Living as if Nature Mattered* (Salt Lake City: Peregrine Smith Books, 1985), p. 7.
29. Warwick Fox, 'Approaching deep ecology: a response to Richard Sylvan's critique of deep ecology', Hobart: University of Tasmania Environmental Studies Occasional Paper 20, 1986.
30. Richard Sylvan, 'A critique of deep ecology', Canberra, Australian National University Discussion Papers in Environmental Philosophy, no. 12, 1985.
31. Fox (1986), p. 85.
32. David Pepper, *The Roots of Modern Environmentalism* (London: Croom Helm, 1984), p. 124.
33. Quoted in Fox (1986), p. 46.

1

The environmental crisis and the deep ecological movement

1   The gravity of the situation

Humankind is the first species on earth with the intellectual capacity to limit its numbers consciously and live in an enduring, dynamic equilibrium with other forms of life. Human beings can perceive and care for the diversity of their surroundings. Our biological heritage allows us to delight in this intricate, living diversity. This ability to delight can be further perfected, facilitating a creative interaction with the immediate surroundings.

A global culture of a primarily techno-industrial nature is now encroaching upon all the world's milieux, desecrating living conditions for future generations. We – the responsible participants in this culture – have slowly but surely begun to question whether we truly accept this unique, sinister role we have previously chosen. Our reply is almost unanimously negative.

For the first time in the history of humanity, we stand face to face with a choice imposed upon us because our lackadaisical attitude to the production of things and people has caught up with us. Will we apply a touch of self-discipline and reasonable planning to contribute to the maintenance and development of the richness of life on Earth, or will we fritter away our chances, and leave development to blind forces?

A synopsis of what it is which makes the situation so critical could read: *An exponentially increasing, and partially or totally irreversible environmental deterioration or devastation perpetuated through firmly established ways of production and consumption and a lack of adequate policies regarding human population increase.*

The words 'deterioration' and 'devastation' are here understood to mean a change for the worse, a decrease of value. An ethical theory is presupposed, a system which allows one to judge a change as negative.

Chemistry, physics, and the science of ecology acknowledge only change, not valued change. But you and I would presumably agree that a change in the bio-conditions of a river or ocean which excluded most forms of life would constitute a deterioration of value. Our evaluative thinking contends that it would constitute a devastation of diversity. The inability of the science of ecology to denounce such processes as the washing away of the soil of rain-forests suggests that we need another approach which involves the inescapable role of announcing values, not only 'facts'.

We need types of societies and communities in which one delights in the value-creative aspects of equilibrium rather than the glorification of value-neutral growth; in which being together with other living beings is more important than exploiting or killing them.

This discussion of the environmental crisis is motivated by the unrealised potential human beings have for varied experience in and of nature: the crisis contributes or could contribute to open our minds to sources of meaningful life which have largely gone unnoticed or have been depreciated in our efforts to adapt to the urbanised, techno-industrial mega-society.

It would be unwise to suppose that improvement can be achieved for the great majority of mankind without severe political contests and profound changes in the economic objectives pursued by the industrial states. Value priorities are socially and economically anchored, and changes in these priorities continuously interplay with other changes in a boundless, dynamic whole.

It would also be dangerous to suppose that any one group has full insight into and power over the techno-economic systems. The profundity of the crisis is due in part to its largely uncontrolled character: developments proceed at an accelerating pace even though no group, class, or nature has necessarily determined, planned, or accepted the next phase. Built-in mechanisms see to it that the tempo does not slacken. The cog-wheels have drawn us into the very machinery we thought was our slave.

Reaching new objectives for progress necessitates greater insight into this machinery, not only within the elites of power, but also within the populace at large. The latter should participate as much as possible both in the formulation of new goals and in suggesting means to reach them.

2   Production and consumption: ideology and practice

Progress has in all seriousness been measured by the rate of energy consumption and the acquisition and accumulation of material objects. What seems to better the material prerequisites for 'the good life' is given priority without asking if life is experienced as good. But the taste is the proof of the pudding, and more and more people in the so-called affluent societies are finding that its flavour isn't worth the stress. 'I am rich' as an experience is largely, but not entirely, independent of the conventional prerequisites for the good life. High life quality – yes; high standard of living – *tja*.*

The politicians and energy experts speak of exponentially increasing energy *needs* as though they were human needs, and not simply demands on the market. The material standard of living and the quality of life are for all intents and purposes thought to be one and the same. This results in demand for exponential material expansion. It is important to realise that percentage growth is exponential and that a yearly growth of 1% or 2% introduces *increasing* social and technical changes in the course of each year in addition to enormous accumulated changes.

The deep-seated roots of the production and consumption ideology can be traced in all existing industrial states, but perhaps most clearly in the rich Western countries. A great deal of available mental energy within economic life is used to create new so-called needs and entice new customers to increase their material consumption. If it were not, economic crisis and unemployment would soon be upon us, or so it is said.

The dissatisfaction and restlessness due to the artificial tempo and the artificial 'modern' life are conventionally entered on the balance sheet without the batting of an eyelid. A change in the ideology of production and consumption is not possible without considerable change in the economic machinery. At present, the machine seems to require and to produce a distorted attitude to life. Within such a well-oiled system, a revision of value standards in favour of all-round experiential values, life quality rather than standard of living, must sound like a dangerous proposition.

We have 'progressed' to the point where the objectives of the good life must be considered threatening; we are intricately implicated in a system which guarantees short-term well-being in a small part of the world through destructive increases in material affluence. The privileges are regionally reserved because a similar increase of affluence in Africa, Asia or South America is not intended and would hasten the advent of an environmental Armageddon.

The authors who describe environmental problems and agitate for their solutions refer often to certain exponential curves, those which aptly illustrate the crisis situation. Authors who wish to placate an uneasy

---

* A Norwegian expression translating roughly as 'maybe yes, maybe no'.

populace, and who actively endorse a further doubling of economic growth in the rich countries, refer to quite different curves (as an example, see Julian Simon's *The Resourceful Earth*, 1984): the curve for interest in ecology is exponential, as is the curve for new *technical* advancements in pollution abatement. Legislation in favour of the environment was increasing exponentially in the 70s. So, is there really any reason to continue agitation for renewed efforts? One good question deserves another: If positive reactions to agitation are increasing exponentially, is this not ground to cease agitation? Everything is going so well, isn't it . . .?

However, the statement, 'the environmental crisis will presumably be overcome (without our efforts)' belongs to a class of self-refuting statements: the more who rally round, or rather, the more who regard it as true, the less probable it is that the statement will prove to be true.

'Within 100 years, mankind will experience an ecocatastrophe (if neither you or I make an effort)' belongs to the same self-refuting class of statements: the more people rally round, the greater the chances for falsification. And in this case, it is *desirable* that the statement prove to be mistaken.

My conclusion is that many more are needed to agitate for a soonest possible change in direction. Ecologists and other environmental scientists point out that we are still on a catastrophic course, but they do not make firm predictions about what will actually happen. Their statements begin with an 'if': 'If we continue to live in our present manner, so and so will result.'

The crisis of life conditions on Earth could help us choose a new path with new criteria for progress, efficiency, and rational action. This positive aspect of our situation has inspired *Ecology, Community, and Lifestyle*. The environmental crisis could inspire a new renaissance; new social forms for co-existence together with a high level of culturally integrated technology, economic progress (with less interference), and a less restricted experience of life.

3   Our ecological knowledge is severely limited; ecopolitical consequences of ignorance

The ecological movement relies upon the results of research in ecology and more recently in conservation biology (see Soulé (1985)). But to the great amazement of many, the scientific conclusions are often statements of ignorance: 'We do not know what long-range consequences the proposed interference in the ecosystem will beget, so we cannot make any hard and fast conclusions.' Only rarely can scientists predict with any certainty the effect of a new chemical on even a single small ecosystem.

The so-called ecological doomsday prophecies are statements about catastrophical states of affairs which cannot be precluded *if* certain new policies are *not* put into effect very soon. We know little or nothing about the extent to which such new policies will come into being. The fact that the human population is on a catastrophic course does not lead to the conclusion that catastrophe will occur. The situation is critical because we do not know *whether* the course will be promptly and radically changed.

Politicians and others now attentive to the words of environmental scientists are thunderstruck that science itself is proclaiming so much ignorance! It is a strange feeling to have new, politically brazen policies recommended on the basis of ignorance. But we do not know the consequences! Should we proceed with the project or not? The burden of proof rests with those who are encroaching upon the environment.

Why does the burden of proof rest with the encroachers? The ecosystems in which we intervene are generally in a particular state of balance which there are grounds to assume to be of more service to mankind than states of disturbance and their resultant unpredictable and far-reaching changes. In general, it is not possible to regain the original state after an intervention has wrought serious, undesired consequences. And intervention, ordinarily with a short-sighted gain for some minor part of mankind in view, has a tendency to be detrimental for most or all forms of life.

The study of ecosystems makes us conscious of our ignorance. Faced with experts who, after calling attention to a critical situation, emphasise their lack of knowledge and suggest research programmes which may diminish this lack of knowledge, the most natural response for the politicians is to propose that the matter be put on the table or postponed until more information is available. For example, a proposal which would counter the possible death of forests is postponed in order to gather more information on what makes the trees die. It appears that public and private officials who heed ecological expertise must become accustomed to a new normal procedure: the recommendation and instigation of bold, radical conservation steps justified by the statements of our lack of knowledge.

4   The deep ecology movement

The term 'deep ecology' was introduced in an article entitled 'The shallow and the deep, long-range ecology movement. A summary' (Naess, 1973). Some key paragraphs are reproduced here:

> The emergence of ecologists from their former relative obscurity marks a turning point in our scientific communities. But their message is twisted and misused. A shallow, but presently rather powerful,

movement, and a deep, but less influential, movement, compete for our attention. I shall make an effort to characterise the two.

1. *The Shallow Ecology movement:*
Fight against pollution and resource depletion. Central objective: the health and affluence of people in the developed countries. . . .

2. *The Deep Ecology movement:*
a. Rejection of the man-in-environment image in favour of *the relational, total-field image*. Organisms as knots in the field of intrinsic relations. An intrinsic relation between two things A and B is such that the relation belongs to the definitions or basic constitutions of A and B, so that without the relation, A and B are no longer the same things. The total field model dissolves not only the man-in-environment concept, but every compact thing-in-milieu concept – except when talking at a superficial or preliminary level of communication.
b. *Biospherical egalitarianism – in principle*. The 'in principle' clause is inserted because any realistic praxis necessitates some killing, exploitation, and suppression. The ecological field worker acquires a deep-seated respect, even veneration, for ways and forms of life. He reaches an understanding from within, a kind of understanding that others reserve for fellow men and for a narrow section of ways and forms of life. To the ecological field worker, *the equal right to live and blossom* is an intuitively clear and obvious value axiom. Its restriction to humans is an anthropocentrism with detrimental effects upon the life quality of humans themselves. This quality depends in part upon the deep pleasure and satisfaction we receive from close partnership with other forms of life. The attempt to ignore our dependence and to establish a master–slave role has contributed to the alienation of man from himself.

In the later 1970s it was difficult to formulate fairly general views which might be agreed upon among people I would characterise as supporters of the deep ecology movement. Finally George Sessions and I formulated eight points, using 179 words and some comments (see next section). We agreed to call it a proposal for a 'deep ecology platform'. It is expected that others who find the distinction 'shallow' (or 'reform') vs. 'deep' ecology useful, and who identify to some extent with the latter, will work out their own alternative formulations (see e.g. Rothenberg (1987)). Any set of formulations will be coloured by personal and group idiosyncrasies. So several are needed.

In concrete environmental conflicts, deep ecology supporters will tend to be on the same side, but the platform formulations are not supposed to list common views in concrete situations, but to express the most general and basic views they have in common. The views are not basic in an absolute sense, but basic among the views that supporters have in common.

5   A platform of the deep ecology movement

(1) The flourishing of human and non-human life on Earth has intrinsic value. The value of non-human life forms is independent of the usefulness these may have for narrow human purposes.

(2) Richness and diversity of life forms are values in themselves and contribute to the flourishing of human and non-human life on Earth.

(3) Humans have no right to reduce this richness and diversity except to satisfy vital needs.

(4) Present human interference with the non-human world is excessive, and the situation is rapidly worsening.

(5) The flourishing of human life and cultures is compatible with a substantial decrease of the human population. The flourishing of non-human life requires such a decrease.

(6) Significant change of life conditions for the better requires change in policies. These affect basic economic, technological, and ideological structures.

(7) The ideological change is mainly that of appreciating *life quality* (dwelling in situations of intrinsic value) rather than adhering to a high standard of living. There will be a profound awareness of the difference between big and great.

(8) Those who subscribe to the foregoing points have an obligation directly or indirectly to participate in the attempt to implement the necessary changes.

The eight formulations are of course in need of clarification and elaboration. A few remarks:

Re (1) Instead of 'biosphere' we might use the term 'ecosphere' in order to stress that we of course do not limit our concern for the life forms in a biologically narrow sense. The term 'life' is used here in a comprehensive non-technical way to refer also to things biologists may classify as non-living: rivers (watersheds), landscapes, cultures, ecosystems, 'the living earth'. Slogans such as 'let the river live' illustrate this broader usage so common in many cultures.

Re (2) So-called simple, lower, or primitive species of plants and animals contribute essentially to the richness and diversity of life. They have value in themselves and are not merely steps toward the so-called higher or rational life forms. The second principle presupposes that life itself, as a process over evolutionary time, implies an increase of diversity and richness.

Why talk about diversity *and* richness? Suppose humans interfere with an ecosystem to such a degree that 1000 vertebrate species are each reduced to a survival minimum. Point (2) is not satisfied. *Richness,* here used for what some others call 'abundance', has been excessively reduced. The maintenance of richness has to do with the maintenance of habitats and the number of individuals (size of populations). No exact count is implied. The main point is that life on Earth may be excessively interfered with even if complete diversity is upheld.

What is said above about species holds also for habitats and ecosystems which show great similarity so that it makes sense to count them.

Re (3) This formulation is perhaps too strong. But, considering the mass of ecologically irresponsible proclamations of human rights, it may be sobering to announce a norm about what they have no right to do.

The term 'vital need' is vague to allow for considerable latitude in judgement. Differences in climate and related factors, together with differences in the structures of societies as they now exist, need to be considered. Also the difference between a means to the satisfaction of the need and the need must be considered. If a whaler in an industrial country quits whaling he may risk unemployment under the present economic conditions. Whaling is for him an important means. But in a rich country with a high standard of living whaling is not a vital need.

Re (4) Status of interference. For a realistic assessment of the global situation, see the unabbreviated version of the IUCN's *World Conservation Strategy* (1980). There are other works to be highly recommended such as Gerald Barney's *Global 2000 Report to the President* of the United States (1980).

People in the materially richest countries cannot be expected to reduce their excessive interference with the non-human world to a moderate level overnight. Less interference does not imply that humans should not modify some ecosystems as do other species. Humans have modified the Earth and will continue to do so. At issue is the nature and extent of such interference.

The fight to preserve and extend areas of wilderness or near-wilderness should continue and should focus on the general ecological functions of these areas (one such function: large wilderness areas are required by the biosphere to allow for continued evolutionary speciation of animals and plants). Present designated wilderness areas and game preserves are not large enough to allow for speciation of large birds and mammals.

Re (5) Limitation of population. The stabilisation and reduction of the human population will take time. Interim strategies need to be developed.

But this in no way excuses the present complacency. The extreme seriousness of our current situation must first be more widely recognised. But the longer we wait the more drastic will be the measures needed. Until deep changes are made, substantial decreases in richness and diversity are liable to occur; the rate of extinction of species will be greater than in any other period of Earth history.

A legitimate objection may be that if the present billions of humans deeply change their behaviour in the direction of ecological responsibility, non-human life could flourish. Formulation (5) presupposes that the probability of a deep enough change in economics and technology is too small to take into account.

Re (6) Policy changes required. Economic growth as conceived and implemented today by the industrial states is incompatible with points (1) to (5).

Present ideology tends to value things because they are scarce and because they have a commodity or market value. There is prestige in vast consumption and waste, to mention only two of many relevant factors. Economic growth registers mainly growth in marketable values, not in values generally, including ecological values. Whereas 'self-determination', 'local community', and 'think globally, act locally' will remain key slogans, the implementation of deep changes nevertheless requires increasingly global action in the sense of action across every border, perhaps contrary to the short-range interests of local communities.

Support for global action through non-governmental organisations becomes increasingly important. Many of these organisations are able to act locally from grass roots to grass roots, thus avoiding negative governmental interference.

Cultural diversity today requires advanced technology, that is, techniques that advance the basic goals of each culture. So-called soft, intermediate, and appropriate technologies are steps in this direction.

Re (7) Some economists criticise the term 'quality of life' because it is supposed to be too vague. But, on closer inspection, what they consider to be vague is actually the non-quantifiable nature of the term. One cannot quantify adequately what is important for the quality of life as discussed here, and there is no need to do so.

Re (8) There is ample room for different opinions about priorities. What should be done first, what next? What is most urgent? What is necessary as opposed to what is highly desirable? Different opinions in these matters should not exclude vigorous cooperation.

What is gained from tentatively formulating basic views shared today by most or all supporters of the deep ecology movement? Hopefully it makes it a little easier to localise the movement among the many 'alternative' movements. Hopefully this does not lead to isolation but rather to even better cooperation with many other alternative movements. It might also make some of us more clear about where we stand, and more clear about which disagreements might profitably be reduced and which ones might profitably be sharpened. After all, as we shall see, 'diversity' is a high-level norm!

6 How the themes of deep ecology are presented in what follows

As can be gathered from the formulation of the platform, the deep ecology movement touches every major contemporary personal, economic, political, and philosophical problem. A selection must be made and I have tried to concentrate on central issues which seem to be insufficiently clarified or elaborated in texts already published.

The first three chapters of the book concern two inescapable components: valuation and emotion in thinking and experience of reality, and how they lead to the ability of a mature, integrated human personality to act on the basis of a total view. The strategy and tactics of the deep ecological movement depend upon drawing the consequences of these necessities.

Chapter 2 begins with an unavoidable discussion of terminology: what is the relation between ecology, ecophilosophy, and ecosophy? The central issue is that of transcending ecology as a science, looking for wisdom through the study known as ecophilosophy, striving for an *ecosophy* – a total view inspired in part by the science of ecology and the activities of the deep ecological movement. A social movement is not scientific; its articulation must be permeated throughout with declarations of value and value priorities – norms, rules, imperatives – indicated in my terminology by exclamation points.

This leads to a rather philosophical theme: is not the value-laden, spontaneous and emotional realm of experience as genuine a source of knowledge of reality as mathematical physics? If we answer 'yes!', what are the consequences for our description of nature? The deep ecology movement might profit from greater emphasis on spontaneous experience, on what is called the 'phenomenological' outlook in philosophical jargon.

Chapter 3 deepens the thrust towards value- and decision-related thinking. Like all scientific reasoning, the chains of arguments in value *a priori* thinking are based on premises that are not conclusions reached from other premises. This does not mean that ultimate, often manifestly intuitive ethical and other normative pronouncements are 'subjective'.

Deep ecological philosophy insists that every non-ultimate argumentation must be tested against its ultimate basis: those value priorities which guide the decisions of mature persons or responsible groups. The limitation of the shallow movement is not due to a weak or unethical philosophy, but due to a lack of explicit concern with ultimate aims, goals, and norms. So a considerable part of the work of the philosophically articulate supporters of the deep movement is to question narrowly utilitarian decisions: how do they relate to the ultimate?

An important instrument for this activity is the *normative system*. The concept is illustrated in chapter 3 by a brief mention of various possible systems of ultimate values. 'Self-realisation!' as an ultimate norm is introduced in a preliminary way.

The three next chapters are less philosophically oriented, tracing the consequences of the philosophical issues within the vast realms of technology (chapter 4), economics (chapter 5), and politics (chapter 6).

Technical progress is never purely technical: the value of technical change is dependent upon its value for culture in general. To assess change in technology within a lesser context than the ultimate cultural aims undermines the very existence of the culture. 'Advanced' technology is what advances the ultimate ends in life. Rationality is relational: rational is rational only in order to reach human ultimate ends, whether in terms of happiness or perfection. The position of technology in our society should be taken more seriously, not less, because of its importance for ultimate ends.

Classical economics concerned itself with a substantial part of human needs. The perspective was both philosophical and practical. Modern economics tends to narrow down the perspective and to substitute demand on the market for human needs. Ecosophy asks for a re-establishment of the classical perspective, adding insights from cultural anthropology. A major job for the leading industrial nations is to help the developing nations to avoid the pitfalls of the 'over-developed'. This implies among other things a shift from measuring the success of an economic policy in terms of average standard of living to that of life quality, especially that of the underprivileged groups. Ecosophical reflection tends to support an economic ideal of simplicity of means and richness of ends.

Chapter 6 concerns itself with the political dimension of the deep ecological movement. Active supporters of the movement and their forerunners, like John Muir, have run into depressing political struggles. The movement is long-term, politics are short-term. Nature is no pressure group, politicians yield only to pressures. 'Green' parties and groups cannot so far point to enduring victories. But the tripartition blue, red, and green is manifest in the political life of many countries. Green technology, green economics, green population policy, green community life and green peace movements are all pillars of support for the richness and diversity of life.

Some supporters minimise the inherent value or effectiveness of green lifestyles, while others announce that we cannot but start with ourselves, changing our lives. It seems, however, that we must acknowledge that the frontier is long and that supporters may find their place somewhere along the front – among the political activists, the social reformers or among those 'hating' politics and appearance before the public.

The last chapter returns to fundamentals and is more narrowly coloured by my own variant of ecosophy, Ecosophy T. Here historical evidence is gathered to support the view of a nature with value in itself, and suggestions are put forth as to how to shape a world-view in harmony with a true respect for nature. Finally the most basic norms and hypotheses of Ecosophy T are tied together in a systematic sketch, followed by a short commentary on the prospects for the future of the deep ecological movement.

2

From ecology to ecosophy

The first part of the chapter introduces a way of formulating the essential traits of a total view which could be of help to all who wish to verbalise their basic attitudes and compare them with others' – especially those who seem to oppose vigorous ecological policies. This portion is methodological, and not limited to my own particular view, Ecosophy T.

The second part attacks problems of ontology, 'what there is'. Rather than talking about reality or the world, ecophilosophical thinking proceeds in terms of nature, and humanity's relation to nature. An attempt is made to defend our spontaneous, rich, seemingly contradictory experience of nature as more than subjective impressions. They make up the concrete contents of our world. This point of view, as every other ontology, is deeply problematic – but of great potential value for energetic environmentalism in its opposition to the contemporary near monopoly of the so-called scientific world-view.

1 The terms ecology, ecophilosophy, ecosophy

Those who come across these three terms should ask for precise definitions – but in the disorderly terminological situation we are placed in today, both descriptive and prescriptive definitions are somewhat arbitrary. In this work, the three words will have three very distinct meanings adapted to our purpose. Others, however, with other purposes, may disagree somewhat on these precise meanings.

(a) Ecology

Biology is central in today's world: three fields of biological research infringe upon the future of *Homo sapiens* in a dramatic way which concerns us all – biological warfare, genetic engineering, and ecology. These fields cry out for evaluative thinking: what do we want and how can it be realised? Is the 'we' invoked here a collective with unitary basic value, or is it a constellation doomed to unquenchable strife occasioned by irrevocable interests in continual opposition?

The expression 'ecology' is infused with many meanings. Here, it will mean the interdisciplinary scientific study of the living conditions of organisms in interaction with each other and with the surroundings, organic as well as inorganic. For these surroundings the terms 'milieu' and 'environment' will be used nearly interchangeably.

The preceding formulation is not especially informative. A great deal depends on one's attitude to the study of one particular animal species – *Homo sapiens*. Do all possible studies of humankind's relations with all possible kinds of surroundings belong to ecology? Hardly.

In the following, the aspect of the science of ecology that is most important is the fact that it is concerned first of all with relationships between entities as an essential component of what these entities are in themselves. These include both internal and external relations. Example: when a bird eats a mosquito, it gets in an external relation to that mosquito, but eating is an internal relation to its environment. (The mosquito is initially outside the bird, but both are within the environment.) This approach can have application in many fields of inquiry – hence the growing influence of the subject of ecology outside its original biological domain.

(b)   Ecophilosophy and ecosophy

The study of ecology indicates an approach, a methodology which can be suggested by the simple maxim 'all things hang together'. This has application to and overlaps with the problems in philosophy: the placement of humanity in nature, and the search for new kinds of explanation of this through the use of systems and relational perspectives.

The study of these problems common to ecology and philosophy shall be called *ecophilosophy*. It is a descriptive study, appropriate, say, to a university milieu. It does not make a choice between fundamental value priorities, but merely seeks to examine a particular kind of problem at the vast juncture between the two well-recognised disciplines.

But such value priorities are essential in any pragmatic argument. The word 'philosophy' itself can mean two things: (1) a field of study, an approach to knowledge; (2) one's own personal code of values and a view of the world which guides one's own decisions (insofar as one does fullheartedly feel and think they are the right decisions). When applied to questions involving ourselves and nature, we call this latter meaning of the word 'philosophy' an *ecosophy* (see Table 2.1).

Table 2.1

	All-inclusive	Concentrating on relations to nature
Field of study	philosophy	*ecophilosophy*
Position, point of view	a philosophy	an *ecosophy*

We study ecophilosophy, but to approach practical situations involving ourselves, we aim to develop our own ecosophies. In this book I introduce one ecosophy, aribitrarily called Ecosophy T. You are not expected to agree with all of its values and paths of derivation, but to learn the means for developing your own systems or guides, say, Ecosophies X, Y, or Z. Saying 'your own' does not imply that the ecosophy is in any way an original creation by yourself. It is enough that it is a kind of total view which you feel at home with, 'where you philosophically belong'. Along with one's own life, it is always changing.

'Ecosophy' is a compound of the prefix 'eco-' found in economy and ecology, and the suffix '-sophy' found in philosophy. In the word 'philosophy', '-sophy' denotes insight or wisdom, and 'philo-' denotes a kind of friendly love. 'Sophia' need not have specific scientific pretensions as opposed to 'logos' compound words (biology, anthropology, geology, etc.), but all 'sophical' insight should be directly *relevant for action*. Through their actions, a person or organisation exemplifies *sophia*, sagacity, and wisdom – or lack thereof. 'Sophia' intimates acquaintance and understanding rather than impersonal or abstract results. Peter Wessel Zapffe's 'biosophy'* does the same: valuation of life, especially the problematic 'human condition'. The more grounded approach of *pro aut contra* dialogue, together with the scientific ethic of respect for the norms of impartiality (in Norwegian, *saklighet*, 'appropriateness to the situation at hand'), serve to help us explore our existence.

Etymologically, the word 'ecosophy' combines *oikos* and *sophia*, 'household' and 'wisdom'. As in 'ecology', 'eco-' has an appreciably broader meaning than the immediate family, household, and community.

---

* Peter Wessel Zapffe is Norway's first ecophilosopher, introducing a connection between philosophy and the biological place of man early in this century. His central point is that Man is the ultimate tragic being, because he has learned enough about the Earth to realise the Earth would be better off without the presence of humankind. His major work, *Om det tragiske* (On the Tragic) has not been translated into English. The only published translations of Zapffe into English are in Reed and Rothenberg (1987).

'Earth household' is closer to the mark. So an ecosophy becomes *a philosophical world-view or system inspired by the conditions of life in the ecosphere*. It should then be able to serve as an individual's philosophical grounding for an acceptance of the principles or platform of deep ecology as outlined at the close of chapter 1.

A conscious change of attitude towards the conditions of life in the ecosphere presupposes that we associate ourselves with a philosophical position in all essential problems of decision-making. Therefore, contextual and systems thinking is to be emphasised throughout this work.

But to have a world-view is one thing, to attempt to give a systematic expression of it is another. A philosophical system has many components. Logic, general methodology, epistemology, ontology, descriptive and normative ethics, philosophy of science, political and social philosophy, and general aesthetics are among the most well known. Ecosophy T says this of this diversity: all are intimately interconnected! You will find a view on all of them intimated in this work. A formal logic cannot be concretely developed without assuming positions in methodology, normative philosophy, etc. Political philosophy is implied in any social development of an ecosophy. Conversely, one cannot develop a political philosophy without presupposing formal logic and assuming standpoints about rhetoric and communication, and thus in the philosophy of language. To assume a position in one scientific discipline presumes standpoints in all the others. A sufficiently profound analysis of presuppositions reveals that a standpoint in any science whatsoever presupposes the assumption of a position in all the philosophical disciplines. To 'have' a world-view or philosophy is not pretentious. We may stress our bottomless ignorance. If anything is pretentious, it is the claim to act as a whole person. If we claim this, I think it is inescapable to admit that we have presuppositions, expressed or unexpressed.

The essential idea is that, as humans, we are responsible in our actions as to motivations and premises relative to any question that can be asked of us. Needless to say, a total view cannot be completely articulated by any person or group. The medieval church and dialectical materialism intended a sort of completeness, but they scarcely achieved enduring success. Yet all we do somehow implies the existence of such systems, however elusive they may be to concrete description (see Naess (1964)).

This book encourages the reader to try to articulate the necessary parts or fragments of his or here own implicit views, in the hope that it will lead to clarification of the difficult process of facing and responding to the challenges of life in our ecosphere.

(c)   *The dangers of 'ecologism': seeing ecology as*
          the ultimate science

All-encompassing philosophical viewpoints have always been more or less inspired by the sciences. In Indian philosophy, grammar was important for Pānini, while, in Greek philosophy, geometry (for Plato) and biology (for Aristotle) were especially inspiring. Ecosophy T is in a similar way inspired by ecology, but it cannot be derived from ecology or any other science.

Some all-encompassing philosophical viewpoints, like Herbert Spencer's social Darwinism, are formed as a generalisation or universalisation of one science or one theory within a science. The conceptual framework and general problem approaches within a given science are then regarded as universal and utilisable within all fields of inquiry. In the Western world, such systematic programmes were introduced when Pythagoras contended that 'everything is numbers', thereby trying to universalise mathematics. Descartes almost universalised mechanics, but he reserved a tiny retreat for God and free will.

Psychological research was enthusiastically welcomed as a general foundation for thought when Fechner established psychophysics. But several events like the attempt to reduce logic to a psychological study of the laws of thought lead to a fiery counter-movement (Frege). The lingering aversion for psychology still prevalent in analytic philosophy is due in part to these attempts. To make psychology absolute – a total system or common framework for all science – has been called 'psychologism'. In debate, to label a standpoint an 'ism' often means it generalises the concepts of a science *too much*. For example: sociologism, historicism, etc.

Many of those who emphasise the tremendous breadth of ecology tend, simultaneously, to limit it somewhat. They conceive of it as a natural science or use primarily examples characteristic of natural science. As long as one retains current concepts of nature instead of Spinoza's *Natura* or other broad, profound concepts of nature, the placement of ecology within the framework of natural sciences favours the shallow ecological movement.

Ecology may comprise a great deal, but it should never be considered a universal science. When concentrating on the relations between things, of course many aspects of their limited separateness are ignored. Ecologism is excessive universalisation or generalisation of ecological concepts and theories. The attempt to fully replace the theory of knowledge with certain ecological theories about behaviour and survival leads to very great difficulties ('labyrinthine epistemology') or, more correctly, one encounters great inconsistency and paradox (Naess, 1939).

Ecologism is not present if one works with ecologically defined thought models which include epistemological phenomena, but which are definitely constrained in accordance with model theory, i.e. with the intention of investigating certain more or less arbitrarily selected aspects ('variables') of the phenomena. A theorem in relation to a model does not necessarily contradict the negation of the theorem if the latter is defined in relation to a totally different model. Thus, no epistemological *model* can compete with the most comprehensive (i.e. philosophical) *theories* of knowledge. The models have heuristic rather than ontological pretensions.

The shallow ecological movement often presents technical recommendations for reform, for example, technical pollution abatement and reduced consumption in the Third World countries. The deep movement is global, and ecologism is then always a threat (see Galtung (1973) and chapter 6) – perhaps not in conscious philosophical inquiries, but in more careless generalisations in the heat of a debate.

2   Normative evaluation

(a)   Objective science cannot provide principles for action

If the term 'objectivity' is meant to imply certainty, intersubjectivity, and stability, scientific texts gain in objectivity when evaluations used as premises are explicitly formulated.

Values are linked together: one thing is good for another which in turn is good for a third thing. A detailed investigation of the evaluations in a given ecological or other scientific investigation will never uncover the values at the end of this process. At the end of the scientific process lie ultimate assumptions of a philosophical kind. For all other values, it is relevant to ask: is it correct that it is good for what it is said to be good for? In what does the good consist in the instance investigated? For example, many people contend that greater productivity is valuable because it increases the general level of material affluence. This is in turn a rhetorically popular value widely considered beneficial to well-being. A critique of the first two values would pose questions like 'Does greater productivity widen or narrow the gap between rich and poor within a country, or the gap between rich countries and poor countries?', 'Is a high standard of material affluence conducive to happiness?', 'What effects do yearly increases in affluence have upon aspiration levels?', 'Are people being encouraged to believe in a constantly receding pie in the sky?' These questions can be approached empirically and probable answers can be suggested on the basis of scientific investigation. Conversely, what can a good life be said to be good for? Both the question and the responses it evokes are certainly philosophical.

The testability of the entire group of statements in question is not necessarily reduced when evaluations are formulated, but it is more complex. Instead of a statement *p*, which comprises a genuine evaluation and a descriptive assertion, we get two statements, *q* and *r*. One of them is the evaluation stated explicitly and the other is the descriptive statement. To the extent that *q* is part of the message which was to be intended by *p*, it is problematic to eliminate *q*. To do so merely masks a crucial aspect of the actual conditions of validity or truth. When the question at hand comprises both evaluations and so-called facts, an impartial inquiry necessitates explicit evaluations.

A large number of the topics labelled as 'ecological' are also 'ecosophical'. This is hardly unfortunate. Without an ecosophy, ecology can provide no principles for acting, no motive for political and individual efforts.

In the early days of the growth of ecological consciousness, ecologists sometimes said things like 'knowledge about what should not be done . . . is derived from the sciences and particularly from ecology.' (K. Caldwell, quoted in Darling (1965)). Statements like this encourage the untenable belief that, if only the grants to ecological and other scientific studies were large enough, the experts could *derive* a conclusion about what we can do. *But we cannot act without norms*! If, because of waterway pollution, we decide that a factory must be shut down or moved, we accept, in addition to the more or less scientific hypotheses about the effects of waterway pollution, a long string of evaluations which are not part of any science: 'waterways *ought* not be poisoned!', 'the employees of the factory *ought* not to go without work'. Both the scientific hypotheses and the evaluations must be precisely formulated, and the respective derivative relationships must be elucidated. When an ecologist says that this or that *must* be done, e.g. 'we *must* reduce the level of human population on Earth!', the ecologist implies that it *can* be done. But to what level? And who are 'we'? This implies that he or she presupposes hypotheses and norms about political conditions and local, national, and global power constellations. And can all this be articulated in words? No, but hopefully enough to clarify the debate.

(b)   *Norms and hypotheses; normative systems*

A particular way of articulating philosophies will now be introduced. It can at least be viewed as an exercise in systematisation. The pieces of the game are two classes of sentences, the descriptive and the prescriptive. In extremely simplified form, they may be arranged in a diagram which shows lines of logical derivation between the statements.

Of the two kinds of statements, the first are called *norms* – prescriptions or inducements to think or act in certain ways. They will be written with an exclamation point, e.g. 'No exploitation!' or 'Be honest!' or 'Don't pollute!'. To justify, explain, and relate such beliefs or pronouncements to one another, a network of supporting non-normative statements is required. These will be written without an exclamation point, and will be called *hypotheses*. The name for this second class of statements is not choosen primarily to suggest uncertainty, but rather a certain tentativeness or revisability.

Throughout this book lists of norms will be presented by letters as N1, N2, N3, . . . and hypotheses as H1, H2, H3, ... Diagrams are presented that illustrate the logical derivations within normative systems.

It has been objected that the term 'norm' and the sign of exclamation make the norm-sentences seem absolutistic and rigid. Actually the function of the general norms is that of tentative *guidelines*. Wise decisions – the aim of normative thinking – are absolute in the sense of being either carried out or sabotaged. In ecosophy, unlike academic philosophy, decisions and actions count more than generalities.

A total view can be systematised in many ways. There is no one definitive way of tracing lines of derivation. It is to some degree arbitrary which norms are chosen as basic, ultimate or most fundamental in the sense of not being logically derivable from any others. And even if the verbal expressions of the norms and hypotheses are arranged in a definite, authorised way, there is still room for differences in interpretation.

There are serious considerations which *favour* a certain vagueness and ambiguity in the outlining of normative systems. Instead of tentatively rejecting one of the norms or hypotheses in favour of a completely different one, it is often better to introduce alternative interpretations of the initial or 'point of departure' wording. The initial vague and ambiguous sentence expressing the hypothesis or norm may then be tentatively given more precise meanings, resulting in new formulations called *precisations*. The concept of precisation is one of the central concepts of an empirical theory of system communications (Naess, 1966). Roughly, a sentence S_1 is more precise than another, S_0, if and only if the latter, S_0, permits (in ordinary or technical talk) all interpretations of the former, whereas the former, S_1, does not admit all interpretations of the latter, S_0. In short, the set of 'plausible' interpretations of the more precise sentence is a genuine subset of that of the less precise.

The choice of a rather indefinite and ambiguous sentence in the most elementary argumentations makes these fairly short and easily understandable and opens a variety of different possibilities for derivation and interpretation. Instead of more or less arbitrarily insisting that your sentence is to be interpreted in a single particular way, options are, as in natural science, kept open as long as this is heuristically convenient.

A highly precise sentence of the kind needed in a fairly abstract and general systematisation is apt to be long and complicated. Therefore, it cannot perform the special function of the less precise. More details and clarity do not render the vague and ambiguous obsolete. We have to work continuously at various levels of preciseness.

When I recommend that norms be made more precise, nothing more is meant than a point-form, fragmentary, or theme-restricted formulation: we erect a fragile lattice of norm and hypothesis relations which at every turn merges with the hazy sea of implicitness. The fragmentary nature of statements must be shamelessly and unreservedly admitted or we sink into the quagmire of sloganised political thought, and veil inadequacies through the agency of words like 'democracy' and 'freedom'.

Communication, we may conclude, is not to be seen as a process of two or more individuals making use of a completely 'shared language', but of each carrying out a personal process of interpretation in their own directions of precisations (see Gullvåg (1983)). So any system which is to serve as a kind of common platform must be articulated at low levels of preciseness.

Returning to practical argumentation, there are several basic points.

(1) A normative system, e.g. an ethic, does not consist only of norms. Most codifications of normative views show a preponderance of non-normative sentences.

(2) Norms are in general derived from other norms and hypotheses, rarely only from other norms.

(3) The existence of at least one hypothesis as a premise for the derivation of a norm establishes the *hypothetical character* of derived norms. Change in hypotheses used as premises normally changes norms. Their *validity* depends upon the validity of non-normative assumptions, postulates, theories, and observations. Example: one does not accept the hostile norms of a systematic racism without accepting certain hypotheses about the peoples in question. The norms are not logically derived from the hypotheses, only psychologically motivated by them.

Methodologically the last point is of decisive importance in argumentation: when the intricate interconnection between norms and hypotheses is left unarticulated, each norm tends to be taken to be absolute or ultimate. This reduces or eliminates the possibility of rational discussion. In harmony with the methodology here proposed, it is always, when norms are opposed in debate, appropriate to ask the opponent: 'Which hypotheses do you think are relevant to the adoption of your norm?'

We should try to uncover the roots of valuations and total systems, in both our own and our opponents' premises and conclusions. The term 'roots' here includes deep psychological and social motivations as well as logically basic norms and hypotheses. But in this book I concentrate on cognitive, especially logic, relations rather than on the conative.

(c)   The generalist in us
When a scientist assumes that there is general agreement about the validity of an evaluation, it is often left unquestioned. Its validity is *presupposed.* He or she does not do this as a scientist, however, but as a generalist and a philosopher. An ecologist may say that ecology shows that we ought to consider the climatic consequences entailed when rain-forests are clearcut. Ecologists may personally deplore the biological effects of deforestation, climatologists warn of its influence upon the weather, and economists stress the *bad* economic consequences these effects would have. But with only *hypotheses* as premises, it is not possible to logically derive these value announcements. Strict consequential ethics is incomplete: a consequence must be judged good or bad. Only these judgements must be justified in relation to fundamental norms of our life. Vast areas of concern are always involved. Therefore, only the generalist in us can set up ecosophical value priorities which conclude with 'we ought' or 'we ought not'. Ultimately a total view is presumed valid.

Only the most cursory of our value judgements are purely instrumental. The more profound are intrinsic, or genuine goals, to be reached for their own sake, rather than as means toward other goals. Without such goals in themselves, there would be an infinite regress. The science of ecology cannot hand you such goals. Things can have both intrinsic and instrumental value. For example, a forest can be preserved for the sake of profit or recreation, but this does not rule out a view of its preservation as a goal in itself. The forest is thus afforded a meaning independent of its narrow or wide utilitarian value.

There are many ways to work out a map of value priorities – the analytical systematising according to norms and hypotheses as presented throughout this work is only one. It is trivial to pretend, though, that such ultimate priorities are determined by society, culture, biology, or economy. We are not thereby exempt from the task of bringing them to consciousness and as integrated persons assessing their validity. Such statements are the backbone of an ecosophy.

We daily decide between conflicting considerations and interests. To work for a more ecologically responsible personal and societal lifestyle is thus not merely the ecologist's job. Nor the philosopher's. We should all do it together, as generalists rather than as specialists. We all have a certain amount of practice in choosing courses of action, and this presumes an ability to make comprehensive value judgements.

Determined efforts to justify these choices on the basis of a given set of premises ultimately lead to the elaboration of a philosophical system, a representation of the contextual associations between all aspects of our existence. Fortunately, we seem to manage quite well from day to day without much stringency. But the ecological challenge encourages attempts at comprehensive value clarification and disentanglement.

An emphasis on *personal* value priority judgements and world-views can be misunderstood to mean that the value priority is only relevant for oneself. Global influence can only be achieved through participation in organised efforts, such as clearly formulated in the important, but neglected *World Conservation Strategy* (1980). The neglect is due to ecopolitical weakness in each country and calls for political activity in each state. But these collective tasks do not make personal value priority judgements and world-views unnecessary. One works in an organisation as a person, not just as a functionary. To act in an organisation merely as a functionary is to renounce human dignity in favour of the anonymity of the automaton.

All this talk is necessary because the aim of supporters of the deep ecology movement is not a slight reform of our present society, but a *substantial reorientation of our whole civilisation.*

(d)   Conservation biology

A new science has developed over the past ten years which combines insights from ecology with normative and generalist aspects to move towards this substantial reorientation. Conservation biology is the spearhead of scientifically based environmentalism. Firmly committed environmentalists with training in the life sciences who use their specialities in direct service of conservation tend to cluster around this new discipline. It is a crisis discipline, like cancer biology, and thus an indispensable instrument of cooperation between nature managers and researchers.

One of the leading researchers in the field, Michael Soulé, whose presentation (Soulé, 1985) I follow in the main, puts forth four norms as the simply worded basis of conservation biology: (1) 'Diversity of organisms is good.' (2) 'Ecological complexity is good.' (3) 'Evolution is good.' (4) 'Biotic diversity has intrinsic value.'

Including these norms in Ecosophy T, I prefer them written as nouns with an exclamation point, e.g. 'Diversity of organisms!' The derivation of the first two norms within Ecosophy T needs no comment. As to 'Evolution!', this norm inserts a long-range perspective characteristic of the deep ecological movement: 'Long term viability of whole systems!'. What goes on today is a destruction of the conditions necessary for *continued evolution*, including speciation, through future millions of years.

Continued evolution is indispensable for the long-range maintenance of diversity and richness of life forms (cf. point (2) of the Platform, chapter 1). This indispensability gets into Ecosophy T in the form of a hypothesis. From point 2 and this hypothesis we derive the third norm of conservation biology. The fourth norm, 'biotic diversity!' is a special case of 'life form diversity!' if we use the broad sense of 'life' used in point (1) of the platform. The conservation biologist has, of course, ecosystems, habitats, and communities strongly in mind.

The normative character of conservation biology results in recommendations and decisions which can be made as hastily as our current political structures require. These have for instance influenced the political decision in Western New Guinea (Irian Jaya) to establish a series of national parks. Recommendations were made *before* biologists had made the usual scientific investigations concerning loss of species etc. if logging were to continue. Political constraints made such investigations impossible, but the normative character of conservation biology allowed the scientists to have a say in the deciding process.

The gravity of the situation is eminently clear from some of the well confirmed 'hypotheses' of conservation biology. Species are a significant part of one another's environment, therefore the tendency towards non-natural (anthropogenic) communities threatens their structure, function, and stability. The extinction of one species of a community may eventually result in the extinction of hundreds of others. Therefore the saving of one may result in saving hundreds. But time is running out!

Another hypothesis: a species has a greater chance of survival in a larger natural area or nature reserve. Examples of reasons for this: sudden considerable growth 'outbursts' of the population of one species can destroy other species. They 'are most probable in small sites that lack a full array of population buffering mechanisms, including habitat sinks for dispersing individuals, sufficient predators, and alternative feeding grounds during inclement weather. The unusually high population densities that often occur in nature reserves can also increase the rate of disease transmission, frequently leading to epidemics that may affect every individual.' (Soulé 1985, p. 730.)

Clearly, moderation of the present extinction rate on this planet requires significantly bigger nature reserves, and also significant decrease of the extent of human habitation:

> Nature reserves are inherently disequilibrial for large, rare organisms. There are two reasons for this. First, extinctions are inevitable in habitat islands the size of nature reserves; species diversity must be artificially maintained for many taxa because natural colonisation (reestablishment) from outside sources is highly unlikely. Second, speciation, the only other nonartificial means of replacing species, will not operate for rare or large organisms in nature reserves because reserves are nearly always too small to keep large or rare organisms isolated within them for long periods, and populations isolated in different reserves will have to be maintained by artificial gene flow if they are to persist. (Soulé, 1985)

Absorption of even a tiny fraction of the information which conservation biology furnishes makes it clear that to conserve a major part of the existing diversity and richness of life forms on this planet requires changes of the basic kinds expressed in the Platform points (4) to (6).

The kind of exposition illustrated through the norms of conservation biology can be generalised and made more sophisticated. We then arrive at normative systems on the level of complex expositions of philosophies or oulines of systematised total views. But these cannot be furthered without an investigation of the various ways of perceiving and experiencing nature itself.

3   Objective, subjective, and phenomenological descriptions of nature

Deep differences in people's attitudes to nature and to their intimate surroundings are commonly called subjective: '*different* feelings and perceptions are induced in different people by *the same thing*'. The thing is supposed to be objective, the perception subjective. What leads one to believe that it is the same thing which we have different attitudes towards? An easy answer: nature and thereby the immediate physical surroundings have a uniquely determined set of characteristics at any moment. These characteristics are considered independently of how individual people comprehend them. They belong to the things *in themselves, Dinge an sich*.

Subjects (human beings) are assumed to face physical and other objects of which they create different pictures or conceptions. The objective conception, the one which describes the object as it is in itself, must be independent of these differences. This way of thinking eliminates, among other things, all individual differences of sense qualities. So the thing in itself cannot have colour, nor shape.

What then remains? Perhaps merely an abstract structure of some kind – in any case recent developments in physics seem to indicate just that. There does not appear to be either world or nature remaining, merely several common *reference points* suitable for mathematical description.

Within the informed public, the dominating answer would in all likelihood be that it is precisely the mathematical natural sciences which supply the approximately correct description of the environment as this *is in itself* (we have learned to admit that the description may never correspond *perfectly*). Are we getting any closer with the long scientific strides built upon the work of Galileo and Newton?

The Russian poet Tiutchev sings of an opposition to this established view (Perminov, 1970, p. 54):

> Nature is something else than we believe
> It has soul, it has freedom,
> It has love, it has language

Philosophers and scientists have attempted to supply understandable descriptions of things in themselves, descriptions *absolutely* independent of their comprehension through the senses or in any other way. I believe we can safely say that all the attempts have failed and that it is the formulation of the problem which is at fault.

A strong philosophical tradition goes from Newton to Kant and his *Ding an sich* about which *nothing* positive can be said. Our textbooks, with impermissible inconsistency, usually stop half-way: form, weight, and certain other qualities are objective whereas colour and smell are said to be subjective.

However, if we take characteristics like 'oblong' and 'square', for example, they cannot objectively be qualities of a table, as the quality cannot be separated from the concepts of time and velocity in the theory of relativity. The mentioned characteristics are not subjective, but, like smell, *bound in an interdependent relationship* to our conception of the world. This is what is meant by calling them 'relational' – rather than 'relative' or 'subjective'. It is justifiable to refer to them as objective in the sense of being independent of a person's likes or dislikes. We arrive, not at the things themselves, but at networks or fields of relations in which things participate and from which they cannot be isolated.

Einstein sought a structural specification which would apply for each and every observer, irrespective of the state of motion of the observer in relation to the observed. The objective can be interpreted as 'that aspect which is common for a large group, or for all observers'. It is important to note, however, that *that which is common* is extremely abstract, completely intangible and *in no way obvious*. (General relatively will never be obvious, I suppose.) The attempt to create a description of the content of the world based upon such conceptions is bound to fail. At best, one arrives at a spectral, wholly inhuman world. An interesting child of fantasy, but useless as actual description.

To believe that what is common for the individuals in a class must be itself an individual in the class is an erroneous idea whose influence in semantics and conceptual learning is lamentable. For example, an expression can justifiably be made more precise in ten directions, and one therefore believes that what is common to the ten directions is an eleventh direction, which must necessarily be the 'most correct'. A good deal is common for all dogs, but the attempt to imagine a dog which has the common, and *only the common* features of all dogs overlooks not only colour but *everything* which distinguishes a bulldog from a terrier. A nature consisting solely of the features about which we are continuously in agreement is like such a spectral dog – therefore any objective notion of nature cannot be seen as that which we all agree upon as being 'there'.

Quantum physics is no more successful in retaining the constant, definitive roundness or squareness we assume to be the form of the table itself. But the physicists need not conceive the content of nature as actually and objectively being so drastically different from the way we (and classical naturalists) experience it. They could be satisfied with saying that, *based on certain models*, a table or the universe should be described in a certain way. Only the study of methodology can facilitate understanding of the function of physical thought models. This relieves us of the many fruitless attempts to distinguish between things and nature in itself, '*an sich*', and nature for me, '*an mich*'. The distinction itself can be gradually eliminated.

Some may have received the impression that I have basically concluded that everything is subjective, and that our original distinction subjective/ objective useless. This impression should be dispelled if one keeps the following in mind: there is a difference between something relational and something which is no more than an expression of one person's personal judgement. When we say 'the Eiffel Tower is on the left', we describe a state of affairs which does not express individual personal judgement. But the statement becomes incomplete, 'elliptical', when it is detached from a particular geographical situation. In relation to other places the Eiffel Tower is to the right. Personal whereabouts are not necessary to justify the relational position of the Eiffel Tower. The relational is not subjective.

In short, there is no single natural science description of nature, only a number of contributions. Physics provides some common points of bearing, for example time and space coordinates, degrees of longitude and latitude. But characteristically enough, these are nowhere to be *found*: There are few who believe that when a ship crosses the equator, a man must stand in the bow and cut it with a knife. A physical equator is nowhere to be found!

Together, these bearing points create a pure structure or form. The structure is 'pure' in the sense that it lacks bodily or other content. One can easily imagine atomic nuclei to be small things with colour and a hard surface, but the scientific content in statements concerning atomic nuclei is abstract and based solely upon structure. Such theoretical science can be learned, understood, and acknowledged to be valid in any culture whatsoever, not because it describes the common reality, but because it describes a structure independent of most cultural conceptions. The structure *belongs to* reality, but *it is not* reality. It can be revised again and again, making possible ever different interpretations of and routes to reality.

So, understanding the world as a collection of things with constant or changing qualities breaks down when one attempts to render it very precise and apply it in natural scientific or historical research. We must strive for greater familiarity with an understanding closer to that of Heraclitus: everything flows. We must abandon fixed, solid points, retaining the relatively straightforward, persistent relations of interdependence. 'Objective descriptions of nature' offered us by physics ought to be regarded not as descriptions of nature, but as descriptions of certain conditions of interdependence and thereby can be universal, common for all cultures. Cooperation along these lines would in any case fulfil intentions of universality and at the same time safeguard the diversity of human cultures.

The designation of 'phenomenological description' is used for quite different psychological and philosophical operations. For example, in psychology, a description of motorists and pedestrians is said to be phenomenological if it clearly and thoroughly describes how motorists apperceive pedestrians and vice versa – in no way questioning whether pedestrians *are* as described (e.g. so careless) by the motorists, or whether the motorists *are* (e.g. so arrogant) as the pedestrians interpret them. Nor is the question raised as to what ought to be, or why or how it has arisen. Philosophical phenomenology (inspired more or less by the work of Edmund Husserl) also attempts to give a description of the immediately apprehended, and of the act of self-apprehension itself.

Phenomenological viewpoints are valuable for the development of consciousness of a non-instrumental, non-utilitarian content of the immediate experience of nature. For example, one may consider colours, without thinking of their wavelengths as a result of mathematical calculation, or what 'signal functions' they have: 'Brown' for some people has the signal function 'dry' and 'poor harvest', which hinders their apprehension of certain qualities of desert landscapes. Each and every painter must develop the knack of seeing colour independent of conventions. Without practice, one sees things as 'das Man' (Heidegger) sees things, in other words, in our society: a utility-conscious, average, or mean, way of seeing them. A joyful experiencing of nature is partially dependent upon a conscious or unconcious development of a sensitivity for qualities.

There are enough qualities for everyone! Those profoundly sensitive to an abundance of diverse qualities are in an excellent position in life, provided they can subsist economically at the same time.

## 4	Primary, secondary, and tertiary qualities: do they exist in Nature?

'Nature is a dull affair,' said A. N. Whitehead, with irony, 'soundless, scentless, colourless.' (Whitehead, 1927, p. 68). The poet should praise *himself* for the scent of the rose. The rose itself cannot have either colour or odour. Whitehead was joking. But some natural scientists and technicians believe in the subjectivity of sensual qualities, perhaps because these cannot be measured by their methods. For them, real nature is something infinitely different from what mankind immediately experiences and appreciates. A dialogue with nature is out of the question. An I–Thou is impossible!

We find the same point of view among some of today's philosophically minded biologists. For example, Bernhard Rensch, leader of the Zoology Institute of the University of Münster. His work in 'biophilosophy' is an attempt to create a scientific philosophical system with a biological groundwork. To the thing 'rose' belong, objectively, only certain chemical and physiological peculiarities which our sense perceptions indicate. The sensual qualities are subjective, not objective (Rensch, 1971, p. 258):

> We are sure that the rose itself does not possess colour, but light waves
> reflected from it generate photochemical reactions in the visual cells of
> our eyes, and specific impulses are passed on through the visual nerves
> to the brain. The sensation of colour is only then coordinated with the
> physiological activity . . .

This 'coordination' is about the most inexplicable thing in Rensch's
philosophy.

Let us look at the matter in a historical light: During the seventeenth
century, the following distinction became generally accepted among
scientists.

(1) *Primary*, geometric-mechanic *qualities* – size, shape, movement.
They were considered to be part of the physical bodies as such, 'in the
objects themselves'.

(2) *Secondary qualities* – colour, warmth, taste, etc. These were
considered to be mere names for the sensations and feelings experienced
as an (unexplained) effect of physical and physiological processes in the
outer, physical world.

Descartes and Galileo established this distinction while Newton lent it
his authoritative approval in his *Optics*.

(3) The term *tertiary qualities* comprises the perceptually complex
qualities, such as the quality of strength expressed by powerful orchestral
chords associated with the visual impressions of an attacking bull, and
qualities such as sorrowful, beautiful, threatening, pathetic. Qualities
like open and closed referring to landscapes can be interpreted as tertiary.
They all have a more or less emphatic complex gestalt character (see later
in this chapter).

With regard to the distinction between (1) and (2), one can say that the
primary qualities were considered objective, independent of every subject which beholds them, while the secondary qualities were considered
non-objective, dependent upon the constitution of the subject, particularly its sensory apparatus. Furthermore, the primary were considered in
reality to be 'out there', in the object, while the secondary only appeared
to be out there and in reality were within consciousness. They were
thought to be somehow 'projected' into nature: the wild, flowering
meadow was in reality in one's head. Remarkable indeed! Out there were
merely colourless atoms, until the idea of atoms disappeared in our own
century into abstract mathematical structures.

An example taken from the great mechanist Thomas Hobbes illustrates how the differences in the shape of a body's smallest parts were
thought to cause differences in the experiencing of taste qualities. He

imagined sweet taste to be caused by round atoms in slow, circular motion, bittersweet taste to be caused by oblong, narrow atoms in violent circular motion, and sour taste to be caused by slender oblong ones in a linear motion, back and forth. Hobbes admitted that this was pure speculation, and said nothing about these extraordinary causal relationships occuring inside people.

Viewpoints hostile to nature and the environment are commonly presented as descriptions of the factual/objective conditions, while the opposing points of view are referred to, analogous to the teachings of secondary qualities, as manifestations of more or less incidental subjective evaluations, 'mere' feelings and sentiments. The tertiary qualities such as melancholic are not accepted as qualities in nature or the environment, but are placed within the person, for example, as an experience or feeling of melancholy which is then projected out into nature. A landscape may in itself be 40 km^2 but not melancholic. But is it possible to stop half-way? It is difficult to understand why it is not also necessary to 'project' length, and all other qualities from within the human subject. If we do, we arrive at 'the thing in itself' as an x about which nothing can be said, while everything is ascribed to a subject who 'creates' the world as it is actually experienced. A very flattering, albeit uninformative conception.

We may find that the smell of pine is difficult to imagine without the existence of olfactory organs. Before there were olfactory organs, how could there be odours in the world? Similarly with colours, we would probably agree that before there were eyes, the glaciers cannot have been white, nor the sky blue, nor the night black, nor the mist grey. We end with something the philosopher Fechner called *Nachtansicht der Natur* – the night vision (nightface) of nature, as opposed to the vision of the day – formless and even darkless, without any of the qualities we know. Nature as it is construed in atomic physics, for example, is neither dark nor light. Through this viewpoint, *human reality is severed from nature proper*. All prestige belongs to the core of reality which is real, measurable and scientific. Inaccessible, calculated probabilities of elementary 'waveicles' (Eddington's shorthand) are supposed to be part of 'actual reality'.

But we see in the words of Norwegian novelist Finn Alnæs that even these 'real' processes excite the imagination and emotions, as one seeks to involve oneself in the attraction and repulsion predicted by the 'objective' mathematical calculations:

> Oh might! Atoms gather, atoms near atom, matter colludes in orderly rhythm, particles unite in a concentrated cloud, the entire mist spins

> about like a gigantic wheel . . . There! The smaller whirls assemble in ring dances around the larger – for such is the law: the largest mass attracts the most . . .

Clearly even this elemental world, *invented* to clothe mathematical entities, is far from being dry and colourless – see what happens when Alnæs in his *Dynamis* draws us into its own romantic possibilities.

Whitehead aptly says (1927, p. 69) that the paradoxical assumption that nature is actually without colours, tones, or odours exists because we have confused our abstractions with concrete realities. That *so blatant* a substitution is possible in our century is perhaps a consequence of the increasing power that abstractions wield over us in our highly technological time – perhaps as many as 99% of all 'experts' are educated to believe that all which is beautiful and lovable (or ugly and 'hateable') is created by humanity, with nature as nothing in itself. But *not man apart*! Could we dispense with nature in a technological utopia? Could machines directly stimulate the nervous system with a simulation of the very qualities of the nature some of us love . . .?

If we give up the belief that our rich world of senses is a projection created by humans, we need to try to get the qualities back into nature. This is problematic, but not impossible, as we shall see in what follows.

5   Protagorean 'both-and' theory

(a)   The relational field

Suppose we have kept one hand in our pocket, and the other in the cold open air. If we put both hands in a bucket of water, the one hand may report that the water is warm and the other that the water is cold.

The well-trodden path to *Ding an sich* paradoxes, and the theory of the exclusive reality of the primary qualities, may begin with a neither-nor response to the question: 'is the water warm or cold?' The reply contends that the water, in itself, is neither cold nor warm. We as subjects project different qualities into the water in accordance with the state of our hands. But, according to Sextus Empiricus, Protagoras replied with a 'both-and'. He said that the basis for all that we perceive is in matter. Thus, matter *in itself* has all the properties which are perceived by each individual. Human beings grasp (understand, perceive) differently, and the same individuals differently at different times.

Accordingly, this theory contends that the water is both warm and cold. When one's hands are in different states, both can be perceived simultaneously.

Suppose now that ten others dip their hands into the same water and all exclaim 'it's lukewarm!' Is this perception better founded? Protagoras seems to have replied in the affirmative. In relation to water, human beings have a natural state (*kata fysin, secundum naturam*). In this state, they perceive *approximately* the same, and they may be said to pronounce the *socially correct* reply, or standard reply to questions about the warmth and coldness of the water. But, by the very fact that the water manifests itself for some as cold and for others as warm, it is both.

Ecosophically, the main points are (1) the secondary qualities are apprehended as genuine qualities of matter or nature itself, (2) that, by the fact that someone perceives a thing as warm, cold, green, or black, it is in itself just that, (3) two different statements about the thing, that it is warm and that it is cold, are not contradictory, and (4) what Protagoras calls the 'socially correct answer' is only the middle of the road response, and thus philosophically uninteresting.

I suggest a continuation and refinement of this Protagorean framework. Instead of matter, I will speak of the relational field. The term 'relational field' refers to the totality of our interrelated experience, but in general not to time and space. Things of the order 'material things' are conceived of as junctions within the field. The same things appear differently to us, with dissimilar qualities at various times, but they are nonetheless the same things. I interpret this to mean that *the relations* which define the thing *conceptually* converge at the same junction.

A thing which is both warm and cold at the same time does not lead to inconsistency, for the thing is a warm thing in one relation and a cold one in another. All statements 'about the thing' are relational statements: statements like 'thing A is B' are in Ecosophy T abandoned in favour of 'thing A is B in relation to C' or 'the relational thing AC has the quality B'. For example, 'water A is warm in relation to hand B', 'the relational thing "B-hand-W-water" has the quality warmth'.

The example illustrates that the relationalism introduced does not always refer to senses, perceptions, soul, consciousness, or subject. The factors it associates are water, hand, coldness and water, hand, warmth. Niels Bohr introduced a similar relationalism in his well-known discussions in Moscow with dialectical materialists: quantum mechanics does not bring a subject into physics, only instruments (see Müller–Markus (1966)). In our example, the hand plays a similar role to the instrument in quantum physics.

An important expression of the principle non-contradiction is that the same thing in the same relation cannot both have and not have the same quality. This principle is not contradicted by the both-and interpretation: 'A is warm and A is not warm' says that A both has and does not have the quality of warmth. This statement violates the identity principle! However, 'A in its relation to B is cold and A in its relation to C is warm' does not.

It is worthwhile to note that, within relational thinking, the identity principle cannot be violated unless negative qualities are introduced, i.e. 'not-cold' or 'not-warm'. These 'absence-qualities' have a rather remarkable status: they do not exist! There are warm things and cold things, and things which are not warm and things which are not cold, but no not-warm or not-cold things. We lose very little by relinquishing these not-qualities. Strictly speaking, we lose nothing at all.

Both-and theory thus reconstructed admits sensory reality with sterling ontological status. The secondary and tertiary qualities are the only ones at hand, if the primary qualities are interpreted as they are in the mechanical world description, namely as mathematical-physical ideal abstract relations (length, curvature, wave, etc.). Such abstract qualities achieve one kind of existence, the ideal, they *are,* but they cannot be *found* hiding under a tree or bush, or anywhere else.

The relational field, like matter in mathematical physics, achieves such a conceptual existence. Relationalism has ecosophical value, because it makes it easy to undermine the belief in organisms or persons as something which can be isolated from their milieux. Speaking of interaction between organisms and the milieux gives rise to the wrong associations, as an *organism is interaction.* Organisms and milieux are not two things – if a mouse were lifted into absolute vacuum, it would no longer be a mouse. Organisms presuppose milieux.

Similarly, a person is a part of nature to the extent that he or she too is a relational junction within the total field. The process of identification is a process in which the relations which define the junction expand to comprise more and more. The 'self' grows towards the 'Self' (see chapters 3 and 7).

The preceding analysis cannot directly serve to criticise Galileo's words: 'nature's book is written in the language of mathematics'. As a structure, the relational net is partially or fully accessible for mathematical, and thereby intersubjective, description. But his dictum ought perhaps, until we know more, be replaced by 'one of nature's books' or 'nature's *book*' or 'nature's book is *written* in this language . . .'

(b)   *The world of concrete contents**
     In short, the both-and answer may be formulated thus: there are no completely separable objects, therefore no separable water or medium

---

* Some of the paragraphs of this section are quotes from Naess (1985a).

or organism. But what are the actual contents of the relational field? Within such a field, any *concrete content* can only be related one-to-one to an indivisible structure, a *constellation* of factors. Concrete contents *and* abstract structures make up reality as it is in fact. It is misleading to call it *real* only *as felt by a subject*.

Concrete contents have a one-to-one correlation with constellations – there is an isomorphism between the concrete and the abstract. When we say that the sea is now grey, the water of the sea is only one part of the constellation. Nevertheless it is somehow the dominant part. We would not say that the air between the sea and us is grey, or that we are grey. The sea has thousands of individual colour hues as inherent properties, but not as an isolated thing. One must take the colour of the heavens, the colour of the plankton, the waves, and the senses of observers into consideration. The colours of the sea are part of innumerable gestalts.

The ontology I wish to defend is such that the primary properties (in a narrow sense) are *entia rationis* characteristic of abstract structures, but not contents of reality. The geometry of the world is not *in* the world.

The both-and answer as elaborated here emphatically rejects the theory of projection. *There is no such process as the projection of sense qualities.* The theory is a clever invention which makes it possible to retain the notion of things in themselves retaining their separate identity in spite of the bewildering diversity of secondary and tertiary qualities. But the price of this conservation of the Galilean ontology is desparately high: there is no evidence whatsoever of a process of projection.

6   Gestalts and gestalt thinking

'All things hang together' is a good slogan, but does not bring us far if we do not form some notions of *how* things hang together. And what about 'things'? Perhaps we need to get away from certain conceptions of the status of 'things'. In our treatment of secondary and tertiary qualities we have neglected the task of suggesting a potent way of describing how they hang together. In what follows I suggest a way that conceives the world neither as a mass of things nor as a mass of qualities.

In our spontaneous experiencing of reality *what* we experience is more or less comprehensive and complex. When we hear the first tones of a very well-known complex piece of music, the experience of those few tones is very different from how they would be experienced if we had never heard the piece. In the first case, the tones are said to fit into a *gestalt*, into our understanding of the piece *as a whole*. The basic character of the whole influences *decisively* our experience of each of the tones.

Take the example of Beethoven's Sonate Pathétique, which has three movements – Allegro, Adagio and Allegro. Many people know only the second movement. This is a genuine whole in itself, and the experience of each tone will be decisively influenced by the whole movement. But normally the experience will be different if people get to know the whole sonata. The movements are subordinate wholes, *subordinate gestalts* as part of musical reality. Within the movement there may be sets of tones forming contrasting wholes. We have therefore a complex realm of gestalts, in a vast hierarchy. We can then speak of lower- and higher-order gestalts. This terminology is more useful than speaking about wholes and holism, because it induces people to think more strenuously about the relations between wholes and parts. It facilitates the emancipation from strong atomistic or mechanistic trends in analytical thought.

Historically, gestalt research began in the psychology of perception, not in ontology and conceptions of reality. Very well-known are the ambiguous visual gestalts that cause oscillating perceptions of pictures; you see one face, then seconds later a different face, and you soon learn to switch back and forth.

Entering a room, there may be a spontaneous experience of it as a whole, even with a strong, definite negative or positive colour. Within the room, the experience of a subordinate whole – an arrangement of chairs around a fireplace – may change the experience of the room decisively, for instance from a definite kind of negative, to a definite kind of positive gestalt. So, within the hierarchy of gestalts, influences may go in any direction. Up or down the hierarchy or horizontally within one level.

The gestalt of a complex piece of music is subordinate to the experience of that piece in a particular situation. The piece may be played in the open or in a beautiful or an ugly building. If we have a particular companion, our relation to the companion in that situation influences the experience of the music. No part of the experience stands entirely alone.

In the same way the gestalt of a flower – with all its parts coming together – is influenced by a higher order gestalt which includes the surroundings. If a 30 cm tall flowering plant is found together with a 5 cm tall one with proportionately large flowers, the former may be experienced as small and the latter as big, because of the gestalts formed through experiencing the two species and knowledge of the average size of the two species.

The most well-known slogan of gestalt psychology has been 'the whole is more than the sum of its parts'. It is a good slogan against mechanical models, but it does not allude to the infusion of the character of the whole into each single part. It neglects what might be called the hologrammatic part, a conception of a part for instance of a piece of music as much more than a fragment getting its meaning from the whole as if the whole could

exist apart. Whole and part are internally related. General gestalt thinking and ontology cannot accept the slogan, but neither would 'the whole
is in the parts' do. This sentence is instructive in so far as it suggests that
you cannot have the whole as something or something that can be shown
except through subordinate wholes.

By 'fragments' we mean something most easily understood as part of a
larger gestalt. A grain of sand might most spontaneously signify a beach.
But of course such an 'atom' may be *inspected* and it will be experienced
as of a definite shape and with definite patterns of colours and light – a
microcosm which supplies us with endless opportunities for discovery.
Then even something so tiny can have a gestalt character. Everything in
nature, as nature, has this ability or potency.

Auditory and visual gestalts are connected into gestalts of higher
orders. Three hills or mountains silhouette the sky, e.g. the lowest on the
left, the next lowest in the middle and the highest on the right, in such a
way that we get a bowed, rising line which immediately gives rise to a
similar gestalt as the introductory, first three crescendos in Beethoven's
Sonate Pathétique (see figure 2.1).

**Figure 2.1 Gestalt understanding of a piece of music (Beethoven's Sonate
Pathétique, op. 13). The initial motif *A* is enhanced through its repetition,
B. As the gestalt, a, they together make up the first part of the initial
phrase of the sonata. Adding the climax and conclusion of the statement,
C, completes the phrase, which is a higher-order gestalt, b. In a similar
way the various sections of the entire *Sonate Pathétique* can only be
understood with full awareness of their participation in successive orders
of gestalts.**

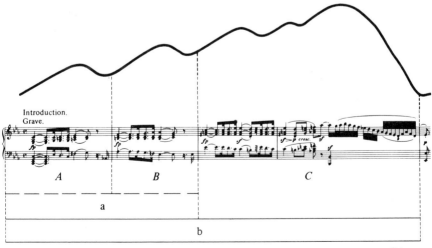

Etc.

The line rises because it comprises a gestalt of movement in which the head and eyes most naturally move from left to right or from lower to higher. The tonal pitch and strength also combine in a gestalt, but it remains a sensory, preceptual gestalt. A line is drawn in the figure and the curve at the edge of the page implies a rise, perhaps because of the way the page is held before us. We speak for example of 'the top of the page'. The thickness of the stroke comprises gestalts of strength, a thin stroke is often called a weak stroke. The 'music and hills' example shows that higher order gestalts can comprise 'things' which conventionally have nothing to do with each other, but are genuine parts of a common reality. What have hills and music in common except rhythm and form? What about content? Does the term 'growth' correspond to a concrete content with gestalt character or does it only furnish abstract tools in our thinking?

A whole book has been written about the gestalts of a line and thereby of symbolic values: Paul Klée, *The Thinking Eye* (1961). When a gestalt synthesises at least two elements into a higher (more comprehensive) unit, and at least one element is from a sensory area and at least one is from a normative and/or assertive area, I will call it an *apperceptive* gestalt. Labour sharing tends to become labour fragmentation in old-fashioned industry and this implies a decline in the superior gestalts, the meaningful things, the purposes – an important class of apperceptive gestalts.

When one's attention is not deliberately focused upon perceptual gestalts, all experience is apperceptive. Its units are apperceptive gestalts, not sensory elements, not intellectual elements. *The distinction between 'facts' and 'values' only emerges from gestalts through the activity of abstract thinking.* The distinction is useful, but not when the intention is to describe the immediate world in which we live, the world of gestalts, the living reality, the only reality known to us.

Gestalts of a very complex character are easily destroyed by attempts to analyse fragments of them consciously. They are very sensitive to introspection. They can scarcely be learned in an ordinary fashion. Some people can distinguish between species of birds in flight at a great distance with great certainty even in dim light. Attempts to formulate precisely the telling characteristics (that is the individual components of the gestalt perception) prove to be futile, however, and can reduce one's ability to distinguish between species under difficult conditions (Lorenz, 1959). We must expect that the application of scientific observation habits to greater and broader fields will lower gestalt abilities if counterforces are not introduced at an early school-age level.

Gestalts bind the I and the not-I together in a whole. Joy becomes, not *my* joy, but *something joyful* of which the I and something else are interdependent, non-isolatable fragments. 'The birch laughed/with the light easy laughter of all birches . . .' This gestalt is a creation which may only incompletely be divided to give an I which projects laughter into a non-laughing birch tree.

The glorification of conventional 'scientific' thought leads to the ridicule of such creations. It tears gestalts asunder.

Quantitative natural sciences must use models for the individual aspects of reality. This intervenes in the gestalt conception of nature as it is formed in day-to-day life. But so-called mythic thought is gestalt thought. Language conforms to the common shared gestalt of a culture. This is the origin of words and expressions for gestalt units consisting of widely diverse components.

The Sherpa people inform us that their great mountain is called 'Tseringma'. We then think that Tseringma is a geographical concept. When we learn that 'Tseringma' is also the name of a wonderful white princess and also 'mother of long life', we believe we have discovered an ambiguity. But no, the word is explicitly stated to be the name for the *same* in both cases. (And are the names of our own culture's geographical features any different?) The unity is said to be 'mythic' and mythic reasoning was characterised as self-contradictory by the young Levy-Bruhl (he later recanted this) and other researchers in the tradition of Auguste Comte. One noted that a stone, which to a European anthropologist was simply a hard stone, was also a spirit, something not hard. This was considered a logical impossibility! If we assume that the name-giving accords with the unit of a gestalt, however, mythic thought becomes more comprehensible. And if the gestalts rather than their fragments are identified as the contents of reality, mythic thought then characterises contents which are largely unavailable in our culture. This type of identification (see chapter 7) is essential in the ontology of Ecosophy T. European anthropologists did not often achieve an experience of the shared gestalts of foreign cultures. Natives were 'alogical'. Gestalt thought furnishes the key to communication between dissimilar cultures. Verbal deterioration of gestalts ('a stone is a stone!') implies deterioration of the culture. This is also true of our own culture.

In non-nomadic cultures, especially agrarian ones, a geographical sense of belonging is crucial. More specifically: rooms, interiors, stairs, farmyards, gardens, nearby trees, bushes – all these things become, on the whole unconsciously, a part of that which is ours, a powerful kind of gestalt. The geographic relationships are of great importance in an appraisal or urbanisation and design and its penetrating transformation of personality.

When a child grows up, the higher order gestalts of the home change gradually. Certain things which were threatening cease to be so as one becomes larger and stronger. Some things which were more distant or mystical move nearer because of the improved ability to cross distances. The essence which remains constitutes the character of belonging, of being at home, an interwoven gestalt diversity with extremely potent symbolic value: A has symbolic value B when A *stands for* B in conceptual experience. (The ancient formula goes '*aliquid stat pro aliquo*'.) Symbolic function must be distinguished from signal function, as A can very well be a signal for B without combining in a gestalt. On the other hand, A has symbolic function in relation to B only if a gestalt is created which includes both A and B. A red light makes us stop, and we *can* develop a gestalt which makes it a symbol for stopping, but more likely, it will continue to be an external association, a *signal* for stopping. In the symbolisation of B through A, A and B are bound together in an internal and not merely external relation.

A description of the home milieu with the evaluative predicates beautiful, good, boring, safe, familiar, etc., sounds artificial to people who haven't been away for a longer period of time, as the milieu gestalts themselves comprise evaluations. A neutral, name-giving description sounds more correct. The point is important as it to some extent explains why many people who live in, and are well-adapted to, a locality do not find it natural to praise nature or the environment. It smacks of tautology – the beauty is 'in', not to be found and talked about.

What remains of our sovereignty? When we go into nature, we often hear that there 'one can be oneself'. This seems to imply that one isn't pressured by nature, one is 'left in peace'. Of course it challenges and presents problems to be solved, but there is an element of voluntarism in the association which is not an essential aspect of social milieux.

In Norwegian rockslide areas, the boundaries can be studied between relations in which nature is pressing, confining, or threatening, and in which it is freeing, expanding, and Self-realising. 'Should we move, or should we stay here where we belong, at home?' Home as a positive, value-weighted place can be defined here in part as the relations with nature. The rockslide relation generates stress and is of course negative. To move from the slide area implies the loss of an appreciable part of one's self – loss of gestalts which comprise 'one's roots', 'my surroundings', 'our surroundings'. New gestalts must be built up at the new location, but after the developmental years it is not possible to recreate the most fundamental gestalts and symbols. One remains a stranger towards or in oneself; or one preserves the old associations, and a self which belongs to somewhere else, an emigrant.

These symbol and gestalt relations are significant because they concern the social cost of centralisation, urbanisation, greater efficiency, and increased mobility. It is easier to take these relations into account in the initial phase of an ecologically responsible policy than in a policy of sustained material growth. For the former, the local community is the natural starting point for political deliberation.

The rising degree of meaninglessness felt by people who have 'done well for themselves' is partially due to such an indifference to symbols. People who have succeeded according to the usual criteria tend to regard everything as a means. In this situation, I believe that therapy to a great extent should be milieu therapy and nature therapy, and that correct milieux have uncharted resources for a meaningful and good life. The concept of nature relevant here implies that nature is not something to be used only as a means for this or any other end, it is something independent which requires our unconditional attention. Ecological psychology and psychiatry take this seriously.

To 'only look at' nature is extremely peculiar behaviour. Experiencing of an environment happens by doing something in it, by living in it, meditating and acting. The very concepts of 'nature' and 'environment/ milieu' cannot be delimited in an ecosophical fashion without reference to interactions between elements of which we partake. Spinoza conceives of knowledge as cognitive acts of understanding/love.

Gestalt formation crosses boundaries between what is conventionally classed as thinking as separated from emotion. The tertiary qualities tend to be separaed from the gestalts and referred to as merely subjective emotions. The overcoming of this prejudice has profound consequences for environmentalism.

7   Emotion, value, and reality
The activism of the ecological movement is often interpreted as *irrational*, as a 'mere' emotional reaction to the *rationality* of a modern Western society. It is ignored that reality as spontaneously experienced binds the emotional and the rational into indivisible wholes, the gestalts. It is often said that to value is nothing more than to express a positive emotional liking for something.

It is not merely in technologically oriented literature that one discovers warnings against emotional emphasis (especially of the religious kind) within the ecological movement. Some ecologists caution against 'religious emotionalism', or 'religious humility in the face of nature' (Watson, 1985). But experience has proven that this very humility is compatible with scientific sobriety. A religious motivation at a deep level can stir up worldwide reaction: Rachel Carson's motivation in writing *The Silent Spring* was partly a feeling of deep humility. Humanity, 'a drop of the stream of life', should not thoughtlessly try to change this stream.

In a discussion of value thinking, it is essential to clarify the relationship between spontaneous feelings, their expression through our vibrant voices, and statements of value or announcement of norms *motivated* by strong feelings but having a clear cognitive function. It is tempting to characterise it as a consequence of value blindness when complaints are made about the expressions of feelings in environmental conflicts. Of course, outbreaks of feeling are not arguments, but evidence that something is felt to be crucial. Examples of statements of feeling: 'It is good to be here', 'NN is a true friend of mine', 'The building is threatening, cold, and hard'.

In these statements, feelings are closely tied to intention. The authors could be mistaken: 'A special atmosphere at the time influenced my statement that it is good to be here.' 'NN can hardly be called a friend – he proved that yesterday.' 'Only a cursory first impression could suggest coldness. I was mistaken.' If the sentences were only reports of feeling, the authors could not conclude later that they were wrong.

The thought content of a statement includes assertive content, and it is useful to clarify the latter by searching for possible mistakes. Naturally, the technique does not work when the statement is then felt to be undeniably correct. In short, value statements are normally made with positive or negative feeling, and it would be nonsensical to ask for neutrality.

It is quite correct that outbreaks of feeling do not supply an adequate guide to a person's system of value. In environmental conflicts, for instance, expressions of love of nature are not enough. What count, or rather, what should count, are the norms and value priorities actively expressed in the conflict. While supporting an infamous hydroelectric project in arctic Norway, the president of the Norwegian parliament said that he loved nature as much as the opposition, but the issues are priorities, and policies – love in action.

Spontaneous positive or negative reactions often do little more than express what a person likes or dislikes. Value standpoints are reflections in relation to such reactions: 'Do I like *that* I like it?' We get a four-way division: positive evaluation – one likes that one likes, or likes that one dislikes; negative evaluation – one dislikes that one likes, or dislikes that one dislikes.

It is thus unwarranted to require that feeling be eliminated in an impartial discussion. If the debate is to proceed in depth, these feelings should be clarified, and made explicit as the need arises. Specific personal, idiosyncratic components must be sorted out if the debate is concerned with more or less general norms. When a statement's assertive and evaluative content is dismissed because the content is strongly emotional, the 'point' is lost. We get a debate which throws the baby out with the bathwater. To avoid this, environmentalists should have training in the explicit voicing of values and norms. Formulate strong, clear expressions of values and norms which the opponent cannot neglect!

8 From emotion to evaluation

Since a main purpose of this work is to relate philosophical and valuative premises with the concrete aspects of ecological problems, I shall draw attention to the following somewhat academic question. Is it proper to say that adjectives which express feelings can be applied to the things themselves, or can such adjectives only characterise the subject who feels? I will describe how the approach is taken within Ecosophy T.

'Look at that high, dark, sombre tree.' Little is gained by placing the darkness or sombreness in the person's consciousness or brain, while the height is allowed to be the tree's own. The tertiary qualities of things have an ontological status which is best expressed by complex relations. These occur between the complex thing-qualities and a field. In symbolic logic, a tree's sombreness S is represented by a relation symbol $S(A,B,C,D, \ldots)$, where A could be location on a map, B location of observer, C emotional status of person, D linguistic competence of the describer. There are formidable number of variables compared to technical height, $h(P,Q)$, where P gives the number of units of height, and Q the type of unit.

Subjectivism need not arise in either S or H, if you are able to specify the exact context in which the quality occurs.

Sombreness is no more 'within' our consciousness than is the height of the tree. This position has been represented within psychology since the time of William James. Consciousness is not some kind of storeroom for the tertiary qualities! As far as the brain goes, it is an inappropriate use of our expensive electron microscopes to look for sombreness there. The qualities can be discovered elsewhere – in the trees, given the relational network.

The identification of primary properties with those of objects them- selves leads to a conception of nature without any of the qualities we experience spontaneously. Now, there is no good reason why we should not look upon such a bleak nature as just a resource, an instrumental value as the cause of our experiences. Every appeal to save parts of nature based on reference to sense-qualities of any kind becomes meaningless. Every passionate appeal that involves deep feelings, empathy, and even identification with natural phenomena must then be ruled out as irrelevant. The sphere of real facts is narrowed down to that of mechanically interpreted mathematical physics.

But this is not the case with the world experienced as a set of concrete contents interpreted through abstract structures. When one is absorbed in contemplation of a concrete, natural thing there is no experience of a subject–object relation. Nor when absorbed in vivid action, whether in movement or not. There is no epistemological ego reaching out to see and understand a tree or an opponent in a fight, or a problem of decision. A tree as experienced spontaneously is always part of a totality, a gestalt. Analysis may discover many structural ingredients. Sometimes an ego-relation, sometimes not. The gestalt is a whole, self-determining and self-reliant. If we call it 'experience of the gestalt', we are easily mislead in a subjectivist direction.

When describing a constellation of gestalt relations it is important not to let the usual stress on the epistemological subject–object distinction dominate the expression. In spontaneous experience there may or may not be any ingredient corresponding to the distinction.

Confrontations between developers and conservers reveal difficulties in experiencing what is *real*. What a conservationist *sees* and experiences *as reality*, the developer typically does not see – and vice versa. A conservationist sees and experiences a forest as a unity, a gestalt, and when speaking of the *heart of the forest*, he or she does not speak about the geometrical centre. A developer sees quantities of trees and argues that a road through the forest covers very few square kilometres compared to the whole area of trees, so why make so much fuss? And if the conservers insist, he will propose that the road does not touch the *centre* of the forest. The *heart* is then saved, he may think. *The difference between the antagonists is one rather of ontology than of ethics.* They may have fundamental ethical prescriptions in common, but apply them differently because they see and experience reality so differently. They both use the single term 'forest', but referring to different entities.

The gestalts 'the heart of the forest', 'the life of the river', and 'the quietness of the lake' are essential parts of reality for the conservationist. To the conservationist, the developer seems to suffer from a kind of radical blindness. But one's ethics in environmental questions are based largely on how one sees reality. If the developer could see the wholes, his ethics might change. There is no way of making him eager to save a forest as long as he retains his conception of it as merely a set of trees. His charge that the conservationist is motivated by subjective feelings is firmly based on his view of reality. He considers his own positive feelings towards development to be based on objective reality, not on feelings. And as long as society is largely led by developers, he need not be passionate in his utterances. It is the struggling minorities who tend to be passionate rather than those who follow the main stream.

It is, I think, important in the philosophy of environmentalism to *move from ethics to ontology and back*. Clarification of differences in ontology may contribute significantly to the clarification of different policies and their ethical basis.

In an analysis that begins with concrete contents, the is–ought and fact–value dichotomies don't look quite as they did from where Hume started, namely at factual and value *affirmations*. Expressions of concrete contents are designations, not declarative sentences.

Expressions of the kind 'object x has value y' immediately lead to the question: Given an object x, how do I *assess* its value y? If we start with designations of concrete contents, for instance 'delicious, red tomato to be eaten at once' or 'repugnant, rotten tomato' the evaluative terms are there from the very beginning of our analysis. And there is no separatable tomato to value!

J. Baird Callicott (1982) says that 'ecology changes our values by changing our concepts of the world and of ourselves in relation to the world. It reveals new relations among objects which, once revealed, stir our ancient centers of moral feeling.' (p. 174) The stirring is part of a gestalt, and as such not to be isolated from the 'objects'. What I have done is to try to explicate what kind of change in concept of the world and status of the subject is at issue.

Between the items of the world conceived as contents in the form of gestalts there are internal structural relations, but they do not add to the set of contents. And we are free to conceptualise them in different ways. The ecosystem concept is used to describe abstract structures, and the deep ecology movement is to some extent concerned with abstract structures. The importance of abstract structural considerations cannot be overestimated, but, like maps, their function is not to add to the territory, the contents, but to make it more visible. The whole Earth is not the Earth *plus* its maps.

So the transition from emotion to evaluation is not so much an actual motion, but merely a shift in emphasis based on an acceptance of feeling as a basic motivation for our diverse and actual world-views. It then remains to investigate just what feelings we can accept as guiding 'stars' to justify our actions, and how to perceive these lights in a coherent system that articulates and explains our beliefs so as to translate them to action.

3

Fact and value; basic norms

1   Announce your value-priorities forcefully

A deep ecological movement envisages a shift in basic attitudes from the dominant paradigm in leading industrial societies. Norms and values again and again have to be contrasted, not with any explicit philosophy which justifies the dominant paradigm (that does not seem to exist) but with its practice.

Therefore, we need an elaboration of our norms and values which correspond to the shift of basic attitudes. This requires the tentative systematisation of those norms and values. This is the theoretical background which sets the stage for this chapter, where philosophically problematic topics will be discussed, bearing in mind their importance to practical ecological debate. I will discuss exactly the same subjects in different ways, because readers with diverse backgrounds have been found to require different approaches to the same topics.

Not everything can be proven – an old thought first emphasised by Aristotle. The string of proofs on any definite occasion must commence somewhere. The first unproven links in such chains of argument are called 'axioms' or 'postulates'. Those which are proven by means of these postulates are called 'theorems'. History of mathematics and logic shows a diversity of systems, but they all have starting points beyond which they do not penetrate. They also have *rules*, some deduced from other rules, but at least one must be simply postulated, without any justification whatsoever.

When value priorities are traced back to the very fundamentals, the validity of the latter can then be questioned. Evidence *always* ultimately rests at any time upon something which is neither proven nor provable, explained nor explainable.

But are not value axioms necessarily more subjective than other evaluations? The situation is in principle no different from that of axioms and basic rules in mathematics. Their appearance without proof on page 1 of a textbook does not render them more subjective. If that were the case, how could one explain the fact that theorems deduced using the 'subjective' axioms and rules of proof can be intersubjective and objectively valid?

In science as in all other fields of communication, we must start somewhere, with explicit rules, norms, implicit valuations and plain assertions. We can say with Martin Luther 'Here I stand, and can do naught else!' We can add: 'It is as thus I see and experience the world!' And the words 'as thus I see and experience' could be parenthesised, bracketed. Face to face with our antagonist, we already know that it is a particular person who presents a view. Why then add 'I think' or 'as I experience it' when expressing evaluations? We don't say 'the bus leaves at two o'clock as I experience the bus'. Some norms and evaluations are just as obvious as bus schedules. Let us forget the modest 'I think that . . .' or 'I cannot but think that . . .' when it is a case of well thought out personal evaluations! *Away with all forms of norm hypochondria!*

But any increase in normative frankness should be accompanied simultaneously by an elimination of absolutisms, arrogance, and 'eternalism' with regard to validity in time and in social and physical space.

To accept a particular norm as a fundamental, or *basic norm*, does not imply an assertion of infallibility nor claim that the acceptance of a norm is independent of its concrete consequences in practical situations. It is *not an attempt to dominate or manipulate*.

As with descriptive statements, we should retain a *principle of revisability*. The cult of obstinacy in the realm of norms renders calm debate practically impossible. Generally, the acceptance of a given basic norm, for example the general repudiation of the use of violence, is *motivated* by specific instances in which the use of violence has been unconditionally rejected. Beginning here, reflection upon other possible situations leads to norm generalisation. Logically speaking, the argument proceeds in the opposite direction, from the generalities to particulars. One *justifies* the specific instances in the light of the basic norm, while the acceptance of the norm is motivated by experiences and reflection associated with the specific instances. A change of derived norms is both logically justifiable and of motivational character, while changes in basic norms are *purely motivational*.

Perhaps we, in our society, and perhaps people in most societies, are influenced by our early helplessness as children when powerful grown-ups say 'you shall!', 'you ought!', or 'you must!'. Later opposition to such manners of speech may be spreading to all straightforward evaluations, even the more neutral: 'it is *right* to . . .'. This is especially true for evaluations presented from the rostrums of our schools and universities. Those present may be reliving an awkward aspect of their childhoods, feeling themselves manipulated and exposed to authoritarian influence.

It seems that many scientists try to avoid direct influence by substituting descriptions for explanatory sentences. But if I were to replace 'it is right to' by 'according to Norwegian law, it is right to' I can still be exerting an influence. Restricting oneself to descriptive statements does not prevent possible influence; on the contrary, it is often made more intensive. The non-normative: 'The critical smoker smokes NN's tobacco' is perhaps more suggestive than 'Smoke NN's tobacco!'

An objection from philosophical quarters has been that impartial discussion has to stop when direct norm collision arises: further advancement is not possible. Absolutism or a lack of training in normative debate may be responsible. This will, especially in combination with non-violence in communication, ensure that the discussion can proceed constructively.

If one admits that evaluations can be substantiated, the situation is no different from that with directly descriptive (non-normative) collisions. 'According to Norwegian law, . . .'. 'No, Norwegian law does not say that . . .'. The disagreement lies in the description of Norwegian law. 'It is right to steal bread from a store if one is very hungry and penniless!' 'No, that cannot be universalised!' In the two preceding statements, attempts are made at substantiation. In both cases basic methodologies are assumed which cannot themselves be substantiated without circular reasoning.

In other words, the assertion that 'the continuation of impartial discussion is impossible in open norm conflicts' is invalid. It can be difficult, but that is also the case with all kinds of disagreement. This is true in mathematics, physics, and all other areas in which such disagreement arises.

If a speaker's norm pronouncement 'It is right to deny x' is answered from the audience 'It is not right to deny x', there is nothing to get in a fuss about. The situation begs to be debated. A debate requires clarification of value priorities. Formulations of the type 'I think that . . .', 'As I feel . . .' may also give rise to debate, but often of a more dishonest, veiled character. There is less face-to-face confrontation, more sneaking about. One doesn't want to hurt anyone, nor stand up and confess anything. It is advantageous to state one's position in a way as direct and concrete as possible.

Care in the expression of norms is closely associated with their directive role for action. Action confrontation develops from norm confrontation, and vice versa. I reach for the gold bar, as does another. If we each regard our position as ethically responsible, the conflict-resolving strategy of Gandhi can be resorted to. We retain our grip on the bar of gold but simultaneously converse with our opponent. Even in such a direct action, there is no limit to meaningful interaction.

What is the relevance of the foregoing pages to the deep ecological movement? Members of the bureaucracy, politicians and their scientific and technical advisers in questions of 'the environment' have a work load and responsibility of such a sort that they search for arguments exclusively based on 'facts'. Anything that does not fit into the established framework is easily felt as a threat. Anything smacking of straightforward valuation is eliminated.

The goals of the deep ecological movement cannot be understood, much less reached, without the forceful announcement of value priorities within wider frameworks.

The most common counterarguments among the powerful groups mentioned consist characteristically in referring to public opinion: the public asks for higher wages, lower taxes, more gadgets, longer vacations, a higher standard of living, less unemployment, more medicines: short-term gratifications!

In social conflicts, the antagonists naturally form stereotyped pictures of each other. Those more or less responsible for detrimental decisions from the point of view of deep ecology tend to have unfavourable and strange opinions about the supporters, especially the activists, of the movement. And the latter tend to have rather stereotyped opinions about the former. The biased opinions may strengthen motivation within the opposing camps, but it makes communication distorted and is not in line with the principles of nonviolent conflict resolution. Openmindedness and fair play could overcome this difficulty.

Earlier in this century, many people believed that politics in a highly developed industrial society would assume the character of – social technology: one could *calculate* what would be advisable. 'The end of ideology' was a powerful slogan. 'Politicians' would die out as a race, and we would get *experts* – administrative, economical, technical – in their place. Decisions would then be made based upon calculations far beyond the average man's capacity.

The faith in the technocracy is still alive and well, and often the argument 'but it is only a technical question' assumes that we live in a society where 'progress itself' is led and must be led technocratically.

Public discussion of ultimate values is simply not thought to be necessary – events ride on their own inertia.

Few things have had a more destructive effect upon candid speaking, and more generally upon personal engagement in the ecological movement, than the claim that 'there's no sense trying to stop progress'. 'Development' and 'progress' are thought of in those terms of techno-industrial growth, and the change to fewer and larger organisation units, centralisation, and ever more 'efficient' processes: 'technical development necessitates ever more and larger airports'; 'progress requires larger industrial units'; 'development necessitates bigger units of government'.

It is interesting but disturbing to note that certain techno-industrial sides to existence are now accepted as unalterable and objective. We don't say 'progress requires that slums be eliminated, there's no sense to try to stop it!' Slums may be eliminated by the time we arrive at commercial space flight, but why do the words 'development' and 'progress' have so little appeal here? Or: we do not say that 'progress requires that each and every one of us has access to nature and agreeable milieux for our children. There's no sense fighting against progress.' Or: 'Progress requires a change from constitutional democracy to a democracy of true living together (*samliv*)'. Just when do we choose to make use of this term 'progress'? Why not speak of progress in life quality?

The strength of the deep ecology movement depends upon the willingness and ability of its supporters to force fact-dependent experts who underpin environmental decision into discussions in terms of values and priorities (Naess, 1986a).

2   Total systems; norm system models in pyramidal form

Systéma is a combination of *syn*, together, and a form of the Greek verb *histémi*, I set up. To systematise is to make something fit together as a whole. In the following, the intention is to get many particulars to fit together, to suggest a total view. The constellations we have to deal with are so intimately associated that the particular components cannot be isolated without resulting in appreciably different constellation characteristics. In other words: the constellations are of dovetailed units. The tendency to see things in context, systematisation *as defined here*, characterises ecological thought. Hence the slogan 'everything is interconnected' suggests the necessity to articulate total views, everything being in principle relevant for every decision made.

'System' is, therefore, here a word with positive value connotations; not negative as in much contemporary philosophical thought reacting against the great system-builders (Aquinas, Descartes, Spinoza, Hegel, etc.). But to encourage systematising does not imply encouraging system dogmatism – the tendency to herald one system as the sole truth, and eternal truth. A system is a structured assemblage of statements, all provisional and tentative. An all-encompassing philosophical system is meant to express all *fundamental (or basic)* premises for thought and action and to suggest some areas of concrete application. This is a minimum. Point for point, the system cannot be extended down to *all* decisions. Jeremy Bentham elaborated his political philosophy to include the preferred colour for a voting box! Other decisions might be more important.

The rules for impartial debate require standpoints on questions of interpretation, definition and clarification. If more than one assertion is presented one must answer for their mutual consistency. In all cases, the consequences of a particular assertion must be envisaged. Furthermore, the path 'backwards', from conclusions to premises, must be visible, enabling one to trace the chains of argument which lead to the assertion. Possibilities for empirical testing must be dealt with when an assertion has at least one empirical component. One must be prepared to assume responsibility for the results or consequences of basing one's actions on the assertion.

Relevance for supporters of the deep ecology movement? They are trained in discussing facts, less in discussion of value, still less in systematic explication of value priorities, and still less in carefully connecting concrete environmental conflict facts with strong basic philosophical and religious positions – their own ultimate premises. These are mostly quite compatible with those of the opponents. What is needed to convince them, or at least to make them a little softer in their resistance, is to actualise the debate on priorities, especially *long-range* priorities – again and again inviting them to state their positions on long-range values, deeply seated values and, even more important, norms.

What about some of their reactions, 'you are too dogmatic, you are simplifying too much', 'you believe too strongly in your system'?

In debate this means that you, if you feel like me, should courageously announce where you stand, but even then full of humility in relation to truth. Admit confusion, but insist that even the confused has to act – even an abstention from taking part has political consequences. Remember: there is something called 'criminal neglect'. Better be active and join the battle. Your opponents have mostly high regard for the combination of personal honesty and integrity with attitudinal admission of frailty and fallibility. But to discuss values in public requires training, some of it (and of course only some of it) being theoretical.

Within life and society, new and unpredictable considerations arise and clash constantly. The situations to be judged are incessantly shifting. Our hypotheses on the effects of our actions and policies, be they public or private, will be more or less mistaken. Norm collisions are inevitable. *Absolute consistency through time is illusory*: you change, things change. Should we consistently recommend an immediate stop to the polluting production of 'useless' articles, or should we consistently first establish new jobs in the vicinity for the workers to be affected by the ceasing of production? Perhaps neither? But we need general guidelines!

Our opinions as to what is or *ought* to be done are highly dependent upon our *hypotheses* as to how the world is organised. Applied to ecological relationships, this implies that our norms are dependent upon our beliefs regarding the interdependency relations within the biosphere.

A set of norms can be arranged in *pyramidal form*, or more precisely, in the form of a frustum of a pyramid with a broad base and a narrow top. The non-derived norms are placed at the top (see figure 3.1). Though this is a useful conceptual device, it can be problematic if one analogises to structures or organisation or implementation: *remember the pyramid is only for purpose of logical derivation*! The upper norms are not to be considered as ethically superseding. We make use of the pyramidal systematisation, but only with our revised conceptual determination of the key terms of altitude and priority. This must be understood fully, so as to avoid misunderstandings of the type that Fritjof Capra (*The Turning Point*, 1982) might criticise – if the image of a 'tree of norms' with the top level of norms as the trunk or stem seems more appropriate, then by all means use it.

Each norm has its particular position. The top norms may concern liberty, equality and fraternity, love for one's neighbour, or the search for truth. All other norms and evaluations within the field to be systematised are then conceived as derived norms in relation to the fundamental ones. The derivation may be called logical. Other uses of the term 'derivation', such as historical or generative derivation (seeking origins) are to be avoided here.

When a value is accented as a means in a given systematisation, this does not *imply* that it lacks *intrinsic value*, but merely that any such prospective intrinsic value does not appear in the systematisation. To illustrate: from 'Choose that which lasts longest!' and 'Honesty lasts longest!' follows (with tolerable logic) 'Be honest!' But the derivation as such does not contradict the intrinsic value of honesty.

A norm which is valid *only* as a means to the fulfilment of another more basic norm is called a *purely instrumental norm*. A *genuine norm* is one which has validity independent of means/goal relations. Its realisation has intrinsic value over and above any possible means value. Being a genuine norm does not preclude its having, in addition, means value. Honesty can be thought to have both intrinsic value and in addition means value in the realisation of the many norms in our social existence. 'Be honest!' is then both a genuine, basic norm and an instrumental norm.

If exam and grade giving norms are regarded as purely instrumental in relation to norms of cooperation, fraternity, and love, the latter occupy a more basic level or plane in the ends/means pyramid. A norm conflict between 'Help your friends!' and 'Don't help anyone in an exam!' is then resolved by ignoring the exam norm.

Remember that the comparison is only in respect to *logical derivation*, never ethical or moral priority. If a basic norm is 'Never use another person simply as a means!' (Kant) and people are divided into yellow, white, red, and black (a rather curious classification), the result is four derived norms: 'Never use a *yellow* person', 'Never use a *white* person', etc. It would be absurd to accord the norms a lesser ethical or other validity because of their derived character. Another example: if we compare 'Do not kill' with 'Do not kill your mother', the first has logical priority because from it we can derive the second, but not the other way round. The second has ethical priority: if somebody accepting the first is tempted to kill his dog *or* his mother the ethical situation should be clear.

Derivations of practical interest require statements concerning actual conditions in the world, our actual inclinations, and much more. Statistically, statements of so-called facts in verbalised ideologies are in an overwhelming majority of the cases made in relation to normative statements. Hitler's *Mein Kampf*, to mention an unpleasant, but central example, consists for the most part of statements which have a descriptive content, hypotheses about Jews. But these are clearly very peculiar hypotheses. They must be accepted or else the entire construction of the book collapses. As most of us today do not accept any of these hypotheses, we are unable to accept Hitler's norms on how to treat Jews.

Enthusiastic participants in the ecological movement may subject everyone else to a veritable hailstorm of norms. Many assume the form of slogans, maxims, and mottoes. They are understandably imprecise, and can appear dogmatic, narrow-minded, or fanatical to the uninitiated. ('Give Los Angeles back to the Condors!!') It is therefore important that those who use them more or less mercilessly are aware that such slogans are in principle meaningless and unjustifiable outside of an extensive normative and descriptive conceptual situation. Even if we are capable of explaining the presupposed normative system, we must be aware of the narrow limits of how much we can communicate in a given situation.

For example, an excellent *slogan* suggests that private cars be replaced by bicycles as a mode of transportation to and from work. But to proclaim to the world a general *norm* 'Bicycle, rather than drive, to work!' entails a hair-raising unreason. If the subject were to be systematised, many factors would have to be taken in to account – varying conditions in hundreds of local communities, various climatic conditions, varying possibilities for public transportation, of course distances involved, pollution of the cyclist's milieu, the dangers of cycling in heavy traffic. In some instances, a changeover to bicycling might mean increased resource consumption – say, if the bicyclist took an oil-heated sauna after each trip. Or such a transition might sabotage the use of public transportation. If one attempts to systematise a conflict-ridden subject, the formulations must be precise and carefully weighed, and the pretentions of the summary of norms and hypotheses must be clearly stated, along with its deficiencies, e.g. inevitable lack of completeness!

It is most advantageous to the ecological movement that as few as possible norms should be purely instrumental. When discussing bicycles, not only the intrinsic values to be obtained should be mentioned, such as being closer to outdoor life, but also the innocent joy involved in pushing a bicycle pedal instead of a gas pedal. Remember that norms against pollution often have a tiresome instrumental character: 'Give a hoot! Don't pollute!' (Woodsy Owl in advertisements of the US National Park Service through the 1970s). A radical way of avoiding this norm is for instance indirect actions against the use of beverage cans. But proclaiming, 'Don't use beverage cans!' is merely the substitution of one strictly instrumental norm for another.

If the norms relevant to particular points were not related to one another, norm conflicts would arise at every turn. None of the norms can apply absolutely or maximally – each of them must take account of or adjust to all the others. Extreme norms against resource consumption would stop many activities such as ecological research and thus hinder the possibilities for responsible global ecopolitics. Extreme norms for local self-reliance would mean that one might achieve no more than providing for oneself alone. There are mediating and qualifying factors on all norms.

The preceding examples illustrate the system context for ecological subjects. When particular norms are isolated and universalised, the result is not ecopolitically responsible politics, but a chaos of incompatible policies.

Unfortunately, there is a tendency to maintain that the ultimate consequences of a norm are unveiled by isolating and universalising it. Those who defend abiding by a norm *as though it were not a fragment of a totality* are praised for being logical and consistent!

Ecological deliberation takes place in the widest possible scope for thought. Therefore attempts at articulation result in the emergence of a philosophical system. Even assuming the least possible dogmatic attitude, say, simply posing questions, one builds on hypotheses and norms. Otherwise we could not formulate specific questions at all.

For each participant in the debate, the starting point is twofold: our own system or world-view and that or those views we find to be meaningful in our surroundings. Our actions take place in a social field and we must and will consider the evaluations and the interpretations of the facts, or the lack of knowledge thereof which reigns in a particular context.

Social philosophy, as it appears in public debate and in particular as it appears in political resolution making, takes a pyramidal form, but the mid-section of the pyramid is generally extremely disorganised or even vacant. In other words: the logical derivations of concrete decisions from the basic norms are often shaky. The road which should lead from the basic principles of democracy, freedom, justice, and well-being to concrete policies for the realisation of these principles is as uncharted as a back-country track! A government statement may include important ecopolitical principles, but they often do not seem to have any bearing on decisions. The more concrete policy statement which mentions specific plans for action does not usually concur with the principles, but follows the well-travelled routes of past political processes.

A system pyramid with hollow mid-section can be dramatically illustrated (figure 3.1). No lines of derivation go all the way from principles to practical decisions.

An example of a complete lack of articulation of the mid-section can be found in the current curriculum plan for Norwegian elementary schools. It states that schools are to be the means for giving the pupils an attitude

Figure 3.1

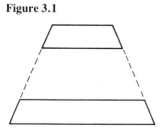

to life which revolves around truth, honesty, faithfulness, cooperation and charity. But no attempt is made to demonstrate how this objective can best be obtained. Can pupils become charitable through studying things, subjects? Are the examinations firmly connected with these values? Why cannot pupils cooperate during exams? Why not teamwork?

Implicit in this curriculum is a conception of schools which is so narrow that it is essentially confined to presenting subjects to groups of pupils in competition with one another. A great number of norms and hypotheses are mercifully hidden from critical views. They belong to the middle section of the pyramid. The top is without them floating in thin air. If a very wide definition is used, a fruitful school debate may be possible, with a much greater interested public.

3   Ecological system thinking

As a wholly incomprehensible number of interactions can occur in an ecosystem, the use of methodological models plays a decisive role, particularly those expressible mathematically. A *selection* of the relations within the ecosystem is specified. The selection simulates 'reality' to *some extent*. A principal concept is 'system state at time t'. Its state is described in a given number of respects, each characterised by a set of variables.

Progress in system ecology is dependent upon the modelling of systems which are built up in levels of scope and detail. For example, one can study and predict how a caribou population is related to and dependent upon the number of predators and certain other factors without studying the individual caribou's relationship to particular predators. Studies of the latter take place at a lower stage in the system of interactions. Similarly, one can study the life and death of a particular animal without studying its individual cells. A cell can be studied in many ways without studying the chemical structure of every single molecule in the cell. One speaks of *planes of integration* where the behaviour of a set of complex system components can be studied without necessitating the study of each component's subcomponents.

The principal point is that *all these studies are fragmentary*: they select and isolate relational nets through abstract analysis. One does not ever attempt to study the total net. According to our intuition, though, there is something we call reality which is in some sense a unity. The idea of totality cannot be discounted.

The fragmentary studies are satisfactory only because the questions posed are fragmentary. The questions are fragmentary because we cannot study everything simultaneously. In our daily work, and our interdisciplinary cooperation, we must, somehow, split up considerations of totality. *But the synthesis must be carried out each time an ecopolitical decision is to be taken*: we are then responsible for all aspects or sides to the question at hand.

Let us consider some of the relatively extreme standpoints on the question of the relationships between wholes and components of wholes – standpoints often called 'holistic' which particularly emphasise the whole.

A living cell can only be considered superficially to be a thing with qualities, as more thorough descriptions lead to field thinking in which the attempt to delimit the cell 'itself' in time, space, or other dimensions is dropped. The entire cell unit's dynamics extend far beyond its observable boundary. Electrical charges and chemical processes occur over an extensive area so that it is meaningless to isolate 'the cell itself' from an environment. The cell walls are not independent of their surroundings – they are not walls in a commonsense way. We are dealing with an 'all-pervasive network' of forces and interactions (Weiss, 1971).

As presented here, it is clear that the whole/fraction distinction is not appropriate for the living cell. The fractions cannot be isolated. Nothing can be causally isolated. Hence the slogan 'The whole is more than the sum of its parts'. This beautifully illustrates gestalt thinking.

The system theoreticians in biology are contributing to a change in the customary conceptual structuring of the relationship between human beings and their surroundings.

(1) A human being is not a thing in an environment, but a juncture in a relational system without determined boundaries in time and space.

(2) The relational system connects humans, as organic systems, with animals, plants, and ecosystems conventionally said to be within or outside the human organism.

(3) Our statements concerning things and qualities, fractions and wholes cannot be made more precise without a transition to field and relational thinking.

About his 'proposed views concerning the general nature of "the totality of all that is"' David Bohm says that at 'any particular moment in this development [of reality] each such set of views that may arise will constitute at most a *proposal*. It is not to be taken as an assumption about what the final truth is supposed to be, and still less a *conclusion* concerning the nature of such truth. Rather, this proposal becomes itself an *active factor* in the totality of existence which includes ourselves as well as the objects of our thoughts and experimental investigations.' (Bohm, 1980,

p. 213). The limitation of what we are doing when asserting our hypotheses and announcing our norms does not reduce our right and our obligation to assert and to announce.

The quotation is useful in making it clear that the work with the 'unfolding' of a view of 'the totality of all that is' is itself a part, a subordinate gestalt, of that very totality. We are when active in unfolding our views creative in shaping and creating 'what there is' at any moment.

4   The search for ultimate goals: pleasure, happiness, or perfection?

'Saltdal wants nature – not hydroelectric power' – front-page headline in Norway. The Saltdalians probably meant that to have both would be best, but what if it were a question of one or the other? 'Pristine nature is of more importance to us than any conceivable concession fees. There is unanimity about this here in the township.'

If material standard of living and general affluence no longer suffice as principal objectives for all politics, what can replace them? Well-being? Quality of life? Free nature as such is neither well-being nor quality of life. Therefore it must be *something which is attained* through protection of free nature – perhaps something which serves well-being or quality of life? But what are the qualities of 'the good life', and which of these should be given priority if they cannot all be attained, at least not simultaneously.

In the following I will deal with some very elementary considerations to illustrate what may be called 'the basic norm' of the problem: what can be established as the greatest common goal, to which all personal and social endeavours should be directed?

Three types of goals which have been and will continue to be mentioned in this connection may be roughly indicated by three well-known terms (table 3.1).

The wise man cannot merely be aware of the consequences of the basic principles these words suggest, but must also think clearly about them and decide how to apply them.

The ecosopher must thoroughly think out, and also 'feel out', what he or she actually wants, not simply as a personal matter, but in a social and ecospheric perspective. The question here is not one of drawing the consequences of a viewpoint already essentially given, but one of clarification of attitudes, of 'finding oneself', not in isolation, but in deep connection to all that surrounds.

The realisation of centrally placed norms in the norm array is dependent upon faith and insight into *how* this can occur, given particular milieu factors. When a human being or a group is convinced about the merits of

Table 3.1

Goal	Norm
(1) pleasure	pleasure!
(2) happiness	happiness!
(3) perfection	perfection!

one avenue over another, appreciable amounts of energy are freed. Characteristic words here are glow (*gløt*), passion, intense engagement, fervour in pursuit of the goal. When someone is passionately engaged in something, other worries and sufferings recede. All defeats are met with a fresh head of steam. If the fervour dies down, however, innumerable anxieties crop up in consciousness. The joys of life become more and more passive. The client and patient becomes the idea. As patients we are served, we are *guaranteed* goods and services.

With the philosophy and psychology of mountaineering in mind, the following 'equation' was propagated and published by me in 1965:

$$W = \frac{G^2}{P_b + P_m}$$

W – well-being
G – glow (passion, fervour)
P_b – bodily pains
P_m – mental pains

The equation is meant to say that the level of well-being is proportional to the *square* of the level of glow. So, with sufficient glow, any amount of pain is overcome.

The usefulness of the equation (which of course could be made much more sophisticated in the milieu of mathematicians and psychologists) depends on its ability to make people try to find out what they deeply and eagerly want and thus to make them risk some pain and discomfort in its pursuit. It is perhaps overestimated to what extent people try to avoid physical or mental pain at any cost. Characteristically, what people then find that could make everything meaningful is *not* pleasure or cosy happiness, but something beyond, something that *might* have such happiness as a corollary, but not with any certainty.

As can be expected, some people react against this 'equation' because they think quantification of such important issues is a bad thing. The equation is nevertheless acceptable, *with a smile*, and that is important.

Basic norms associated with the three listed possible goals can be formulated:

(1) Choose that alternative for action which gives most pleasure! ('hedonism')

Immediately, questions crop up. Most for whom? Most for myself? For Norway? For developed and developing countries? For every living being? For our generation? In the long run? Immediately? – *Any* kind of pleasure?

What if an alternative gives most pleasure, but also some pain? How can the pain be introduced into the calculation? The most romantic response: the attainment of maximal pleasure can be consummated most advantageously by seeking death immediately thereafter. Pessimists – Schopenhauer and others – prefer negatively phrased norms which speak of pain rather than pleasure, e.g. 'choose that alternative which gives least pain!'

Every answer to the above questions gives rise to yet other questions: how do we *find out* what gives most pleasure? What is the appropriate methodology? And, what if an alternative which entails little effort will in all likelihood provide a certain moderate pleasure, while another promises greater and more intensive pleasure, but entails difficult times and a low chance of real success?

Pleasure (or pain) as an obvious and isolatable experience seems to be confined to strictly limited physiological and spiritual functions. A pin-prick on the leg, a swallow of cold water in the heat. A pin-prick near the eye, however, often causes anxiety, even panic if one sees the needle approach. We experience a negatively laden total situation, perhaps of some few seconds duration. The pain is next to nothing, but the situation is unpleasant.

Technocracy and hedonistic philosophy may be said to have certain characteristics which make them good bedfellows. For example, in certain medical circles, it is maintained that our endeavours to eliminate pain have gone too far. The elimination of pain by means of technical aids is an implicit norm which the technology of our cultures seeks to fulfil. But this may destroy good health, thereby bringing about suffering (in a wide sense) which is worse than a given dose of pain.

(2) What about happiness, well-being, and, as an extreme, *joy à la hilaritas* in Spinoza's terminology. These expressions relate, as understood here, to enduring total situations. Gestalt thinking necessarily leads from the pleasure norm to such a happiness norm. Well-being as opposed to, for instance, depression concerns wholes.

'Seek happiness!' is now and then interpreted as 'seek success', defining 'success' as material output or welfare and therefore independent of emotional life. As understood here, happiness, or well-being, has a dimension of positive emotion, primarily of joy.

We can in our context define happiness or well-being as a positively laden, enduring total situation or state. After running twenty miles, a marathon runner *can* still feel good, happy, even joyous although all his sensations are variants of pain. If the runner does much better than expected, he or she feels that something momentous is happening. As a gestalt, the total situation is positive, though a particular fragment may be negative, e.g. the runner might have lost the race, or he might be totally exhausted.

(3) The Spinozist teaching on human nature seems to contend that increase in perfection and joy merge into one totality, a gestalt where the increase is internally related to joy. Joy as a sensation is merely an abstract and perfection is nothing more than an unfolding of that which lies deepest in human nature (see Spinoza, *Ethics* (1949), 3PllSch, and Naess (1975)).

This leads us to a large class of basic norms, the norms of perfection, the term being interpreted on the basis of a main connotation of the Latin verb *perficere*, carry through, do the job as intended. Many tend to set up performance, or achievement as basic values. 'Happiness? Well-being? No, I *want* something. I may become happy if I find it, but maybe not.'

Sir Samuel White Baker was determined to discover the source of the Nile. Suffering was lightly borne, and the thought of his probable death on the trip did not change his attitude. Others have other norms of perfection: to get rich and admired; to base actions on generosity or love; to be just; to carry out one's duties to the best of one's ability; to sacrifice oneself completely for something.

The so-called existentialists assume important implicit norms of perfection. Their answers to 'What is mankind?', 'What is the specific human condition?' are formulated in a descriptive way but *function* as norms. If an existentialist says that something is genuinely human and something else is ungenuine, the statements seem, for them, to be norms.

The perfectionist can value pleasure and happiness highly, but refuse to regard them as ultimate goals. In a purely tactical light, there is little sense in a continual 'bringing to consciousness' of pleasure and happiness norms even when they are posited as basic: the blinkers of self-centredness ('Am I happy?') pave the way for passivity and depression. The pleasure norms in particular have a tendency to lead to complacency and the exclusion of all activities tinged by unpleasantness or pain. The perfection theoreticians maintain that well-being normally results from an active life, even though one's activity can entail much pain.

There are always certain key phrases which indicate the most fundamental goals for further development of a society. It is implied that the individual members can best realise the 'good life' through that development. In Scandinavia, the phrases *well-being, welfare,* and *standard of living* have filled the bill. Within the deep ecology movement, the phrase *quality of life* now has a central place.

But like the existentialists' 'authenticity of life' it leaves very much open. How does it relate to the three main sorts of supreme goals, pleasure, happiness, and perfection? I do not see how we can avoid falling into the third category. This means that personal quality of life somehow is proportional to the degree to which the personal basic objectives (not defined in terms of pleasure and happiness) are reached. The quality of life in a community must then be defined in terms of the quality of life of its members. Again there is a great openness for different conceptions of the objectives, one's own way (*svamārga*).

5   Self-realisation as top norm and key term for an ultimate goal

In the systematisation of Ecosophy T, the term 'Self-realisation' is used to indicate a kind of perfection. It is conceived as a process, but also as an ultimate goal, in a rather special usage of 'ultimate'. It is logically ultimate in a systematic exposition of Ecosophy T. The term includes personal and community self-realisation, but is conceived also to refer to an unfolding of reality as a totality.

Vagueness and ambiguity of important key terms like 'Self-realisation' make derivation in any exact sense impossible. It is therefore necessary to clarify which direction of interpretation, or, better, precisation, is chosen. But in spite of the importance of this one single term, it may not be so wise to assign to it too definite a meaning. The interpretation of the top norm sentence and of the others should be a continuous process, where tentative modification at one level interacts with tentative semantical modifications at others.

The main semantical device used to adapt the term 'self-realisation' to ecosophy T is to precise it in three different directions:

T_0 – self-realisation
T_1 – ego-realisation
T_2 – self-realisation (with lower case s)

T₃ – Self-realisation (with capital S)

This last *kind of* concept is known in the history of philosophy under various names: 'the universal self', 'the absolute', 'the *ātman*', etc. Many Indo-European languages use terms corresponding to the English 'self' in analogous ways.

In the prevalent individualistic and utilitarian political thinking in Western industrial states, the terms 'self-realisation', 'self-expression', 'self-interest' are used for what is above called 'ego-realisation'. One stresses the ultimate and extensive incompatibility of the interests of different individuals. 'One man's bread is another man's dead.'* In opposition to this trend there are others which are based on the hypothesis of increased compatibility with increased maturity of the individuals. Ecosophy T leans heavily on such ideas, excellently developed in the *Ethics* of Spinoza. His ideas of 'self-preservation' (or, rather, self-perseveration) cannot develop far without sharing joys and sorrows with others, or, more fundamentally, without the development of the narrow ego of the small child into the comprehensive structure of a self that comprises all human beings. The deep ecology movement, as many earlier movements before it, takes a step further and asks for the development of a deep identification (see chapter 7) of individuals with all life forms.

The development of life forms, especially since the Cambrian era, shows an extreme degree of expansion of life space and a corresponding diversity of forms making use of different climatic and other conditions. There is no merely passive adaptation, no mere self-preservation in any narrow sense. There is rather a 'creative evolution' in the sense of Henri Bergson, a creativeness expressive of the formidable *élan vital*. The term self-expression or -realisation is therefore better suited than self-preservation. If the term 'self' is felt to be unfitting, we can concentrate on life-unfolding or life-expansion. But then the essential relation between self and Self is lost.

Inspired by Kant, one may speak of 'beautiful' and of 'moral' action. Moral actions are motivated by acceptance of a moral law, and manifest themselves clearly when acting against inclination. A person acts beautifully when acting benevolently from inclination. Environment is then not felt to be something strange or hostile which we must unfortunately adapt ourself to, but something valuable which we are *inclined to* treat with joy and respect, and the overwhelming richness of which we are inclined to use to satisfy our vital needs.

* Norwegian proverb.

Assuming that we wish benevolent action to flourish, some of us stress the need for teaching about the moral law, others stress the need for more understanding of the condition under which people get to be benevolent and well-informed through natural inclination. I take this process to be one of maturation as much as of learning. If the conditions for maturation are bad, the process of identification is inhibited and egotisms of various sorts stiffen into permanent traits.

So the norm 'Self-realisation!' is a condensed expression of the unity of certain social, psychological, and ontological hypotheses: the most comprehensive and deep maturity of the human personality guarantees *beautiful action*. This is based on traits of human nature. We need not repress ourselves; we need to develop our Self. The beautiful acts are natural and by definition not squeezed forth through respect for a moral law foreign to mature human development. Increasing maturity activates more of the personality in relation to more of the milieu. It results in acting more consistently from oneself *as a whole*. This is experienced as most meaningful and desirable, even if sometimes rather painful.

One is said to cultivate oneself when acting egotistically and when one develops oneself through traits conducive to 'winning': What I suggest in such cases is that people underestimate themselves. Our personality is not as narrow as we think. The sources of joy go deeper and farther. We need not cultivate the ego and the notion of winning over others in order to realise our potentialities. Nor need we ignore or suppress the ego in order to broaden and deepen the self in contact with the Self.

It is my feeling that such a way of thinking and teaching is more conducive to well-informed benevolent acts than appeals to moral laws.

Why should anybody try to make a single term, 'Self-realisation', cover all this? I am not inviting anybody to pursue such a goal. But if we, instead of one, employ ten or twenty key terms on the same ultimate level, we may get into trouble: the complication of proving consistency, and of priority in case of norm collisions.

A determined rejection of the single term construct reflects an overestimation of the aim and function of models as tools. If too much is demanded from them, it is better to work without them. But the increased clarity and possibility for communication that come with such simplification and constructing should not be ignored.

Now let us examine what the elaboration of such system models can reveal. We return to the further elucidation of the notion of Self-realisation in chapter 7.

4

Ecosophy, technology, and lifestyle

1   Ecosophical consciousness and lifestyle

How would mankind's present role on this planet be evaluated in the light of philosophical world-views of the past? *No matter which one of the great philosophies one considers to be valid, our current role would be evaluated negatively.* It is in opposition to value priority as announced by these philosophies. This applies to Aristotelianism, Buddhism, Confucianism, and other great philosophies of the last two millennia.

In the great philosophies, greatness and bigness are differentiated. Greatness is sought, but it is not magnitude. The importance of technology is recognised, but cultural values get priority of consideration. The good life is not made dependent upon thoughtless consumption.

In the great philosophies, people are required to attempt to evaluate the distant consequences of their actions and the perspective used is to be universal in time and space. None of the great philosophers regarded market relations and modes of production as the source of norms for state, society, or individual. The importance of economic relations is recognised but seen as a fragment within the web of social relationships.

My conclusion is that there is no articulated world-view which endorses mankind's current role in the ecosphere. Environmentalism has no articulated philosophical system to fear.

But this does not furnish any potent consolation in the situation characterised in the opening of the book. The question must be raised: how are the ecologically destructive, but 'firmly established ways of production and consumption' (p. 23) to be changed?

Large segments of the European public are now aware of formidable destruction. The death of German forests is well known. But the same segments have not been able, and partly not even willing, to change the ways of production and consumption. These are secured by the inertia of *dominant ideas of growth, progress, and standard of living.* These ideas, manifest as firm attitudes and habits, are powerful agencies preventing large-scale, long-range changes. In this chapter questions of mentality and technology are reviewed, in the next I shall discuss the growth and progress ideas in economics.

A central slogan of ecosophical lifestyle: 'Simple in means, rich in ends.' It is not to be confounded with appeals to be Spartan, austere, and self-denying.

The ecosophical lifestyle appreciates opulence, richness, luxury, affluence. But the joys are *defined* in *terms of quality of life, not standard of living.* When circumstances force people with a high quality of life to retreat to a mere high standard, the transition can be painful and dangerous for their self-respect. The abundance, richness, luxury, and affluence are within the framework of quality of life defined in such a way that personal experiences of these states are central, whereas standard of life requires the goods and goodies which are accepted socially at the moment to define 'the good life'.

The retrogression from quality to standard leads soon to the inordinate attention to the budget. 'How much can we afford? There is now a still better car, video, etc. being sold. Can we afford all the things to keep up with *what is the best?*'

What is ecosophically 'best' for somebody relates to *their* total view. If a camera is said to be much better than yours, it may nevertheless be much worse for you. It may not be sensible to buy it, and the ecosopher will then not feel any regret at not possessing it.

2   Mutual help towards ecosophical lifestyle: 'The Future in Our Hands'

Ecological consciousness manifests itself today on the level of personal lifestyle through ways of living in dramatic and conflict-arousing contrast to the dominant way of life in our industrial societies. Because of the conflicts and confrontations which individuals trying to live differently inevitably encounter, it is *indispensable to have centres of information and organisations for people working upon alternatives to assist each other.* There are many such organisations around the globe, but few have affected as great a percentage of a country's population as the movement called 'The Future in Our Hands' in Norway, initiated by Erik Dammann in 1973. It includes both an information centre in Oslo and numerous decentralised active groupings. One of its basic principles is quoted here:

> . . . preservation of the natural and whole biological environment, with
> humans as an integrated part, is a necessary condition for the

development of the life quality of mankind, and its maintenance in the future.

It is elaborated as follows:

> . . . quality of life is here considered to be something incompatible with
> artificial, material standards above that necessary for the satisfaction of
> fundamental needs, and secondly, that ecological considerations are to
> be regarded as *preconditions for* life quality, therefore not outside
> human responsibility. . . . The life style of the majority should be
> changed so that the material standard of living in the Western countries
> becomes *universalisable* within this century. A consumption over and
> above that which everyone can attain within the foreseeable future
> cannot be justified.

In 1975 a poll was undertaken which indicated that three out of four Norwegians believed the standard of living in Norway was too high. 'More than 80% of those questioned expressed the opinion that further growth in production, income and consumption will mean more materialism, more unnecessary goods, more stress and danger to health, at places of work, more pollution and more inhuman cities.' (Dammann, 1979, p. xiv.) In 1975 the concept of quality of life was largely unknown, but the answers illustrated the need of such a concept.

The Future in Our Hands is actively associating consciousness and lifestyle change with direct action. Attempts at a change in lifestyle cannot wait for the implementation of policies which render such change more or less required. The demand for 'a new system' *first* is misguided and can lead to passivity. The same applies to personal lifestyle change *first*, and consequent isolation from political action. These two changes must proceed simultaneously. Changes have to be from the inside *and* from the outside, all in one.

Debate as to the importance of a change in 'consciousness' is clouded over by the failure to *differentiate between change and that strategy which is best suited to bring about such change*. There can be complete concordance with regard to the urgency of change, while attempts at *direct* change, by moral harping, for example, may be considered ineffective. In the following, change in consciousness is taken seriously, although the direct approach, i.e. appeals, information, humanitarian action and education, is not assumed to be the sole or most effective method. The change must essentially be interpreted as a 'dependent variable'. Perhaps changes in certain variables which subsequently influence consciousness are the most effective, e.g. a direct change in economic policies. But the *political will to change* can only be developed among the people and politicians through increased awareness of the unreasonability of the present state of affairs.

Some Marxists have maintained that The Future in Our Hands' talk about reduced consumption serves monopolistic capitalism, and that it is therefore reactionary: waste is a product of the present economic system, and only the replacement of the system can change the pattern of consumption. This critique has been disclaimed by others who espouse dialectical materialism. Steinar Bryn writes in *New Lifestyle*:

> It is correct to maintain that it is our economic system which is the cause
> of our pattern of consumption, but to conclude therefore that the
> consumer is powerless is clearly reactionary. To assert that it is
> ineffective to separate the contest against the present consumer patterns
> as a legitimate point of contention in its own right in political activity
> ends easily in a mechanical cause/effect theory with regard to societal
> and material conditions and human actions. One then disregards the
> people themselves as the creative driving force in history. Individuals
> and groups of individuals are capable of leading a struggle to change
> themselves, their lifestyle, and their living conditions.

The Future in Our Hands does not 'privatise' political problems, but rather fights the underevaluation of personal initiative and the power and abilities of the individual. The movement is *oriented towards* the individual. If we are to hope to reverse the current trends, we have to create a common front between the individual-oriented and the system-oriented activists.

A person can free themself from the profit and consumption consciousness, in spite of the non-stop pressure from the mode of production which depends upon such mentality. Opposition groups rely on possibilities of the new freedom, and lend great importance to the individual's thoughts and feelings. Dammann maintains that *only blaming the system is pacifying*:

> I have heard innumerable times when discussing the difficulties of the
> underdeveloped countries: 'It is the system which is at fault . . .' What
> good does it do to assert that? Of course the system is bad. It is so bad
> that it is quite unbelievable that it is still in existence in spite of the fact
> that everyone says a change must take place. But who has the power to
> maintain conditions as they are in our democratic countries? It is too
> simple to claim that capitalists, industrial magnates, bureaucrats, and
> politicians alone have the power to preserve the system which our
> society and our standards of living have as a foundation. In the majority
> of the rich countries, the people are free to instigate changes if they so
> desire. It goes without saying that democracy often lacks a great deal,
> but that is no justification for doubting that changes would occur in
> Norway if Norwegians really desired them. (Dammann, 1979)

Stated briefly, it does not follow from the norm 'the system must be changed!' that 'consciousness need *not* be changed!' and the hypothesis 'the system changes everything' does not lead to 'consciousness changes nothing'.

The change of consciousness referred to consists of a transition to a more egalitarian attitude to life and the unfolding of life on Earth. This transition opens the doors to a richer and more satisfying life for the species *Homo sapiens*, but not by focusing on *Homo sapiens*. This attitude arises through a truer picture of our existence.

3   Effects of change of mentality

Without a change in consciousness, the ecological movement is experienced as a never-ending list of reminders: 'shame, you mustn't do that' and 'remember, you're not allowed to . . .'. With a change in mentality we can say 'think how wonderful it will be, if and when . . .', 'look there! what a pity that we haven't enjoyed that before . . .'. If we can clean up a little internally as well as externally, we can hope that *the ecological movement will be more of a renewing and joy-creating movement*.

It is dangerous to rely only on a political process leading to decisive green influence on governments. The early Marxist critique of 'classical nature conservation' was valuable as long as it stressed the importance of political engagement. It is clear, however, that many nature magazines and associations should be kept largely free of political and moral propaganda. They foster and encourage nature-lovers, but membership tends to fall unduly if a stern political line is enforced with pages of distressing news, and long, tedious meetings are required.

For the worker within the ecological movement, it is important not to spread oneself too thin, but to make concentrated efforts at one or a very few tasks. Some then concentrate essentially upon increasing awareness, and deliberations concerning mentality and ideology, while others choose to work for direct changes of social and economic conditions in industry, fishing, agriculture or other areas of practical life. *Devaluation of each other's efforts within the total movement is an evil which must be avoided at all costs. No sectarianism!* The Future in Our Hands is aware of the main problem in the development which places economic growth and increase of production before all else. The movement encourages the reduction of individual total consumption, and will through information, increased awareness, and mutual influence attempt to free the individual and society from the consumer pressures which make it very difficult for politicians to support better policies and a healthier society.

The necessity of efforts to change mentality is closely associated with the necessity of organised efforts for profound changes in the structure of society. These two kinds of effort must be coordinated, not polarised against one another.

Let us imagine that just one of the lifestyle and consciousness changes encouraged by Erik Dammann took place: if waste was reduced by 50%, hundreds of firms would immediately have sales problems. Within a year, unemployment would perhaps double. This and other unfortunate consequences can only be avoided if these changes are combined with other changes. The most important in this case is revamping production to dispel the spectre of unemployment. To avoid undesirable consequences, it is useful to consider the personal reduction in consumption as part of a total pattern of life which also includes political engagement.

After considerable changes in lifestyle have been carried through the *everyday* glaring contradictions with dominant lifestyle invite public outcry. One feels like the victim of an occupier ruining the country. But it is also seen that to carry out considerable change is a long and difficult job as long as dominant trends are shaped to resist such change. It is practically impossible not to 'go public'.

4   Technology and lifestyle

The technological developments in modern industrial societies have resulted in continuous pressures towards a kind of lifestyle repugnant not only to supporters of the deep ecology movement but to those in most alternative movements (Elgin, 1981). Some of the reasons for such a confrontation are fairly obvious: modern industrial technology is a centralising factor, it tends towards bigness, it decreases the area within which one can say 'self-made is well-made', it attaches us to big markets, and forces us to seek an ever-increasing income. The administrative technologies are adapted to the physical technologies and encourage more and more impersonal relations.

Those who resist such modern developments have technological symbols in common: the bicycle, home-baked bread, the recycling of goods. In what follows I shall only mention some principles but otherwise refer to the growing body of important literature covering parts of this enormous and complex field of inquiry: technology, lifestyle, economy, politics. The deep ecology movement confronts issues in this realm daily.

Energy consciousness means consciousness of using limited resources, delight in being able to satisfy needs for energy, concern about waste, and concern about the poor and underprivileged for whom energy requirements are a major threat. Where we, who are not poor, live in close and direct relation to nature, and where we are active in providing energy from natural resources, energy consciousness adds to the feeling and experience of richness of the Earth.

In modern industrial life, hot water is tapped in quantities without the joy of being fabulously rich and without the joy of sometimes enjoying extravagance. This holds even among those who work for water conservation, and are fully, even if rather abstractly, aware of the crisis due to thoughtless misuse of a limited resource.

In Nordic countries energy consciousness was developed even from childhood through life in cabins as part of classical *friluftsliv* (see chapter 7, p. 177). When returning from the cabin to live with 'ordinary' ways of using energy, the lack of joy of richness and the unbelievable waste have always had a strong impact. Clearly the cabin tradition is one of the ecosophically most potent sources of permanent alertness towards the destructive misbehaviours of modern life. It is scarcely an overstatement that the private consumption of energy in Norway could be reduced by 80% without affecting the satisfaction of needs, and with an increase of *joyful* energy consciousness. To be realistic, the change must be seen as one that takes many years, even generations, and there is at the moment no strong trend in favour of life quality comprising energy joys.

Within an ecologically interested minority in many industrial countries the use of wood for heating has been rapidly increasing. Especially if the wood has been collected personally, it favours joyful energy consciousness. In this situation as in many others, a certain amount of knowledge is required in order to avoid an unecological result: undue pollution of the atmosphere. Again, an active interest is required: one has to reflect about the proper use of ventilation.

The above ecosophical critique of 'average' industrial lifestyle applies with heavier emphasis to the average lifestyle of the economic elites. The fashionable lifestyle we can learn about under the heading 'Living' in *Time* magazine might more appropriately have the heading 'Dying' in so far as the universalisation and implementation of the norms imply a catastrophic decrease in living conditions of most kinds of living beings.

(a)   The non-existence of purely technical advance

When a so-called 'purely technical' improvement is discovered, it is falsely assumed that the individual and society must regulate themselves accordingly: technique, in part, determines its own development. It is treated as if it were autonomous. Certain subordinate areas of technical development can be favoured and others hindered through political means, but when a 'breakthrough' takes place, we are expected to conform and adjust society appropriately as soon as possible.

It 'ought to be relatively simple' to solve, for instance, the social problems of automation 'through reschooling and planned retraining within the framework of the extensive public welfare organs'. Certain pressure groups are said to attempt to stop or delay this 'natural development'. The use of the word 'natural' is typical of an interpretation of society as subject to laws of *man-made* nature to which mankind must submit. When a technical 'advance' is made in a leading industrial country, is it *natural* that the thousands of cultures and sub-cultures on this globe ultimately adapt themselves to one group's 'progress'?

Within Marxist literature, the assumption is sometimes made that technical development of the means of production essentially determines all other development. The mode of production can come out of step with the means of production: the 'contradiction' must and will be resolved by reworking the *mode* of production (a broad Marxist term which encompasses social relationships), not the *techniques*.

Even in a traditional society with technical tasks it is 'unnatural' (in many senses of the word) to stop the search for technical improvements. It is against our active nature, our personal and cultural unfolding. However, the *evaluation* of a technical change in such a society is relational: it is relative to social and cultural goals. If a technician points to a specific machine part and says: 'there, now you can *see* the purely technical advance!' this can only be interpreted as a highly condensed lecture. To prove that progress has been made, the technician will naturally not limit the substantiation to the anatomy of the machine part. He or she will point out saved labour time and other social consequences.

Improvement of technique implies improvement within the framework of a cultural pattern. That which threatens this framework should not be interpreted as improvement, and should thus be rejected. In the industrial societies, these social consequences are not given enough consideration. *There is no such thing as purely technical progress.*

Those who maintain that technological development must run its course whether we like it or not are mistaken both historically and empirically. Why didn't the advanced technical inventiveness of old China change the social structure, for example? A society is capable of rejecting a more 'advanced' or 'higher' technique on account of its social and other consequences. The Chinese rejected banking and certain agricultural tools for this very reason. A lack of critical evaluation of technique is the harbinger of a society's dissolution. A technique has to be *culturally* tested.

Technique in the industrial countries is guided by narrow economic considerations by a small elite of the population. Technical 'development' is driven in widely dissimilar directions in response to prices for different raw materials and energy, and the cost and make-up of the labour force. Our helplessness in questions of technical 'development' is a myth – a very useful myth for those introducing expensive new technology. Technology is chosen, but not by consideration of society as a whole.

One speaks of *laws* for technical development which are independent of other factors. Weighty objections to such a view have been advanced in recent years. In today's capitalist countries (including Russia, with its state capitalism), large profit margins in agriculture are intimately associated with a technology which entails excessive demands on the environment, ruining the soil in the long run.

Technical development is a fragment of total development, and it partakes in an intimate interaction with a host of factors. Social anthropology and related areas of study supply instructive examples of how ideological, and particularly religious, attitudes influence the directions taken by technical change. The subject is neglected in our technical schools, but the breakthrough of ecosophical thought implies a renaissance for the idea of technique submitted to the ideals of a world-view. The idea can be restated as *technique submitted to evaluation in normative systems*.

If a technique is said to express an improvement or a technical advance many tests are relevant. Here are some questions that must be raised. (See also Devall and Sessions, 1985, p. 35.)

(1) Is it conducive or dangerous to health?

(2) How meaningful, capable of variations, conducive to the self-determination and inventiveness of the worker?

(3) Does it strengthen cooperation and harmonious togetherness with other workers?

(4) Which other techniques does the technique require in order to be effective as part of greater units of technology? What is the quality of these techniques?

(5) Which raw materials are indispensable? Are they locally or regionally available? How easy is the access to them? Which tools are indispensable? How are they obtained?

(6) How much energy does the technique require? What is the amount of waste? What kind of energy?

(7) Does the technique pollute directly or indirectly? How much and what kind?

(8) How much capital is required? How big must the undertaking be? How vulnerable in times of crisis?

(9) How much administration is required? How much dependent upon hierarchical arrangements?

(10) Does it promote equality or class differences at the place of work or more generally?

Langdon Winner opens the first chapter 'Autonomy and mastery' of his book *Autonomous Technology* (1977) with a quotation from Paul Valéry: 'So the whole question comes down to this: can the human mind master what the human mind has made?' An excellent opening, but it may be added that the general trend of modern technological developments has perhaps *not* been masterminded by anybody, by any group or any constellation of humans. It may have developed largely 'by itself'.

(b)   'The environmental crisis can be technically resolved . . .'
A widespread assumption in influential circles of the industrial countries is that overcoming the environmental crisis is a technical problem: it does not presuppose changes in consciousness or economic system. This assumption is one of the pillars of the shallow ecological movement.

Opposition to further economic growth in the industrial states is unnecessary, it is said, and continued growth is often simply taken for granted. Technical development will reduce pollution to tolerable levels and prevent serious resource depletion. Present forests may be dying, but we can find or create new kinds of trees that thrive on acid rain, or we can find ways to live entirely without trees.

Our governments are incessantly asked to provide good, liberal conditions for centralised, highly technical industry which obeys the 'laws' of the world market and the political pattern of the dominating Eastern and Western industrial lands. The 'concise, factual, professional manner' is on a level *isolated from a discussion of values.*

Those who believe in the possibility of a technical solution often refrain from discussing a radical transformation to soft technology. There is little demand on the market, so why bother? The market suggests a preference for hard technology: tremendous new energy sources, a more extreme 'efficiency program' based upon centralisation, or technical solutions to population growth.

W. Modell, MD, New York, has indicated to a group of pharmaceutical manufacturers that, by studying organisms which live in the poisonous atmosphere of volcanoes or the near boiling waters of a geyser, we can find substances which could render future conditions on a devastated Earth livable for mankind (Modell, 1973, pp. 153ff). The animals which now live in sewage may supply us with knowledge so that we too could survive in sewage-like conditions. Dr Modell concludes with the hope that none of these possibilities will need to be realised. The approach is characteristic of the one-sided technical approach to our crisis, but I am glad to say that Dr Modell is not entirely serious about his solutions.

The essential ingredients for a technocracy are present when the individual and the organisations in which the individual functions become more occupied with means than with ends, and more occupied with subordinate ends (buildings) than fundamental ones (homes). The more the ability to dwell upon intrinsic value diminishes, the faster consciousness turns from immediate experience to planning for the coming times. Although the intrinsic values are ostensibly still the central themes, the procurement of effective means is the principal occupation. The undesirable consequences of this become more and more aggravated as the individual consumer has less and less to do with production. The techniques are 'improved' constantly, requiring great sacrifices of time and energy. Unnoticed, the time spent upon goals withers away. The headlong rush after means takes over: the improvements are illusory.

A crucial objective of the coming years is, therefore, decentralisation and differentiation as a means to increased local autonomy and, ultimately, as a means to unfolding the rich potentialities of the human person.

The great representative of intermediate technology, E. F. Schumacher, spoke of 'production of the masses' as opposed to 'mass production'. The expression 'local production' is also appropriate, as 'the masses' is often associated with many people in a homogeneous milieu. There are masses of small communities, but the techniques will vary greatly if the message of ecosophy is taken seriously. In the same light, 'advanced technology' should be seen as *technology which advances the basic goals of each culture*, not anything more complicated or difficult for its own sake.

Schumacher emphasises that production of the masses mobilises the inestimable resources which ordinary human beings possess: brains and skilled hands. And the means of production of the masses assist them with first-class tools. The technology of mass production is in itself violent, ecologically harmful, ultimately self-destructive in its consumpton of non-renewable resources and stupefying for the human person (Schumacher, 1973).

(c)   Soft technology and ecosophy

'To tread lightly on Earth' is a powerful slogan in the deep ecological movement, and slogans such as 'soft technology' are obvious corollaries. Which technologies satisfy maximally both the requirements of reduced interference with nature and satisfaction of human vital needs? Clearly the requirements cannot both be maximally satisfied without getting into conflicts. It is a major concern to find a kind of equilibrium, and the proposals are dependent on geographical and social diversity of life conditions.

A widening circle of technically proficient people are devoting their attention to the discovery of ecologically satisfactory techniques. The increase in interest evidenced by those who direct research in industry and governmental machinery is proceeding more slowly, and grants are minuscule compared with the amounts received by projects indifferent or blatantly irresponsible to ecosophy.

There are many useful works outlining the distinctive qualities of soft technology. What is often missing in such overviews is a discussion of the *transition path* between our present society and one which would make full use of soft and appropriate technologies. Johan Galtung (1978) outlines a way to utilise both *alpha* structures (big, centralised, hierarchical), and *beta* structures ('small is beautiful') as instruments for a composite change to a way in which the former will be phased out gradually, as structures move slowly from the vertical to the horizontal. He asks for a *mix* of technologies, thus a realistic and immediate alternative: see table 4.1.

In spite of the comprehensive nature of the list, the confrontation between standardisation and diversity could be further highlighted. Decentralisation, and emphasis upon local resources, climate, and other characteristics would result in variations of a technique within the same ecosophically sane technology. The same applies to the products of the techniques. Diminishing standardisation and increasing diversity follow.

The demand for expert aid to carry out planned transitions to softer technology is greater than the supply in Great Britain and elsewhere. Work procedures are being reworked. Volvo's experiments with smaller factories, improved external milieux, more all-round tasks and more responsible decision making on the job are well-known.

But the dark outlook for an early transformation to soft technology in Europe may be especially associated with three restraining political factors: the fear for reduced industrial-economic profitability, the fear for reduced material standard of living, and the fear of unemployment. The last factor would appear to be paradoxical, as there seems to be universal agreement that a transition to soft technology would increase the demand for labour, and improve the opportunities for workers. The counterargument reveals a vulgar empiricism: it is said that historically the development of non-soft technology over the last fifty years has occurred simul-

Table 4.1

	Alpha	Beta
Food	build down trade in food, drop cash crop practices; build down agribusiness	try to restore the old system that the food is grown within the horizon – local autarchy; also local preservation and storage; collectivise ground that can be used for food
Clothes	build down international textile business	try to restore patterns of local handicraft: symbiosis with food production
Shelter	build down housing business; transfer more work to homes to help dissolve centre-periphery distinction	try to restore local building patterns with local materials; collectivise ground that can be used for housing
Medical care	rural clinics, control of drugs	positive health care: participation, less separation between healthy and ill
Transportation/ communication	less centralised, two-way patterns, collective means of transport	try to restore patterns of walking, talking, bicycling, more car-free areas, cable TV, local media
Energy	better distribution of centres for large-scale energy production	solar/wind/wave/biogas networks
Defence	democratised armies, better distribution of commanding positions	local defence patterns, non-violent groups
Comprehension	maximum transparency through citizen participation and reporting	small-size units comprehensible by anybody

taneously with a decrease in unemployment. But where is the substance of such a connection?

In technical circles, it is often said that a radical transition to soft technology is politically unrealistic and unnecessarily drastic. But the importance of the many *small* changes in the environment caused by hard technology is presently underestimated. For example: even if we totally avoid large oil catastrophes at sea, the many completely 'normal' small leaks can result in a multitude of tiny detrimental effects upon organisms which will ultimately be catastrophic for living conditions. The minor spills and leaks are calculated to release between five and ten million tons of oil into the seas each year. If the consumption of oil in the Third World increases to the European level within thirty years, living conditions will degenerate ten or more times faster than the present rate.

(d)   The invasion of hard technology in the Third World
    Faced with the dominance of hard technology, some are proud of the fact that it is necessary to ask if it can be universalised. Can all countries follow in our footsteps? Will people in poorer countries and the generations of the future have a chance to live in our (seemingly) magnificent way?

If not, should we not subscribe to the following norm: 'Choose a level of standard of living such that you realistically may desire that all fellow humans reach the same level if they want'? With the rate of destruction of woods and degrading quality and quantity of good soils, and the prospect of human population at least reaching 8000 million, there is no universalisability present, no planet available for that. The average level in rich industrial countries is unjustifiable and irrational considering its very uncertain relation to level of life *quality*.

One central question in the Third World is: how much industrial techniques can we import from the leading industrial nations without being obliged to open the doors to undesirable characteristics of their social structures? Do we have to develop a weapon industry like that of the industrial countries to prevent our domination by them? Is it necessary to develop a western technocracy in order to survive as a self-determining nation?

For many years, the answers were overwhelmingly optimistic. The leaders of these countries would say: 'We can assimilate whatever we find technically useful, if we take care to retain our own ideology and our own value priorities. Our cultures will remain unharmed.' This could be termed the 'skim the cream' theory.

The military and administrative elite of the Third World has since 1945 to a great extent been educated in the industrial countries and has adopted our predominant ideology, including a distaste for local traditions and cultural diversity in general. The optimism in this case ultimately rests upon an evaluation about how little there was to lose if the ideologies of the industrial countries happened to be introduced together with the techniques: the integrated notion of technology, remember, includes both.

Today, they have made a near total about-face. If one adopts a technique from the leading industrial societies, e.g. a specific method for treatment of cancer, experience has shown that it cannot be imported in isolation – it presupposes much more importation. And this supportive import is not purely technical. New patterns of human association, and other subcultures of work are assumed. In short: cultural invasion and increased dependence. One's own culture is gradually eroded.

In Tibet, Sikkim, and Bhutan, among other until recently isolated places, the leaders throughout the ages have been aware of the 'domino theory'. Tibet is a dramatic example. Tibet managed to remain isolated for many years. When the leaders of Tibet felt themselves threatened by the new China, they sought contact with the industrial states, to increase their chances for a military defence of Tibetan society and culture. Too late! Their cultural sovereignty has been destroyed. But in Bhutan in the 1980s the government is considering technology and influence from the outside only with extreme caution. For example, any students who go abroad for higher education must, immediately upon their return, spend six months travelling through the countryside for a *re-education* on the actual conditions and values of the people of their own country.

The transfer of technologies from the industrial countries to the Third World has included dramatic, often tragic episodes. *The Careless Technology* (ed. Farvar and Milton, 1972) illustrates the importance of regarding a culture as a whole, and supplies crystal-clear examples of actual results of thoughtless exportation of technology to the Third World. This thoughtlessness is implicit in the 1940s concept of 'underdeveloped countries'. One imagined that *all* cultures would and should develop technology in the same manner as the leading industrial countries.

A widely unnoticed, but, in the history of the world, meaningful, clash between spokespeople for hard and soft technology took place in India in the years following the Second World War. On one side stood a group of politicians with Nehru in the fore. They were inspired by the industrialisation philosophy of the Soviet Union. On the other side was Gandhi. His social philosophy, *sarvodaya*, 'to the best for all', emphasised the importance of decentralised industrial life and extensive self-sufficiency in India's 500,000 villages. His greatest goal was the elimination of direct material and spiritual destitution. His propaganda for weaving looms is particularly well-known, but he also supported other artisan crafts. Centralisation and urbanisation were, for him, evils. The emphasis on large industry and all technology which deepened the division between a technical elite and workers stripped of their culture would lead to a proletarisation of the cities, and increase in violence, and opposition between the Hindus and Muslims.

The contest revolved around the extent to which free India's politics would be based on the red or green dimensions (see chapter 6). Both

Nehru and Gandhi were aware of the implications in the choice of technology. After independence, the opposition blocks led to compromises between the red and the blue factions. It has been said that the two greatest catastrophes in India have been the elimination of Buddhism and the deaf ear turned towards the green teachings of Gandhi. This may be an exaggeration, but had priority been given to the technical development of the local community, India's material needs would in all likelihood have been met in the 1950s.

(e)   Ecosophy and technology: a summary

(1) Objects produced by labour of a technical nature are in intimate interaction, not only with the means and the mode of production, but with all essential aspects of cultural activity.

(2) Therefore technology is intimately related directly or indirectly to other social institutions, e.g. the sciences, the degree of centralised government, and beliefs about what is reasonable. *Change in technology implies change in culture.*

(3) The height of technical development is primarily judged by the leading industrial states in terms of how the techniques can be assimilated in the economies of these states. The more advanced Western science, e.g. quantum physics or electronics, a technique presupposes, the higher it is regarded. This untenable criterion of progressiveness is applied not only to our own technology but also to the technology of other cultures. This in turn leads to the general depreciation of the viability of foreign cultures.

(4) The ecosophical criteria for progressiveness in technology are relative to ultimate normative objectives. Therefore culture-neutral statements of the degree of advancement cannot be formulated.

(5) The ecosophical basis for an appraisal of technique is the satisfaction of vital needs in the diverse local communities.

(6) The objectives of the deep ecological movement do not imply any depreciation of technology or industry, but they imply general cultural control of developments.

(7) Technocracies – societies to an overwhelming degree determined by technique and technology – can arise as a consequence of extreme division of labour, and intimate merging of technologies of a higher order, combined with extremely specialised, centralised, and exclusive education of technologists. Although neither politicians, nor clergy, nor other groups with authority in the culture can test the explanations granted to the public, they can to some extent determine the political development. The extent of this influence is dependent upon many things: how much

technical counter-expertise can be mobilised, and how willing the mass media are to present these counter-reports in a generally understandable form.

(8) When a technique is replaced by another which requires more attention, education, and is otherwise more self-engaging and detached, the contact with the medium or milieu in which the technique acts is diminished. To the extent that this medium is *nature*, the engagement in nature is reduced in favour of engagement in the technology. The degree of inattentiveness or apathy increases and thus our awareness of the changes in nature caused by the technique decreases.

(9) The degree of self-reliance for individuals and local communities diminishes in proportion to the extent a technique or technology transcends the abilities and resources of the particular individuals or local communities. Passivity, helplessness, and dependence upon 'megasociety' and the world market increase.

5

Economics within ecosophy

1   The contact with total views

It has been said in the first chapter that what makes the ecological situation especially serious is that there is a deeply grounded ideology of consumption and production which is unecological. This kind of diagnosis makes it essential to analyse economic conditions and to consider a science with great influence, namely economics.

There is another motivation, namely that economics has traditionally a broad contact with total views with normative content.

Economy comes from the Greek word *oikonomos*: one that takes care of the household, a normative undertaking. So to be a good and wise economist is in this sense nothing terribly exciting, or special. *Oikonomos* is a word that may be put in contrast to *cosmonomos*: the nature and world administrator that very few beings can live up to. But already Xenophon, Plato, and Aristotle treated the household problems for the community as a whole, for *polis*. Xenophon was the first in a long series of thinkers who looked at economics from a rather narrow point of view. They became the ideological advocates primarily of the people who had property, the landowners.

Economics is, in the European tradition, often defined as the science of how to satisfy human needs. But since it clearly does not talk about every kind of need it becomes necessary to define 'economic' needs. What are these? It is said that they are those that have to do with external means and how to obtain those external means, especially in relation to community or nations. Thus there is no very sharp demarcation between economics in a traditional sense and other activities of human society. Looking into the pages of economics treatises you see however that practically every aspect of society gets a section. But most of the authors try to avoid too much contact with political problems, saying that the ultimate *goals* of economic policy are decided by the politicians. In this way economists avoid taking wisdom into account. They play the role of servants to whoever happens to have political power. Economists as contemporary scientists do not judge political goals but only advise on how best to realise goals announced by people in power. Unfortunately this is largely unrealised by the public who get the impression that economists personally endorse the goals of their clients. If the scientists announced their persoal view more often in mass media, this impression would weaken.

A feature of economics important for ecosophers is the highly developed study of influences of one factor on other factors in society. The famous Norwegian economist Ragnar Frisch said that 'economics is like an infiltrated maze of mutual influences that runs in all directions'. If you make a change of conditions in one place in one way you have to look for the consequences of this in a vast number of ways and places. It is for instance quite common in economics to require the consideration of a hundred variables. As ecosophers we have something to learn!

It is not uncommon in traditional economics to admit that questions of ethics are relevant in every consideration. There are always ethical requirements which influence the practical arrangements of economic affairs. Any analysis of economic activity presupposes that there are certain norms which have to be satisfied in the analysis. The most prominent economists until this century, including François Quesnay, Adam Smith, John Stuart Mill, and Karl Marx, have been engaged as much in moral philosophy as in detailed economic affairs. In this century there has been a dangerous narrowing of the scope of textbooks in economics so that very little of the normative philosophical basis of the field is left. Economics is dried up. We are left with a kind of flat country of factual quantitative considerations, with no deep canyons or impressive mountain peaks to admire. Fortunately this is changing – in part owing to the impact of environmental concerns.

2 The neglect of economics within the deep ecological movement

Especially among activists within the ecological movement, people have been so fed up with unecological policies that the term 'economics' itself has become a kind of nasty word. Economists have been looked at as inevitable enemies to the green cause. What is especially annoying to many environmentalists is this: in the papers and books of economists *nature* is practically never mentioned, and, if it is, it is only in very shallow argumentation as resources or as obstacles. So nothing can be expected, think activists, from a study of economics – the economists are to be fought.

Every time there is a conflict about policies in economic matters there will be conclusions or decisions more favourable to sound ecological policies than certain others and it is relevant for people supporting the deep ecological movement to point out what is the best alternative when decisions are made in economic terms. This means sometimes to propose solutions which are from a deep ecological view not the best or even good but which are much better than the others under consideration. If the supporters of the deep ecology movement are to take part in politics at all, they have to have opinions on economic decisions, but they should always make clear if they personally are advocates for the decision, or, if it is not completely satisfactory, how they would, if they had power, decide otherwise.

What I am driving at is that we need in society *even as it is now operating* people who are competent to take part in economic decision making and take part in informing the public about the consequences of different decisions. It is highly destructive to the deep ecology movement for supporters to be silenced because they cannot stand up in discussions with people who are well acquainted with economics.

3   'as seen from a purely economic standpoint . . .'

Social activity in non-industrial countries includes economic activities. These have a high degree of complexity and are mostly directed towards household needs of local communities. Much was ceremonial or related to kinship. The economic mores of industrial countries have ancestors in non-industrial cultures, the mores of hucksters. The essence of economic activity tends now to be abstracted from the social matrix. Expressions like 'from a purely economic standpoint' are instructive here.

Non-normative development of household wisdom has made it easy to speak of 'pure' economics and to say by implication that every other consideration such as social costs of an economic decision cannot be relevant within economics. It is, however, clear that in practice it is impossible for economists to avoid such questions. For instance, when it is a question of employment and economists are asked to give advice on how to diminish unemployment, they cannot say, 'All right, we can transport people to those places in the country where there is some kind of work and that would get rid of half the unemployment.' The politicians would then say this is a completely valueless suggestion because it is against the law to force people to move to such places where work is available. Implicitly, economists must take values into account and must themselves think up ethical solutions to their problems. There is no practical point of view that could be called purely economic.

It is often said that the need for so-and-so is so big, where the need is taken to be something we can measure by seeing what the demand for it is. But it is clear that in economics (if economics has to do with the satisfaction of needs) demand on the market is only one of many factors suggesting a need. There are in international economics questions such as how to meet the needs in certain areas of Africa where people are starving. The demand there is practically zero because they don't have any money, so if demand is taken to be the main criterion they need much less than we do. Are starving people without needs!? Demand criteria lead one to say that there is a maximum need for foodstuffs in certain parts of, say, the US, where there is a great demand for the feeding of *animals* essential for the modern human diet. Household policy will never be determinable by pure consideration of such demand.

In modern economics texts there is much talk about rationality and rational choice. In economics as in other sciences, rationality has to be measured in relation to basic norms. If there is a non-basic norm in relation to which something is expedient this does not imply that it is also rational in relation to more basic norms. Whenever we bring questions of rationality into economic life the *ultimate norms of economy* have to be considered. When it is said that it is economically more rational to transport heavy goods from A to B by means of trucks than by means of horses, it does not exclude the possibility that it is unwise to transport any heavy goods from A to B. Higher household norms than cheapness etc. may be involved. Elimination of normativity in economics turned a great deal of attention in the name of 'progress' towards irrationality or something completely neutral in relation to rationality. Economic growth in the Third World is still conceived largely in terms of non-normative economics, the 'experts' being unaccustomed to reasoning from the maximally wide and deep perspective of a total view.

4   An economic policy system fragment

We can illustrate a way of approaching normativity in economics with the method outlined at the beginning of chapter 3. Fritz Holte gives in his book *Sosialøkonomi* ('Economics', 1975) an example of 'a set of fundamental and derived goals for economic policy' (p. 241). What is expressed 'according to Holte' has been the accepted view in Norway from 1945 to the present day. Such goals were, characteristically enough, not explicitly accepted by *him*.

Using the normative system technique, the set of fundamental and
derived norms may be formulated as follows:

Basic norms in economic policy:

B1   Full employment!

B2   High consumption now! (i.e. within the present electoral term)

B3   High consumption in the future!

B4   Much leisure time now!

B5   Much leisure time in the future!

B6   Reasonable distribution of consumption! (public vs. private,
private vs. personal)

Derived norms:

D7   High national product now!

D8   High national product in the future! (rapid economic growth =
high growth rate in GNP)

D9   High investment!

D10   Reasonable distribution of investment among different
industries

D11   Balance foreign trade!

D12   Hold prices stable!

The diagram of derivation (figure 5.1) illustrates three levels in the
system fragment. In order to reach the level of concrete decisions more
levels would, of course, have to be added. A normative pyramid is
formed. A derived norm (or goal) has the character of a means in relation
to the norm (or goal) it is derived from. Therefore, all the goals in the
system except the top six have the character of mainly being 'means to
ends'.

By saying that economics can concern itself only with means but not
with goals, one neglects the central things it should be concerned with.

Figure 5.1

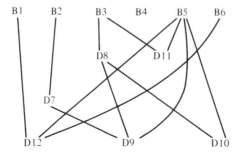

Such a proposition is clearly untenable. But it does point to the fact that all human actions are goal-directed and work within a hierarchy of goals which correspond to a hierarchy of *gestalts*. If one does not work with goals one does not work with human actions. Model thinking is thinking in terms of models. If one is not concerned with the goals, such models are useless.

The aim of the diagram is to provide an easily perceivable skeleton fragment of a complex system. Vagueness in formulation goes together with the fact that the goals suggest broad guidelines for policy goals rather than precise directives.

The decisive weakness of this fragment from an ecosophical standpoint is the fact that a vast number of hypotheses are required to logically derive the norms D7–D12 from the 'fundamentals' B1–B6. None of the required hypotheses appear in the fragment.

An example: from 'Much leisure time in the future!' (B5) is derived 'High investment!' (D9). But in Ecosophy T 'voluntary simplicity' is taken to be necessary to achieve much leisure time. High investment is incompatible with voluntary simplicity. The derivation of D9 is only possible with 'High consumption in the future!' (B3) as a basic norm. From B3 follows D8, 'Rapid economic growth!', etc. With such anti-ecosophical norms, the comparatively attractive 'leisure time' norm gets absorbed into a total economic system which is decidedly un-ecosophical.

In short, the postulated relation of derivation between a norm of more leisure time and a norm of more investment *presupposes hypotheses* about how leisure time is to be increased. The fragment is one-sided and reveals according to ecosophy the gigantic illusion that modern industrial society guarantees leisure time.

A second weakness of our system fragment is that the basic norms are not placed deeply enough: the justification of leisure time and norms of distribution are already beyond the reaches of current economic science. A kind of philosophical welfare theory seems to be assumed. Without such, the choice of basic norms B1–B6 must be considered highly arbitrary. *Why should a wise household need high consumption as a basic norm?*

Norms can be divided up between those which function as rules and those which function as guidelines. Economics as a social science is by nature coloured by guidelines: one cannot by pure deduction come to the solutions as they are generally given. The estimations of economists will therefore only be one set of economic opinions. A set of norms together with a series of evaluations will therefore lay the ground for results. Economic tradition since the 1890s has put systematic weight on the presuppositions of the models used. An example of what this means is here found in Holte (1975, p. 37):

> Many of the reasonings which were put forth in this book are built on the following presuppositions. Every businessman has the goal of obtaining the greatest possible profit from his business. Every businessman knows how the possibilities of selling the business products vary with the price. Every businessman knows how the costs in his business vary with the level of production.

Those kinds of presuppositions make it possible to construct quantitative economic 'laws' which we know cannot hold as strictly as the economists would like. In modern economics quantitative formulations are taken to be necessary and superior to make economics a 'science' (in a narrow sense). Such presuppositions still dominate. We may get a high-level methodology, a high level of deduction, a high level of precision, but a certain barrenness from the point of view of norms, barrenness from a point of view of humanity, and extreme danger from the point of view of ecosophy.

5   Gross National Product (GNP)

In this section I shall give a rather detailed critical comment on GNP for two main reasons. People supporting the deep ecological movement need to be able to discuss 'economic growth' because unecological policy tends to be supported by referring to the necessity and desirableness of such growth. But because of the disinclination to study economics by environmentalists the economists' critique of GNP is largely unknown.

The notion of economic growth which is most often talked about is GNP growth. Calculation of the GNP is done by listing and adding up the national accounts every year. The many entries in this enormous product are published by the national bureau of statistics or its equivalent.

Production is the making of real objects by means of other real objects. What are made are called products, and the real objects which contribute to their creation are called production factors. Under the classification 'real objects' we include goods and services. Real objects are distinguishable from finance objects, such as shares and paper money. Production includes therefore services of all sorts which can be bought on the market. A certain equation ought to be mentioned:

$$\text{GNP} + \text{imports} = \text{consumption} + \text{gross investment}$$
$$+ \text{increase of stocks} + \text{exports}$$

However, goods stands for the value of all goods and services which are used as production factors. Holte says: 'in the production of milk, production factors include among the other things hay, labour costs, services from the cows, services from the workers, protection of the cows against the weather, etc.' (Holte, 1975).

Independently of the ecological movement, economists have in recent years introduced a vigorous critique of economic growth and 'national goal setting' as an indicator of welfare growth in the industrial countries. But the key word 'economic growth' has continued to have great importance in politics, in spite of the growing evidence that it has negative influence on contemporary quality of life in the rich industrial nations. As to future generations their life conditions are heavily threatened.

It is a grave error within the ecological movement to fail to utilise economists' own criticism of the economic growth propaganda. Every day, every week of the year newspapers and television programmes continue to mention economic growth as measured by GNP as if it were a decisive ingredient of a successful economic policy. People engaged in the ecological movement rarely protest at this. I suspect that if, in private and public discussion, we had systematically inserted some of the economists' own critique we would no longer have economic growth as a kind of 'superstar' in our overdeveloped industrial society. This is one of the worst instances of our neglect of economics!

6   Arguments for ignoring GNP in the industrial countries

(a)   Historical background for the overevaluation of GNP

In the years immediately following the Second World War, it was imperative to get wheels moving again. Experts assumed that it would take a very long time to rebuild Europe. To the surprise of all, it took only a few years' time for Germany to become an economic giant with a high material life standard. In other lands (perhaps not the UK), growth was more rapid than expected. The technological possibilities for enormous industrial production became and perhaps continue to be underestimated.

What happened from 1945 to 1965 in Europe was an economic growth in the sense of building up and moving forward. Obviously GNP was relevant. Unhappily it became such a popular notion that people sought to clarify and explain economic progress in a wide positive meaning by means of the narrow and ambiguous indicator of GNP.

Doubts made themselves felt already when talking about all the strange things which began to turn up on the plus si:e of national accounts: industry focusing on the elimination of pollution and first aid to victims of traffic accidents, prisons, and absolutely everything which the industrial countries need to repair the undesirable sides of this society are included. The cost of the growth itself gets into the positive side of GNP accounting!

GNP is therefore in a certain sense a value-neutral quantity: a measure of activity, *not of activity of any kind of value.* A first argument against continued growth is just this. The GNP does not give any guarantee of meaningfulness of that which is created. Growth in GNP does not imply any growth in access to intrinsic values and progress along the course of Self-realisation.

Obviously any kind of economic growth which is not related to intrinsic values is neutral or detrimental. The measure of GNP is somehow related to the *fierceness* of activity in the society but this fierceness may very well have more to do with a lack of ability of the members of the society to engage in meaningful activity than a measure of something humanity should look upon with joy. There is no clear relation to life quality.

It is worth while to discuss GNP because in politics it is actually used as if it has an intimate relation to life quality or the three kinds of ultimate goals suggested in chapter 3, §4. In short GNP tends to be treated as Gross National Quality of Life, Gross National Pleasure, Gross National Happiness, or Gross National Perfection. The term 'gross' is important because the same GNP is compatible with any distribution, for instance 95% of people in utter poverty and 5% in extreme opulence, or all people having the same standard of living.

(b)   GNP is not a measure of welfare: why not?

An essential argument against GNP growth concerns its difference from welfare growth. The editor of the specialists' magazine *Sosialøkonomen* ('The Economist') put it in this way as long ago as 1972:

> 1. The national product comprises fewer goods and services than even the average person has use of.
> 2. The valuation components for the single entries in national accounting do not respond to the effect of welfare on the components.
> 3. The national product says nothing on the distribution of goods between persons.
> 4. The national product shows running activity yet doesn't reflect over time. It says nothing on the tapping or elimination of limited resources and irreversible changes.

Elaborating an example used by Hazel Henderson (1981, p. 300) we note that an increase of £1m to £2m spent on anti-smoking educational measures combined with a decrease from £80m to £70m on advertising and promoting tobacco represent a 'lamentable' decrease of £9m pounds in GNP. Any increase in self-reliance, eating at home rather than in restaurants, choice of work near home – practically everything signifying progress towards sane, ecosophically justifiable life, may result in 'lamentable' decrease in GNP and will be noted as 'worrying' decline of economic growth. Ecology is suspect (see Jansson (1984)). Life quality itself is suspect. Every use of anti-depression pills is a plus in GNP.

The tapping of unrenewable resources and other milieu-destroying irreversible processes stand in intimate connection with the level of welfare, globally and in the long run. The expression 'running' activity indicates time neutrality and is different from creative activity. Perhaps 'galloping' activity is a little more apt. *Sustainability* is completely ignored.

GNP cultivation adds to the distraction from problems of distribution. The platform of any green politics contains the elimination of skewness in the distribution between the centre and the periphery as one of its goals. Concentration on GNP favours still more development of the already strongly industrialised and centralised areas.

(c)   GNP growth favours hard and distant technologies

GNP increases not so rapidly with soft and near technology as with hard technology and technology which requires long transportation times and distances. In the short run, this just fits into the following motto of the paradigm of economic growth: if something can be done in a complicated way and thereby generate more profit, why do it simply?

(d)   GNP growth favours wants, not needs

In GNP there is no place for a distinction between waste, luxury, and a satisfaction of fundamental needs. The difference here, which is so essential for wise communal living for our household, between what one has desire for and what one needs, is ignored. Desperate attempts at continuing GNP growth favour the unlimited nature of desires. They also favour, therefore, the belief in the necessity of market expansion.

People have tried to measure to what degree economic growth has increased the satisfaction of basic needs. The conclusion has on the whole been that any positive effect at the outset is now steadily decreasing. Poverty, especially relative poverty, is not seen to be eliminated with increasing GNP. GNP growth tends towards increasing the distance between the individual's material aspiration level (world of material desires) and the individual's actual economic possibilities.

(e)   *GNP discriminates against people working at home*

From the entries in GNP calculations it is clear that an important part of all present-day work is neglected: unpaid work in the home. Housewives' or househusbands' work is not taken into account in spite of the fact that it is relatively easy to calculate how many millions it would cost if all housework were paid at the usual rates. An important traditional component of the working man's or woman's welfare thus does not come into the GNP: that someone works for him or her at home.

In less traditional family structures such things are twisted about quite a bit, but still there is certain work that must be done in the home. And whoever does it, it still does not get considered in *any* of the entries leading up to the GNP. What counts tend to be complicated means to reach poor goals.

(f)   *GNP growth supports irresponsible and unsolidaric*
    resource consumption and global pollution

When the industrial lands' wealth and level of technology lay the ground for the measuring of the resources of the globe, one gets the usual conclusion that they are practically unlimited. Experts hired by governments of the technically most 'advanced' nations reckon that, with the use of a small percentage of the national income, we can shape new technologies to solve any ecological problem. Even if true, this conclusion is not worth much because it does not take up the relation between developing and industrial countries. That which is a usable resource for Britain or Norway may not be usable in a developing country.

(g)   *The irrelevance of economic growth*

How ought an ecologically responsible policy to be carried out? Should GNP grow rapidly, show decreasing rate of growth but still grow, remain stationary, or decrease? There is no simple answer. In principle, GNP is irrelevant. What counts in the economic policy of a *state* is *each entry* which is summed up in the form of a single number – GNP. And the nation state is not the most important economic unit in an economy of needs, the economy of communities has precedence.

If green policy does not support a reduced GNP but a programme for the change of the individual entries, exactly which changes are to be suggested? The answer will not be simple.

There is no economic philosophy of zero growth. It is the defenders of the actual growth increase who have postulated fictional zero-growth philosophies as comfortable but non-existent opponents. A state council minister has, I think, accurately called zero-growth philosophy 'lunatic moonlighting of a spinning brain'. But which brain did the spinning? – Someone in opposition to the deep ecological movement. The term 'zero growth' has a clear meaning in the study of populations. When a population holds itself at a constant level it is said that there is zero growth. There is no reason for economics to take over this term.

The attention on GNP continually focuses on the *aggregate size* of practically everything. *Sosialøkonomen* (**2**, 1973) has laid down this issue editorially:

> The thought itself that it should be possible to come to a single quantity for a country's welfare or national happiness shows a certain naïveté and lack of insight into the aggregation problem. Even if one comes up with such a number, so what? One number cannot be any foundation basis for a concrete policy. The policy must start and end with individual activity.

GNP's lack of import for green politics also stems from the fact that it does not move attention away from the state towards the two essential extremes: the economics of local communities and the global economic links. The average growth in GNP in Norway of 3.47% from 1950 to 1962 indicates mainly the transfer of production factors from branches with low productivity to those with high productivity. Such transfer is very suspect from the green political standpoint. The next most powerful cause is increasing capital input per worker, per working place. The third is named 'progress in technology and organisational knowledge', implying mainly a movement to centralisation and 'high tech'. The fourth is increasing size of businesses.

The statement of causes must of course be used with care but they show with decisive import that attention must be directed at every single entry. If decentralisation and small businesses are to seek strength and to be strengthened one cannot at the same time look for growth in GNP.

(h)   Misplaced attempts at salvation of GNP

Many would like to reform the GNP measure so that it gets to be an expression for *good* things produced. From this follows advice on discount entries in calculation of a company's gross product. If the method of work in a company is associated with stress and this leads to exceptionally large public health expenses, these must be deducted. In the same light, if the workers travel a long way to reach work this increases traffic, accidents, pollution, etc. If the company releases gases into the atmosphere or pollutes in other ways, this must also be deducted from GNP. In short, all the costs for society must be deducted. If we destroy something for future generations this must also be put on the minus side, for people still are interested in children.

But estimates of the social cost of pollution vary expectedly with political philosophies and ethics. The same holds true for other factors which we give as *shadow prices* – prices that cannot be observed on markets. We move away from seemingly clear quantitative measures to systems of value priorities. If the term 'GNP' is to be revamped and given a positive meaning, we are led towards a measure of *progress relative to a normative system.*

So we are back into philosophy. To talk about reform of GNP is then sheer evasion of the issue.

(i)   Employment and growth

It is taken for granted, especially in Europe, that there is a rather definite correlation between level of employment and economic growth. But economics does not at all support this hypothesis. If you change the economic policy, for instance, from capital-intensive to labour-intensive ways of production, economic growth will stop or decrease (measured by GNP) but level of employment will improve.

Then there are the notions of economically 'good times', high consumption, and high demand. High demand, in a society, means there are a lot of things which are felt to be *lacking*. It does not indicate a higher degree of satisfaction or higher degree of happiness or perfection, nor does it say anything about distribution or sustainability. This is not to say that trade or demand is something completely neutral in terms of Self-realisation. Our main conclusion is, however, that any estimate of general economic progress presupposes a set of values or norms, some of which have to be basic. The professional economist has to relate his estimates to such sets.

7   Basic notions in economic welfare theory

(a)   The notion of economic welfare

In this century a very sophisticated branch of economics has developed in Europe, namely welfare theory. By 'welfare' is here meant, in a very gross manner, the satisfaction of a need. Higher welfare is higher satisfaction of needs. Specialists generally do not use the term 'satisfaction' but instead 'utility'. We should remember that increase of utility means increase of satisfaction of a need by means of a good or a service.

How then do we study increase of satisfaction? It is in welfare studies generally done like this. We may register actual true choices of a person NN between two goods A and B in a situation S. If NN chooses A before B this person is said to *prefer* A to B and if we then get hold of A we note down that it is a plus for satisfaction, a plus in utility.

But what we can collect of data in this way is very limited. The person can, of course, be observed on the market but for instance it is very difficult to observe his choice between A and B when choice A is 'living in the city' and choice B is 'living in the countryside'. And if there are five hundred goods on the market his choices will not of course cover all five hundred. So it is necessary to introduce a notion of 'conjectured' choice, or hypothesised choice, about how A *would* act, not in a real situation S but in a *constructed* situation. We can ask in an interview: 'If you were to choose between A and B what would you choose?'

This is how satisfaction is introduced, simply as another term from what is chosen among relative choices, in definite real-life situations or in conjectured situations.

We must also look into another case. If you think of getting hold of one kind of good A, and more and more of it, the rate of satisfaction of each unit of this would generally diminish after a point. If you have then six units, one may ask what satisfaction the addition of a seventh unit would give you. This is called the *marginal utility* of the good A when a person NN already has some acceptable number of such units.

Now another notion, namely *profile* of goods and services. You have, for instance, questions of where to have your home, where to have your place of work, and to what extent you will *need* free nature in the neighbourhood of where you live, and more generally what kind of society you prefer. Then the choice between A and B would imply choice of economic policies, even choice of ways of democracy. The choices of individual things will then depend on one's choice of profiles. The term 'profile' is used because you then have to compare a tremendous number of goods and services, put into the various classes of such things. This leads to other important notions, namely individual welfare, international, global welfare, and then something very important for environmentalists: the welfare of *any living being which can be said to experience satisfaction or have preferences*.

Most of the welfare theories so far have thought of human beings exclusively, whereas if you use the theories of classic utilitarianism (Bentham, Mill), then utility is related to every living being capable of experiencing satisfaction or dissatisfaction. Individual human welfare is then only one, rather narrow, application of welfare theory. The equations of welfare can be related to any kind of *social* unit and also of course the ecologically important extremes of local community and the biospheric whole.

The last notion of relevance is *welfare optimum*. Clearly if you have a hundred people there will be different kinds of increase of satisfaction, such as an increase of one member's which requires the decrease of another's, or one which is favourable to the increase of others'. It is of course only the latter which is compatible with an increase in Self-realisation.

A society's realistic welfare optimum depends among other things on production. If resources are taken as a given, it is then the highest norm of the economic policy to realise the kind of production and the production quantity which will increase *overall welfare* in the society with the least possible work of the sort which does not have intrinsic value. To give good advice, especially with regard to quantities, it is clearly desirable that the welfare profile itself be quantified. This implies an attempt at measuring preferences. It is admitted by economists that this involves enormous difficulties. Many think it is impossible.

There is a great difference between the higher level of abstract thinking in the more or less axiomatic theory of welfare and the rather low level of applications to real problems of society. This has primarily to do with the rather basic characteristics of people as they make choices: their choices are not like atoms but they are in actuality part of very large packages of choices, such as how to live at a given place and how to care for children. Preferences vary with their intended validity in time.

We will come to place great attention on the term 'satisfaction'. It is implied in welfare theory that one has notions of satisfaction and there philosophy is only a help. Some people will have more or less *hedonistic* views. Others have utilitarian, and again you have the perfectionists. One's choices will depend very much upon what kind of philosophy one espouses; not so much on individual quantitative choices (which are of course preferred by economists because they can get so much data from markets). So welfare theory is not philosophically neutral.

When pleasure/displeasure is brought in to the marginal utility usage notions, welfare is accused of being hedonistic/pleasure-philosophy. When utility/disutility is brought in, it is accused of being utilitarian. When choices or decisions are laid at the base, it can be called voluntarism/will philosophy.

Evidently, welfare theory requires that we choose beforehand whether the society we are talking about is to be seen as a hedonistic, utilitarian, or voluntaristic society. Of course such a welfare theory would largely be an indirect application of normative systems and be very far removed from practical economics.

A much deeper criticism is that welfare theory seems to suppose that the population knows its possibilities for choice. This may not be the case.

(b)   From welfare theory to normative systems

When conclusions are practical in the form of real green or red lights for definite incursions into the business, the point of departure must be normative, not simply a 'toothless value priority point', but an expression using deontic expressions like *ought, shall,* or *must*. It will not be enough to say 'If we are going to give high priority to the increase of economic growth then . . .'. It would be necessary to say 'We should give high priority to economic growth! Therefore . . .'. There should be statements with exclamation marks, not only public opinion references and technical economic analyses!

Hard econometric welfare theory takes as its starting point a normative system following Debreu and Rader: an economic system is composed of (1) a specification of two possible states in the world A and B, (2) specification of a value system with optimisation norms, (3) optimisation of the value system within the possible world states. It is easy to see that what is here taken to be a point of departure is a normative system as defined in this book, but in practice the normative character is somehow put under the carpet. There are, of course, reasons for that: if you really go deeply into a particular normative system, you see that there can be no *science* built up from it as a whole. But if value priority *postulates* are laid down, parts of the system may satisfy scientific methodology.

That this is so is, in an instructive way, clear from economic thinking in the Soviet Union. A gigantic central bureau with big data machinery tries to keep in contact with lesser bureaus all over the vast country and the highest goal is optimal long-range national economic planning (Fedorenko, 1972). The stated normative system has one and only one top norm: consolidation and development of the socialistic system! Thanks to the vagueness and ambiguity of this formulation it is not difficult to see then that the lesser norms further down in the pyramid of norms can be taken care of by the lesser bureaus. The interpretation of the top norm is from time to time altered by pronouncements in the Politburo by top economists of the country. In practice this means that it is not really a completely stable top norm through history, but a flowing development of interpretations of the meaning of socialism, revised through time.

From this top norm a long list of lesser norms are derived. N4 has the key term: 'Increase welfare for the members of the socialist union!' Derived from N4 is N4.1: 'Increase material welfare!' and N4.2 is 'Increase social welfare!' The whole pyramid is explicitly called the '*tree* of goals'. Very instructive for a student of norm systems!

From these norms politicians get tentative projections of what ought to happen in the near future. There is always at least a formal argumentation from the top norm. In short, a philosophy is ostensibly implied which is thought to be invariable from an ideological point of view. In fact there are different interpretations when it is seen in a historical light. And individual interpretations in different departments? We can speculate on the extent to which the system allows for such. Obviously semantic manipulation is important.

The kind of solution tried out in the Soviet Union is not the same as the mixed economy of Scandinavia, but whatever we wish, whether in blue, red, or green politics, we have to admit that there are no solutions, no decisions to be taken, *except from within a total view*, including norms which are accepted as basic without justification. We do not avoid fundamental value priorities and we are only making things less clear if we forfeit the forcefulness of exclamation marks! We simply have to admit that we as humans have to try to act as integrated persons, and societies must be integrated societies even if they are to be pluralistic. A philosophy is pre-supposed. In this book, I have proposed as an example Ecosophy T.

(c)   Welfare to Self-realisation: from W to T
        In what follows there is a suggestion of how to transform welfare-theoretical sentences into Self-realisation sentences. The indication illustrates the dissimilarities between the viewpoints of contemporary economists and those of ecosophers. It is our hope that the future will bring with it fruitful cooperation.

Let us take as the starting point of welfare theory sentences of the following kind: NN would choose A before B if NN had the opportunity to choose. Here A and B are situations characterised by two different profiles or qualitative sets of goods and services. From the point of view of Ecosophy T which has 'Self-realisation!' as the most fundamental norm, such a sentence will be taken as a sign and only as a symptom that situation A would imply better conditions for fuller realisation of NN's norms within his system than B. The choice of A harmonises better or is in better conformity with NN's philosophy than choice B, or choice A creates better conditions for the carrying out of NN's philosophy than the choice of B.

How successful the choice will actually turn out to be depends not on relation to one single norm – there will always be many norms relevant and the consequences of the choice will spread like waves and contact the validity domain of many norms. With this as a starting point, we can offer for inspection three kinds of propositions with the same basic meaning:

NN's Self-realisation would reach a higher level in, with or by A than in, with or by B.

= A implies better conditions than B for Self-realisation (not just of NN, but of the ātman)

= NN's total Self-realisation increases when NN attains or obtains an A and does not at the same time lose some other positive.

The two goods or services, or profiles of goods and services A and B do not therefore *define* Self-realisation but can be said to have a positive or negative import for Self-realisation.

What is now said to be decisive is a hierarchy of norms and hypotheses in a Self-realisation philosophy: the conclusion that A is better than B is built upon a set of hypotheses of actual relations, for instance, resources, but also including hypotheses about oneself. If there is a norm N1 which together with hypothesis H1 implies that one should choose A over B it is clear enough that NN's as well as the social scientist's task is to investigate H1's tenability and relevance.

If a norm runs 'Seek security against unemployment!', it is mostly clear that NN's security depends on the economic policy of his community and on many other things outside the world NN knows fairly well. NN will therefore try to support a policy which he thinks secures him, or adds to the probability that he can secure himself against unemployment. NN is not totally egocentric, and will think of the security of others against unemployment as well, and this makes NN's opinion about which policy is the best quite important for the whole society. Any purchase of goods and services must be seen in the light of at least one such norm, fairly high up in the pyramid of norms.

It may be necessary for NN to take a job which is higher salaried but more insecure. We are led to quite different kinds of investigations from the usual kinds within practical economics.

8 Life quality research: deep interviews

People relate their value system to that of others by comparing how they see family life, the importance of job or profession, the level of economic security vs. economic risk-taking, how they value interesting or useful work vs. well-paid work (where such a contrast ensues), the relative importance of education. But, they are also willing and able to go into more abstract matters such as what they find especially meaningful, worthwhile, or representative of an ethically justifiable lifestyle.

Insofar as an interviewer can get a clear view of the various value judgements of a subject, the road is open to find out to what extent the subject considers themself in a position to live in accordance with these judgements. The higher the attained harmony between ideal and reality, the higher the life quality.

The question of economic policy enters: what economic policy does the subject consider favourable to the realisations of their value priorities? *What economic policy is most favourable to the level of life quality?*

The relevant new social science here is called *life quality research*. The term life quality is introduced more or less in opposition to the economic notion of standard of living and to the confusion of demand on the market and needs. For literature see e.g. Chamberlain (1985). Relation of income to quality of life is central, see e.g. Duncan (1975).

A research technique in these investigations is the *deep interview*. If we are in positions in which we are responsible in some way for people in our community, we have to try to map their normative systems by means of in-depth interviews and relate these results to the resources as we see them and as the people see them.

Life quality has a strong centre in psychological life quality: you investigate how men and women *experience* their life situation, whether they feel threatened by something and what they are threatened by, whether they feel uncertain about something and what they feel uncertain about, whether they feel inferior in some way and what they feel inferior to, and what kinds of frustrations they have in general. In other words, an empirical investigation of normative systems by continually asking the question 'why?'

Of course, some people then feel threatened by things that a social researcher doesn't think exist and on the other hand it can happen that they are not threatened by things the researcher thinks should threaten them, and they feel secure in spite of insight that they may lose their job or be hurt in some other way. So the social scientist must weigh his or her own hypotheses against those of the person being questioned – the discrepancy between the hypotheses themselves is in itself of interest and should be taken into account by decision makers.

It is up to the people who are responsible for the policy of the community to decide whether and to what extent to take the sayings of each person at face value. They have to plot a policy in part on the basis of the different hypotheses. This also holds true for the norms. If the person clearly acts on the basis of a felt threat, thereby hurting other people, one has to try to influence the norms of how people behave towards other people in the community.

It is clear that the data that one gets from deep interviews in life-quality research are a much better basis for policy than what one gets from market research. The term 'deep' here is used because the interview should take place in the natural milieu of the person being interviewed, and take at least several hours and proceed in a relaxed and natural manner, hoping to reach ultimate value priorities and outlooks on life. One needs say on average at least half a day's work before any useful information can come out. This may be a very costly affair, but results so far indicate that the real norms, and real satisfactions people experience, are different from what researchers have supposed. The money is well spent. We discover great differences between conventional views as to what people want, and what they really want.

In Ecosophy T it is of basic importance to realise that the minorities, that is to say groups with very different normative systems from the majority, are helped to retain those conditions for life which they think are essential without destruction by majority voting and prioritising. On the whole, the democratic ideal of the majority is undermined quite a bit by life-quality research. People are diverse! Too many decisions are made on the basis of majorities which tend to coerce the minorities in their most vital interests.

Concluding, it should be clear that, whatever the usefulness of welfare theory and the kind of empirical data obtained from its conceptualisation, it remains superficial, and it hinders the necessary move from the descriptive to the normative point of view. As soon as normative impact is acknowledged, the theoretical tools should be changed from welfare terminology to the terminology of normative systems, defining level of welfare as the level of agreement of actual life with a life in harmony with one's norms and values.

9   Shadow-pricing nature

In cost-benefit analyses and in many other investigations, economists handle prices found by observing markets. The value of certain goods and services which are not exchanged on markets is estimated in other ways – they get their 'shadow prices'. So why not consider pieces of free nature, for instance, the value of *not* developing a certain river? If it should and could be done, conservation projects might be said to create vast monetary values and thus be economically on a par with industrial production.

There is not much data on the question, but I guess social scientists, and among them economists, are on the whole less favourable in their attitudes towards environmentalism than natural scientists, humanists, and medical scientists. There are, of course, exceptions. And among these it is a natural goal to work for environmentalist causes using the professional tools of their trade (Rolston 1985). One goal is clearly to find ways to get protection of nature into the framework of quantitative economic analysis. After all, if this is impossible, concern for the environment will not appear in this analysis except as concern for fisheries, fur trade etc. Concern for fish, wolves, and wilderness in themselves cannot appear in the calculations.

In March and April 1985 two investigations were made by means of questionnaires (Hervik (1986)). In March, a representative sample of 1000 persons were asked what they would be willing to pay in increased cost of electricity if this payment would protect a certain class of rivers from being developed (including making dams, etc.). It was made clear that the abstention from developing the river systems might perhaps lead to higher prices per unit electricity for household purposes. Definite amounts of money were suggested in a somewhat complicated and methodologically sophisticated manner.

In the April investigation it was said that the development of the rivers might presumably lower the price of energy (with the amounts of money corresponding to the amounts dealt with in March). People were asked what would be the minimal reduction of price which would make them favour the development of the river systems.

It would require considerable space to discuss the methodological refinements. Here I propose to discuss the normative problem: whether such investigations should be supported by people in the deep ecological movement.

The intuitively clearest denial of the value or even meaningfulness of the investigations has been worked out under the heading 'you cannot slap a price-tag on nature!'

An expert on energy problems of international repute and a firm supporter of the deep ecological movement, Paul Hofseth, has summarised the main normative arguments against 'pricing nature': if somebody A asks a person B what he or she will pay in order that A does not break B's arm, the amount suggested by B cannot, says Hofseth, be taken as a measure of the price or value of the arm. B has a right to his arm. It is not permitted to break human arms. Analogously, access to free nature is a right.

If a government A asks a population B what price it will pay for protecting a part of nature, the price is not the price of that part of nature as $5000 is the price of a certain car!

Suppose the 'disutilities' brought about by destroying a part of free nature get the price tag $5000, and the utility for the population at large is placed at $10,000. The government should nonetheless *not* be permitted to destroy it. It corresponds to breaking the arm of person B because A, representing the population at large, has calculated the utility being greater than the disutility. The parcel of nature in question is part of his or her Self!

A price of $5000 for a car on the market implies that you can change $5000 into a car or a car into $5000. At least in the case of irreversible or irreparable *damage* to nature, there is no such relation.

Hofseth compared access to free nature with 'access' to education. For some well educated groups within a society it may be of great desirability that certain other groups are not offered decent education, but this is not right. Cost–benefit analysis breaks down in the case of rights.

An article by two environmentalist journalists is witty and superbly well illustrated ('Crosscountry skiing with Uncle Scrooge', *Miljømagasinet*, 1985). Wherever they go skiing, tiny bureaucratic creatures crop up and start to interrogate: 'How much would you give to save this?', etc. If 'a million' is the answer, the interviewer immediately prints out that the amount *must* tally 'with the income of the skiers'. Prices are obtained for everything.

Of course pained, frustrated environmentalists, who practically every day are seeing or hearing or reading about new destructions of free nature, relish reading such articles. They also, at least hopefully, read about actual environmental decisions at least in part based on estimates of the money, the expenditures, people who go fishing, hiking, or otherwise 'use nature' actually give out for equipment, travel, etc. This is then compared to income obtained if a hotel were built or a parking lot or a dam.

Enough along these lines. How do economists specialising in environmental conflicts defend their efforts? Having 'objectivity' as a high ideal, one cannot expect such amusements or catchy phrases. As social scientists, they also tend to avoid ethical pronouncements.

Whatever the actual defence tactics, I think the authors of methodologically sophisticated empirical investigations should state and repeat that they are *not* placing any price-tag on nature! Furthermore they should remind the environmentalists that the way decisions today are taken, the *lack* of quantitative data in support of protection often, or at least sometimes, functions as if quantitative data actually were offered, namely the price zero. Thus the economists may claim that what they try to prevent is the price zero from being used in the decision-making process.

Both March and April 1985 investigations end with the conclusion that to develop certain categories of not yet protected rivers is non-economic

– the disutility is greater than the utility measured in money. The same conclusion may turn up in every other environmental conflict. People are more willing to protect than politicians believe.

But, says the concerned environmentalist, what if the quantitative treatment in serious cases goes in disfavour of free nature? The economists think they have convincing answers to that. Their conclusions should never be taken as the only basis for a decision. The report of their studies should be delivered to the decision makers as only one set of relevant material, and the weakness of the methodology and the limited relevance of the conclusions should of course be made plain. Environmentalists tend, they conclude, to misconceive both methodology and conclusions.

Some environmentalists I suspect will answer that the quantitative nature of the conclusions will impress decision makers, and rarely will they have time to study the methodology. They will be glad to give up 'subjective' and 'intuitive' evaluations in favour of 'objective data'. Their responsibility will be lighter. In the long run a question of principle should be faced as the most important: the surveys conducted in March and April 1985 are explicitly used in decision making on the highest levels, supporting the view that we may interfere with free nature *without limitation* so long as people of the present generation indicate little interest in protection. The ethical and philosophical problem is evaded. And this would be fatal.

To all this the economist may answer that it is based on the premise that politicians are already used to 'quantifying everything'. A mother asks for a sign 'Children at play' to be placed in her street, and gets the answer 'It would cost too much if everybody in your situation were offered such a sign. The price is $1000.' The mother says: 'Shame on you! Putting a price-tag on my son!' As it is now, disutility of an intervention is measured by a listing of interests interfered with. Examples: fishing, regional economy, pollution, cultural heritage. With no weighting it is tempting to count each alike. If careful weighting, and thus quantifiability, is introduced it may support protection of nature. In one study (Wenstrup, 1985) the economist author finds that a sample of people attached weights which, if plotted from 10 to 100, give the following results arranged from 100 and down: protection of nature 100, agriculture 90, *friluftsliv* 70, protection of cultural heritage 60, ... The big pressure groups which seem strongly to influence decisions are in rich democratic welfare states very unlikely to arrive at a favourable ranking.

With increasing awareness of the tremendous exciting and awe-inspiring past, reaching back 3500 million years, the conviction strengthens that the role of *Homo sapiens* cannot possibly be to destroy on the present scale. Furthermore the awareness of the vast time scale of the past strengthens the conviction that our concern cannot be only for our children and grandchildren but must be for remoter generations and for the planet as a whole. Nuclear waste problems have at least the plus that we now feel responsible for pollution a thousand years from now. Can this concern be quantified?

Accepting the inevitable concern on a geological time scale, the so-called discount of future values must be considered anew. Now the diminished concern for the nth generation after us is very roughly similar to a function like $1/n^2$. That is, the negative value our children will experience because of contemporary misbehaviour counts only $\frac{1}{4}$ of the negative value for us (putting $n = 2$). The total negative value has then only risen from 1.0 to 1.25. The negative value for grandchildren will only add $\frac{1}{9}$ to the total. In short, with increasing remoteness our concern vanishes more and more. The possibility of the disruption of nuclear waste containers after 500 years can be ignored – practically no concern is required according to the adopted function.

Against such a cold view of our responsibilities for what is happening even in the geologically and evolutionary close future, a different view should become predominant. The concern for the future should add up towards infinity. Putting first generation concern equal to 1, the concern for generation n from now might be symbolised by $1/n$. The total concern will then approach the infinite (sum equal to $\frac{1}{1} + \frac{1}{2} + \frac{1}{3}$ . . .). Those who think that *Homo sapiens* is 'programmed' to eventually destroy life on the planet should perhaps advise that we leave it before it is too late. There is, however, no good reason to believe that there is such a programming. And the great uncertainty about the remote developments of *Homo sapiens* and its technologies makes it natural for us to concentrate on possible effects of our behaviour for the first thousand years to come. (Population reduction towards decent levels might incidentally require a thousand years.)

The above crude quantification can of course be refined. But this does not change the conclusion that, whatever quantification is chosen, it will be of limited direct help in the decision-making process.

Quantification plays a dominant role in shaping the policies and attitudes in modern industrial society. Before the Second World War, to calculate 'everything' in dollars was ridiculed in Europe and considered degrading, but after the war the tendency, for instance in the branches of entertainment and sport, has been to calculate more and more in monetary terms. It is therefore natural to find more or less generalised negative attitudes towards calculation within the deep ecological movement. There are many kinds of qualitative studies which are valuable for the movement, for instance the distribution of environmental attitudes, and the studies of factors increasing or diminishing concern for the planet.

The March and April 1985 statistics furnish some highly relevant materials. People in Norway living in the three biggest cities are willing to pay much more to avoid development than people in thinly populated areas. People's attitudes of this kind ought to be included among the data utilised by decision makers.

The dramatic criticism by Paul Hofseth of the willingness to pay and willingness to forgo makes it natural to ask what he would recommend. In short he favours the boundary or *limitations* strategy. That is, a good time before any big pressure group casts its eye on a piece of free nature to push for legislation against any 'development'. A key term here is 'enduring protection'. A list of river systems in Norway should be declared inviolable by the government. This idea is the basis of the 'Master Plan' of protection which the government of Norway has now (1986) endorsed. The question is: how operative and binding will the legislation be? What Paul Hofseth and other environmentalists hope is that the 'ideology of the broken arm' is taken seriously. Nobody is entitled to break the arms of fellow humans, however useful this may appear to be, and nobody is entitled to destroy any part of the protected river ecosystems.

Whatever the outcome of the Master Plan approach, thousands of environmental conflicts in the years to come will not be influenced by the Plan. Therefore the efforts of economists to quantify may still be worthy of discussion. Economists clearly on the side of strong environmental policies tend to be pessimistic: the initiative has been taken away from the environmentalists and remains with the economists. The latter envelop quantitative methods which suit the bureaucratic and political leadership. As long as environmentalists look upon economists as enemies instead of people to cooperate with, economists will sway towards unintended, one-sided cooperation with people in power, and easily find financial support for their efforts. It is to be hoped that this situation will change.

This brings us back to the motives for writing this chapter.

10   Summary

(1) The debate in economics in the 80s has *not yet* in all seriousness taken into account the ecosophically valuable contribution of economists like Georgescu-Roegen, Fritz Schumacher and Kenneth Boulding.

(2) Environmentalists contribute to a change in this situation by acquaintance with the work of some of these green economic classics.

(3) This implies also, however, acquaintance with the kind of economic doctrines they (sometimes rather rhetorically) criticise, perhaps even an acquaintance with the quasi-philosophical welfare theory.

(4) Humans' gross interference in nature mirrors our economic activity. Protection of what is left of free nature depends largely on the way humans are willing and able to change their ways of production and consumption – and the ideologies justifying the present economic misuse of the planet.

(5) The development of the Western science of economics has stressed value-neutrality and quantitative relations, but its insights into the complicated web of contemporary existing economic factors are of importance in any environmental conflict. In many questions, like that of the relation between GNP and economic progress, some economists hold critical views useful to environmentalists, who cannot avoid partiality in discussions of an economic character.

(6) Because so many major destructive projects carried out by state or private capital have been judged and found profitable by some hired economists, it is natural that the profession is looked upon with suspicion by environmentalists. But there is a growing treasure of economic literature which supports environmentalists' views.

6

Ecopolitics within ecosophy

1   The ecological movement cannot avoid politics

(a)   All is politically relevant, but not
all is politics

All our actions, and all our thoughts, even the most private, are politically relevant. If I use a clipped tea leaf, some sugar, and some boiling water, and I drink the product, I am supporting the tea and sugar prices and more indirectly I interfere in the works and capital conditions of the tea and sugar plantations of the developing countries. In order to heat the water, I may have used wood or electricity or some other kind of energy, and then I take part in the great controversy concerning energy use. I may use water from a private source or a public source, and in either case I participate in a myriad of politically burning questions of water supply. I certainly have a political influence daily in innumerable ways.

If I *reflect* on all these things along ecological lines and make my opinions known, I contribute to the strength of the politically conscious ecological movement. If I do *nothing* instead of drinking the tea I normally drink I may contribute to the difficulties of the developing countries because then their export becomes smaller. But perhaps not: I may think that they should not export tea but rather produce more food and therefore I make it easier for the politicians of the developing countries to change their economic policies in the direction of self-reliance.

But to say that every action and every thought is politically relevant is not the same as to say that 'all is politics'. Nothing is only political, and nothing is not at all political. Ecopolitics is concerned not only with specifically ecological activity, but with every aspect of life.

In principle, it is desirable that everyone in the ecological movement engage in political activity. Many people whose vital need it is to live in nature, by nature, and for nature, do not make themselves felt in political life. This is a great obstacle for those politicians who try hard to satisfy to some extent the needs of people engaged in conservation of the planet. On the other hand there are plenty of jobs in environmentalism which do not require any political participation beyond mere voting and similar tasks.

(b)   Power analysis is necessary

The force of democratic institutions in our time in determining policies is gradually decreasing because powerful pressure groups take over much of the influence on the decisions. Also, if we consider the big multinational firms, we discover they can have a greater power than small states, and within the states the department of energy, say, may have great influence and will of course tend to support decisions to use more and more energy, whatever the actual need. In environmental conflicts, it is therefore important to *map out the power structures* relevant in pushing the decisions and determining the different stages in the conflict. Even in a small country like Norway, in one relatively minor conflict on the development of a river, the map of power sources included more than twenty power centres. Each stage of the conflict could to some extent be predicted through mapping out the relative strengths of all these centres.

This kind of activity, to map out power structures in a cold and detached way, neither over- nor underestimating the strengths of the opponents themselves, is mostly uninteresting for people who are engaged in conserving nature. So there has to be an intimate cooperation between conservationists, journalists, people knowing political ways and means, and all those who are vitally interested in the workings of big societies.

One of the most important points in conflicts is this: people in the conservation movement do not know enough about how production and consumption are determined so that they try to effect change on society by changing their own lifestyles through a decrease of private consumption instead of using political means. Both ways are of course necessary and complementary but Galbraith (1973) was wise to point out that 'the thought that individual choice determines kind and quantity of production is wrong'.

There has been a change in the 1970s and 1980s in thinking about analysis of power, and analysis of propaganda, and analysis of the power of the mass media. Before this time, there was, especially among people interested in nature, such strong aversion to these themes that they were shunned completely, whereas the new generation is more used to harsh realities, and there is a hope that this will lead to a greater interest in green politics in the near future.

(c)   The politicisation of conservation
Until the fight against uncritical use of pesticides started in the early 60s and the international ecological movement burst forth it was widely held that attitudes towards nature could be significantly changed through direct work on these very attitudes. The pesticide conflict revealed in a clear and dramatic way that ways of production and consumption had to be tackled straight on. E. F. Schumacher describes in a dramatic but simple way what we are up against. Slightly condensed and modified we may formulate it this way. A system of production has immanent forces or implicit aims which mould society. Society accepts the aims as if they were its own and becomes captive to the system. Consequently society cannot adopt different aims and values unless the way of production is altered. Even when captive we may form ideas about a different system, but these are but expressions of wishful thinking without efforts to alter the dominating system (Schumacher, 1974, p. 132). This implies that unless the ideas are acted upon through politics there will be no major changes.

As an example of the politicisation of subjects formerly being isolated from politics, one might mention the conservation of spectacular animals in Africa. When it became more and more clear that a number of species were in danger, the policy was first just to tell people not to hunt, then to make it illegal. But one didn't think much about the sociopolitical implications of this. Through research in cultural anthropology, knowledge about the very interesting and highly developed cultures of these regions was increased, and it was clear from individual observation that through the protection of the spectacular animals we were at the same time contributing to the destruction of certain cultures of which hunting was an integral part.

The opponents of the deep ecological movement try to keep the question of saving this planet from destruction of various kinds away from politics. It is clear that there are very strong forces trying always to show that questions having to do with ecology are cleanly scientific – confinable to physics, chemistry, mineralogy, and resource research in general. A strong slogan in Europe is therefore 'fight against de-politicisation!'

Governments try to hire experts from every natural science discipline so as to avoid the question of how to change our societies in order to make sane ecopolitics possible. The researchers and the experts then publish conclusions which are highly compatible with continued economic growth. By selecting this type of expertise the general public is influenced in the direction of slackness and acceptance of 'development' as it is now commonly understood.

2   The three poles of the political triangle –
the blue, the red, and the green;
the limitations of triangular analysis

One convenient way of naming main contemporary currents and parties in some industrial countries is to present a political triangle (figure 6.1). It illustrates three main political poles. These colours are familiar symbols in European discussion.

Essential for supporters of green policies: to maintain and to show that they cannot be placed on the line between red and blue. A second dimension is needed.

Also essential: political abstractions such as green, red, and blue are dangerous if taken as being merely points. They are more like magnetic poles: dynamic pulls in more or less definite directions. They must be distinguished, then, from particular parties or platforms. These are definable in relation to the poles, not placed at them.

So we can try circles (figure 6.2).

If circles are used, they should be overlapping. Most supporters of green politics see a greater affinity between green and red than between green and blue. But from a wide historic and systematic point of view it is prudent to let the circles overlap equally, rejecting any quantitative interpretation of the overlapping areas.

Examples of similarity between green and blue: stressing the value of personal enterprise (overlapping the blue private enterprise). Very high priority of fighting bureaucracy.

Similarity between green and red: stressing social responsibility. Very high priority of fighting undesirable ethical, social, and cultural consequences of the unrestrained market economy. Equality, opposition to hierarchical structures.

Political parties in many countries can roughly be located within or along the borders of the political triangle. More accurately (but still in a rough way of course) in three dimensions like a cartesian coordinate system (figure 6.3).

But is green to be seen as merely another alternative of *the same kind* as red and blue? No – the essential point here is that green is *not merely another point, circle, or dimension*. It is a dynamic wave-like force which

Figure 6.1

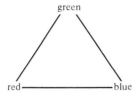

Figure 6.2

Figure 6.3

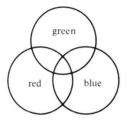

Figure 6.4

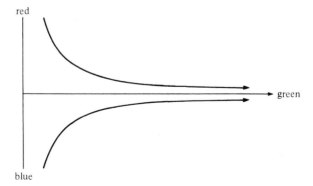

should affect all points along any shallowly conceived spectrum or frontier of political opinions. Hence the British Ecology Party (now renamed the Green Party) makes it clear that its own existence will be rendered unnecessary by its success, as 'all parties will in time become more or less ecological' (Porritt, 1984). A quite ecological attitude about one's own existence!

So probably the most satisfactory diagram would be one which indicates clearly the dynamic and asymptotic nature of the green influence (figure 6.4).

Every political decision has green relevance. A consequence: green parties must be big enough to have people well-versed in each of the major issues. (No single politician can really be well-informed on all.) It is thus not enough to take up the problems which people in general perceive as being typically ecological (nuclear energy, acid rain, etc.). An instructive survey is found in Devall and Sessions (1985), p. 18.

In industrial democracies, the supporters of green policies must keep track of how the politicians of the various parties talk *and vote* on specific matters, evaluating them as seen from the green outlook. Their ecology 'score' should be widely publicised. The same holds true for party platforms, but experience, at least in Scandinavia, suggests that every party platform can look as if a responsible ecological policy is being taken seriously, while decisions may nevertheless turn out to be consistently anti-green.

People have reason to be suspicious about societies planning to implement green policies: do they not ask for still more regulations (laws, coercive rules, etc.) than we already have? The answer is 'not necessarily!' But, in order to avoid suspicion, keeping down regulations must constantly be in the minds of green organisers. A typically blue attitude? Yes and no. Private industry is, in spite of its official 'free and competitive' nature, shot through with internal regulations, mostly unknown to the general public, but no less coercive for that. The smaller-unit industry of green societies will, because of less hierarchical power structure among other reasons, need less regulation. Much depends on change of mentality: the less mental change in the green direction, the more regulations.

3   Checklist of ecopolitical issues and their expansion

It is easy to become lost in absorbing ideological currents and counter-currents in place of concentrating on the following definite question. At what points and how much would ecosophically responsible and justifiable political programmes be different from the present political programmes in the industrial states? In what follows I shall mention some areas of major parts of political platforms which would have to look quite different if the deep ecological movement became influential. We begin with a checklist of the basic areas of ecopolitical interest, and expand them in several directions.

Questions: What is the proposed politics of *x* in regard to subject *y*?

   x – a person, an institution, a nation, a group

   y – any of the subjects listed below

(1A)   Politics of pollution of human environment
   (a)   short vs. long term perspective
   (b)   local vs. regional vs. national vs. global perspective
   (c)   class aspect: local vs. regional vs. national vs. global perspective

(1B)   Politics of pollution of the habitats of other life forms
   (a)   short vs. long term perspective
   (b)   local vs. regional vs. national vs. global perspective
   (c)   discrimination: favoured vs. unfavoured life forms
   (d)   politics related to specific species, ecosystems, landscapes

(2A)   Politics of resources for humans
   (a)   short vs. long term perspective
   (b)   local vs. regional vs. national vs. global perspective
   (c)   class aspect: local vs. regional vs. national vs. global perspective

(2B)   Politics of resources for non-human life forms
   (a)   short vs. long term perspective
   (b)   local vs. regional vs. national vs. global perspective
   (c)   discrimination: favoured vs. unfavoured life forms
   (d)   politics related to specific species, ecosystems, landscapes

(3A)   Politics of population of humans
   (a)   short vs. long term perspective; stabilisation or reduction?
   (b)   local vs. regional vs. national vs. global perspecive
   (c)   class aspect: local vs. regional vs. national vs. global perspective

(3B)   Politics of *population* of non-humans
   (a)   short vs. long term perspective
   (b)   local vs. regional vs. national vs. global perspective
   (c)   discrimination: favoured vs. unfavoured life forms
   (d)   politics related to specific species, ecosystems, landscapes

What is the basic aim of the above pedantic enumeration? It is to contribute to the turning of the shallow ecological debate into deeper channels. We have a formidable task of communication and need techniques to solve it. The above list facilitates intervention in debates of the following sort: 'Yes, I agree about the short term question, but what about the long term?', 'Yes, but don't we at present just leave the problem to future administrations?', 'Yes, GNP is increased, but look at the deplorable ecological consequences!', 'Sure, the protection of nature here is not a local or regional responsibility, it is national and international!', 'Yes, but you have not taken into account the protection of these living beings not for our sake, but for their own sake.' 'Sustainable population? You mean of humans? What about the sustainable population of others?'.

These three classes of issues constitute the core of ecopolitical issues in a narrow, standard sense. The above list may be helpful. But there is a wider, and in my terminology, deeper sense in which ecopolitical issues also directly cover problems within traditional politics.

In relation to 1A–3B, green politics opposes the red, and especially the blue, in the following ways.

> (1) Long time perspective. We intimately feel that we are parts of an emanation of life where a million years is a short time. We are concerned with soils that can be destroyed in 5 minutes but which would take a thousand years to restore. We are unimpressed by short political election periods and reject the superstition that a few years of research and technical development can solve any major ecological problems of any kind. Nevertheless, we must be alert and try to anticipate the next move of our governments, and main unecological agencies such as the so-called forest services.
>
> (2) Green politics combines local and global perspectives, trying to tone down the excessive role of national and international structures. What is known as 'national identity' is based on local communities. Inter-local communication largely supplants international. Assistance to the third world, for instance by the organisation The Future in Our Hands, is done through direct contact between local communities, and help is conceived to be mutual. It is difficult to avoid governmental institutions, but nearly a thousand global non-governmental institutions have their seats in Geneva and can be used to facilitate *inter-local rather than international contact.*

The main arguments used in Norway when rejecting membership in the European Common Market (EEC) in 1972 were mainline ecopolitical (issues 1A and 3B). We rejected centralism endangering local and 'peripheral' communities, forced worker mobility, increased competitiveness on the world market. We said 'no thank you' to the EEC's introduction of four times as many officially accepted medicines, and we said no to opening still wider our gates for immense multinational firms.

(3) Green politics supports the elimination of class differences locally, regionally, nationally, and globally.

The global aspect makes it clear that the majorities in the rich industrial states belong to the global upper class. This is easily forgotten by trade unions, and by some Marxists–Leninists who still unilaterally focus on the liberation of the workers of their own rich countries.

The core of class suppression may be seen basically as a cross-generational suppression of life fulfilment potentials in relation to fellow beings. (Or in my terminology Self-realisation potentialities.)

The politically significant *green–red alliances* in Scandinavia use this name because green political issues are mostly conceived rather narrowly as comprising *only* issues 1A to 3B. Using such a narrow concept a great many political problems seem to fall outside the green framework. But every main political issue can be considered in a green way, using green value priorities.

In the 80s the deep ecological movement has been enriched by increased consciousness of the uniqueness of our planet. It is not a 'use and throw away' planet. It may take more than a million years to fly to a new one of the same incredible beauty and richness. The Gaia-hypothesis of James Lovelock – whatever its scientific worth – has not only opened new areas of research, but evoked a new wave of reverence and pride (Lovelock, 1979). What has Mother Earth done to stay alive and keep evolution going! She has got more friends than ever – people who gladly would pay higher taxes and whatever else is needed to support efforts to conserve what there is still of wilderness and areas in general, big and undisturbed enough to let mammalian and other evolution continue. (About minimum requirements see Soulé (1986).) But clear, forceful signals from the grass roots are necessary for politicians to permit themselves to put forth programmes of real significance.

4   More comments on the basic ecopolitical areas of pollution, resources, and population

(a)   *Pollution*

Pollution is the oldest and best-treated subject of ecological/political concern in the industrial states. But there is still great ignorance of what is really involved in combating pollution with adequate intensity.

First of all, there is of course a tendency to try to get rid of pollution where it is visible and where it is politically dangerous. It is tempting to place heavily polluting industries along the border of one's state so that all the bad air will leave the state. Furthermore it is less dangerous politically to pollute in areas of low density of population or those with poor people and low power consumption. Consequently it is politically wise to place polluting industries in developing countries.

In Hong Kong, by chance, there was an oil spill just in front of the place where there was to be an international competition in sailing. Powerful rich people were exposed to pollution problems. Chemicals were immediately used and the fishing population and the fish themselves were exposed to the ill effects of both the oil and the chemicals. They had to pay for it: the water looked clean but the fish were killed.

Furthermore it is politically dangerous to be responsible for pollution that will clearly show itself within an election term, but it is much less politically dangerous to arrange things so that it will be the next generation or the generation after that who will suffer the real effects.

Regarding pollution of the oceans, some people who own the ships or who are otherwise in the midst of shipping proclaim quite honestly that they are in favour of strict rules about oil spills and cleaner tankers, but as long as these rules are not acknowledged by their competitors they will not be able to compete. This may sound like ducking the responsibility. But for the future we may envision global institutions with some power not only to criticise certain states or companies but also to implement certain measures against the states which violate the rules. We need such international institutions with more than the simple power of criticism. But how to establish them?

In the shallow movement pollution is mainly thought of as relating only to Man's dominion, that is to say polluting human values, whereas in the deep movement one has to look for room for every living being and the ecosystem. Polluting for whom? For this or that species or system?

(b)   Resources

Politically, resources in a narrow context are now a main issue. But the experts appointed by governments of the rich countries have nevertheless not realised that there are ethical problems attached to the industrial countries' consumption in relation to developing countries, future generations, all living beings, and what is left of free nature. There is not a sufficient distinction between usable and nonusable resources as Georgescu-Roegen (1971) and others have tried to point out. Neglecting wide contexts, governments can continue resource waste and use professional resource optimists to powder their conclusions.

Neither the ideals of private economic profitability (USA) nor those of volume of production (Soviet Union) have had implications unfriendly to resource waste. A close relation between political growth ideology and producers' interests makes a green resource policy extraordinarily difficult.

Without a broad rejection of the struggle–growth ideology, there can be no effective criticism of the dominant policies of resource waste.

On the other hand there has been a tendency among the supporters of deep ecology to underestimate oil and other resources because it is good for their political stance to be among those who are shouting loudest about dwindling resources. This has decreased their credibility. It is better to take a *normative stand* that you shouldn't do so and so than to propagate prognoses of doubtful character which will be publicly disputed by experts who know many more facts about the resource situation for humans.

(c)   Population

In the beginning of this century, the terms 'empty' and 'desolate' were frequently used to refer to land without *human* settlement. If the land seemed to be capable of development it seemed to cry for humans, longing only for exploitation by humans. With the human population doubling again and again, and with increasing alteration *per capita*, explorers, tourists, and naturalists use a considerably different terminology now at the end of the century. The term 'free nature' is used about land with no settlements or major signs of present human activity. Because of the steadily shrinking areas of free nature, human attitude towards their own imprints is radically changing. Until recently, it was generally assumed that people born and raised in cities would not develop love of free nature. That has turned out wrong. Free nature is seen by them no longer as empty nature, but as full of life and other marvels.

Earlier in this century there was also vivid interest in how many people the Earth can support – its carrying capacity. In an excellent textbook this is said to be like asking how many cigarettes you can smoke before you get cancer (Miller, 1975, p. 107). The question of optimum population is now found more relevant, but unhappily the general term is used in a narrow way, referring to only one species, *Homo sapiens*, and the mature human need of a superbly rich planet is ignored.

According to Richard A. Watson and Philip M. Smith (Watson, 1970) a United Nations study poses the following question: 'Given the present world-wide industrial and agricultural capacity, technological development, and resource exploitation, how many people could be supported on earth today with the standard of living of the average American? The answer is just 500 million.' The authors think that 500 million would not result in a uniform, stagnant world and refer to the seventeenth century. Agreed, but the question raised refers only to humans. How about other living beings? If their life quality is not to be lowered through human dominance, for instance agriculture, are not 500 million too many? Or:

are cultural diversity, development of the sciences and arts, and of course basic needs of humans not served by, let us say, 100 million? A questionnaire in Norway suggests that there is a minority who think 100 million are enough. (Naess, 1985d). But many more do not really answer, but brush the question away as 'academic', 'utopian'. They immediately think of the difficulties of reduction in a humane way.

Maps with colours showing distance from nearest road are made to make people see how little is left of the planet still free from major, manifest human interference and domination. Extension of agriculture into new areas has lost its function because only little of the present areas is used directly for vital human needs. With present natural parks being slowly ruined through excess numbers of visitors, policies are changed, new areas must be found. But there is also an increase of respect for the 'empty' areas without any prospect for income from tourism. Politically slogans like 'Let evolution continue!' and 'Earth first!' are increasingly appreciated. With greater and greater requirement of space *per capita* in rich industrial countries it is seen that a similar development elsewhere is physically impossible and a total failure of conservation. The overpopulation in the rich countries is manifest from a global viewpoint.

'Untouched' nature was a rather popular term in the 60s and early 70s; with increase in knowledge both of the history of landscapes of the past and of the ubiquitous pollution of soils, air, and oceans, the term tends now to be used with a sad smile. The increasing negative reaction towards the increase of human population is not to foster any animosity towards humans as such – on the contrary, human fulfilment seems to *demand* and *need* free nature. 'Homocentrism' and 'anthropocentrism' which so often have been used in a derogatory way should be qualified by an adjective, 'narrow homocentrism' etc. Gradually the prospect of protecting the planet as a whole and for its own sake is seen as one of the greatest challenges ever. And it certainly is a specifically *human* task. A deep human need is involved, we realise a unique potentiality in revising political decisions so as to satisfy such a need. The time is ready for political realists to permit themselves to refer to that need.

5   Strengthening the local and the global

(a)   Self-determination

Implicit in a system with a basic norm of Self-realisation is the assumption of a capacity for self-determination, a capacity for realising potentialities.

Preliminary studies of attitudes among 'experts' and politicians who participate in decisions on environmental problems (Naess, 1986a and 1985d) indicate a positive attitude – rarely or ever announced in public –

towards not only stabilisation of the human population, but major reduction of the human population. It is of course a very long-range problem and politically today a non-existent issue. It is important, however, that such attitudes should be known by people at large. Otherwise there is little prospect that the groups with a reduction as a distant goal will press for appropriate changes in taxation and other tools of influence.

One of the strange misconceptions which make people reluctant to support a policy of reduction is the view that the immense number of humans testifies to an immense love of children. Consequently, that reduction implies lack of enthusiasm and of love of children. Who would like to be declared enemy of children! Realistic studies of how the population of humans got out of balance do not support any romantic general view of why people get many children.

Social conditions may be good or bad for the development of self-determination.

This implies that, in as many as possible of the essential aspects of life, one should be able to resist coercion. These freedoms are diminished every time there is a centralisation of a decision in the sense that some actor at a distant centre contributes to the decision in a way that must be felt to come from the outside, unduly narrowing one's own freedom of choice. Therefore ecological policies will be on the side of decentralisation.

For instance, in energy. If you centralise energy then anything happening to the central sources makes you more or less helpless and any disturbance which affects the distribution and intensity of the energy you get will pose problems where you are not able to do much. On the other hand, strongly decentralised sources of energy may be less profitable from a narrow economic point of view and require a little more work for the consumer, but you have it inside your own sphere of action and power.

It is common in our industrial states to talk about periphery and centre of the society. Centralisation means also that you have certain places, mostly big cities, where creativity is acknowledged to be highest and this determines conditions in the periphery. In the music you choose, in the clothing you wear, and in a hundred other ways there are centres which determine to a large degree how people in the periphery will live. This centralisation tends to lower self-determination. Yet it must be stressed that self-determination does not mean ego-trip. Being together with others is essential to the realisation of the Self.

In Scandinavia decentralisation and the support of small units in the economy is something that the politicians say they are in favour of. But in practice it is clear that such political opinions have not stopped the continued tendency towards bigger units. And the greater the size of the units as a whole the less possibilities exist for individual creativity. There is less possibility for each member of the unit to have a comprehension of what is going on.

But again one should warn against absolutism. A worker in a big firm with a strong central authority may have better conditions of self-determination in work than one in a small firm. 'Small' is not always 'beautiful' as Schumacher himself clearly announced.

(b)   Self-reliance
The economics of the industrial states has tended to favour *any* increase in trade between nations, and the main thing here is that certain places on the Earth can produce certain products more cheaply and one should always then import from places where they can do things in the cheapest way, and one should export enough to pay for this import. It is very difficult to counteract the force of such argumentation.

The positive effects on material standard of living from international export/import relations are obvious. Some trade has been going on for thousands of years while enhancing cultural diversity. But social and cultural costs *may* be staggering. Lifestyle and entertainment import has led to a dependence upon international economic fluctuations, leading to uniformity, passivity, more consumption, less creativity.

The likelihood for continued cultural diversity diminishes on a global scale. This undermines the independence of different cultures but mostly what it does is make it very difficult to be self-reliant, that is to have the possibility of maximum self-*activity*: creating, rather than consuming. Doing, not being done to. The basic ecosophical terms here would be activeness, inner and outer, in reaching goals.

In some of our industrial states like Norway, we are clearly to a high degree dependent on the resources of other countries, and one district or community is dependent on others. What is suggested through self-reliance is not that all kinds of such communication should cease, but that they should be carried out only if favourable for Self-realisation, and not done as a necessity for satisfying needs that could be satisfied locally just as well.

Self-realisation is not against cultural communication, but it favours intrinsic values, material and spiritual. For instance, if you make a journey that you do not feel has any intrinsic value to a distant point in order to get hold of a good or service, the communication has been a minus, if it would have furthered you better to get the thing locally. On the other hand, if you have friends or if you have something at a distant point which you cannot furnish locally, or if the travel itself is a valuable experience, then of course the communication is acceptable from the point of view of Self-realisation, and therefore Ecosophy T.

Unhappily, increase of self-reliance requires individuals to be very conscious of their values, the obstacles, and what might be done politically to improve conditions. So it is natural that only a minority have had the opportunity to work for a very high level of self-reliance. It is only possible within a coherent, local, logical, and natural community.

(c)   The realisation of local communities
In European sociology, a distinction is made between community and society, *Gemeinschaft* and *Gesellschaft*. Locality and togetherness in the sense of community are central key terms in the deep ecological movement. There is, so to say, an 'instinctive' reaction against being absorbed in something that is big but not great – something like our modern society. It is, however, not easy to make quite clear what are the essential characteristics of a desirable local community.

The so-called green communities have over the last twenty years developed certain properties which are considered positive.

(1) The members are not so numerous that they cannot know each other by acquaintance and there are inherent stabilising factors that keep the population at a fairly constant level.

(2) Decisions in areas which affect all the members are taken through direct communication, so there can be a direct form of democracy.

(3) Counteracting antisocial behaviour is done directly with friendliness. There is little direct influence from the outside which interferes with that order inside.

(4) The ways and means of production relate most strongly to primary production. This has as a result a high economic self-reliance.

(5) Technology is essentially soft. We could also use the term 'near', because what things are made of must come from the neighbourhood, or at least from areas as near as possible, preferably not from outside the country.

(6) Culture and entertainment have to a high degree local colour and this holds for work as well.

(7) Schooling is directed towards acquaintance with technology needed in the local area but of course the possibilities for formal literary and artistic education should be present.

(8) Differences in income and wealth are small. Those at the bottom and those at the top are sufficiently near in ways of life that they can go together and work together.

(9) The geographical extension is small enough so that personal transport such as bicycling is sufficient to go from one end to the other.

(10) In some of the communities there may be institutions which belong to a greater unity, such as hospitals and international research, law, and technical institutes. Some local communities must take care of the central institutions necessary for the function of society at large. *This fact is not incompatible with the notion of local communities.*

A number of political obstacles remain for the conservation and further development of green local communities.

(1) Economic policy is strongly centralised nationally. It sets the goals for the whole state under it. This has as a result a steady stream of ordinances and demands issuing at the centre and determining behaviour in the districts and townships. For instance, the requirements for sewers and building size. All these ordinances tend to make the local administration units indebted and bankrupt. This has a sharp demoralising effect: when there is a possibility of some kind of economic gain, they tend to jump at the chance without criticism. Local communities are thus fragile and easily destroyed.

(2) Cultural politics are centralised through the mass media, especially TV.

(3) Entertainment is standardised through the centralised media and the international culture market. It has not been possible to counteract this tendency even if the undesirable and detrimental results are clearly seen by many politicians. Economic growth is furthered by the standardisations, but it leads to much less variable creativity at the grass roots. Entertainment at the grass roots is not priced on the great market.

(4) Health authorities and social policies are centralised and specialised and more weight is placed on symptoms than on causes. The traditional generalist doctors disappear. Local communities feel they need money to protect themselves from illnesses and this also makes it difficult to avoid passivity towards the central authorities.

(5) Competition, especially on a world market, seems to necessitate rather big firms and hard and distant technology. A greater mobility of workers is needed in order to move according to markets which again destroys local communities, especially the continuity between generations so essential within them.

(6) Economic policy in the international markets is such that self-reliant or soft technology is unprofitable. In many places local resources are misused by the society and firms are introduced from other nations.

(7) Generalism in the sense of developing skills of a large number of different kinds is discouraged because of its unprofitability. Top levels of artists, scientists, technicians, stars in sports and trade from all over the

world set levels which are completely unattainable except through professionalism. *Panis et circenses*! Material standard of living and professional entertainment make the active use of one's own creative potentials seem unnecessary. Local achievement and ability are unknown centrally in big societies and near the local subcultures.

Without strong counter-measures the destruction of local communities and non-industrial culture will continue.

It is also important in the ecological movement to counteract the tendency to equate local community with local administrative unit. The pressure from the central administration down to local administration units is so hard that we often find, especially in northern Europe, local administration units continuously on the verge of economic collapse. This leads them frequently to an anti-ecological stance, even when the community whom the administration is supposed to serve has conservation as a high priority.

6   Direct action; norms of Gandhian nonviolence

Under this heading I think of the special, visible, nonviolent ways in which the environmental grass roots try to fight in public, collective ways. In conflicts concerning the environment there have been hundreds if not thousands of direct actions and most have been nonviolent in the Gandhian sense.

One of the first things to remember when starting to plan direct action is that decisions of an anti-ecological kind usually come after long plans on the part of industry or bureaucracy and that direct action which is performed late in the planning process has much less chance of being successful than a direct action which proceeds at the early stages of planning. The reason is primarily that the planning costs a lot of money, millions of dollars, especially if it includes investigations of feasibility (however perfunctory these may be). When a lot of money has been already used there must be quite a strong argument before anyone will say it was wasted. The project will 'have to' proceed. This point makes it imperative to get as many people as possible acquainted with the plan at its earliest stages. And they must know the plan thoroughly before they speak out on its dangers.

The Gandhian approach is such that the plan to do something *illegal*, against the laws, should occur as rarely as possible. Most actions can and should be made within the sphere of legality.

In the US more than any other nation lawyers have been able to mobilise laws against unecological decisions. In Scandinavia the lawyers have been rather passive, but what should be remembered is that the question of the legality of the decision should always be looked into.

Another point I would like to mention is the necessity of having a very clear, concrete, easily understandable goal for an action and that the opponent should be told very clearly what the goal of the action *is*. And the opponent is hardly ever the visible police, but usually people of high standing in the pyramid of power. Here a couple of distinctions are relevant: an action for instance stopping a road or work on a dam is an action dated for a definite time and there is a precise activity limit for what will or could happen. But the action may be part of a larger campaign, say for instance to save a river, a large number of rivers, or a forest. The action itself may be unsuccessful but this does not destroy the possibility of the success of the campaign, which may contain and comprise many actions. Its success does not depend on total success of every single component action. A main aspect of actions is to attract the attention of the public. The condition of success is then dependent on the tenability of the hypothesis that, if the public *only knew*, the majority would be on the right side.

Not only is the distinction between action and campaign important but also the distinction between campaign and movement. A movement may be for instance to protect a large landscape, making it into a national park after years of campaigning. Such a movement may require a hundred years before eventually reaching its goals.

One of the most important uses of the notion of campaign is to counteract the frustrations after an unsuccessful direct action. Most actions are unsuccessful, and perhaps have to be. It does not reduce their importance. *The campaign continues!* Most campaigns are unsuccessful, but perhaps they need not be so in the future. But certainly, in so far as they are unsuccessful, it is important to see them as part of a movement. As a movement, deep ecology is psychologically and culturally based on fundamental attitudes. To stop support means to negate these attitudes – or to find a different, better expression of them.

Experience from Scandinavia and many other places shows that the possibility of success is highly dependent on the *level of nonviolence* in the actions, campaigns, and movements. It is for instance essential to take the initiative to contact the opponent before a demonstration or a direct action. In the Alta demonstration in arctic Norway the powerful opponents were continually contacted for at least nine years of the campaign, and at the direct action any opponents present were treated with coffee and were immediately invited by the demonstrators to discuss the action and thus avoid misunderstanding. In the Mardøla action the police were treated with fresh mushrooms (but those who were standing near the chief of police didn't take the risk of accepting).

It is a central norm of the Gandhian approach to 'maximise contact with your opponent!' Nonviolent direct actions must be *a part* of the fight for sound ecopolitics, but on the other hand those actions must not result in neglect of the daily, weekly and yearly type of struggle of a far less spectacular kind. And one must plan exactly what influence the direct action is trying to have on the politicians. If not properly handled, politicians may move from being moderately in favour of an anti-ecological decision to becoming fierce defenders of that same decision.

To avoid such misunderstanding, in what follows we shall give a systematic account of the rules for Gandhian nonviolence as interpreted in Naess (1974).

First level norm:

N1   Act in group struggle and act, moreover, as an autonomous person in a way conducive to long-term universal, maximal reduction of violence!

Second-level hypotheses:

H1   The character of the means used in a group struggle determines the character of the results.

H2   In a group struggle you can keep the goal-directed motivation and the ability to work effectively for the realisation of the goal stronger than the destructive, violent tendencies, and the tendencies to passivity, despondency, or destruction, only by making a *constructive programme* part of your campaign and by giving all phases of your struggle, as far as possible a positive character.

H3   Short-term violence contradicts long-term universal reduction of violence.

Second-level norms:

N2   Make a constructive programme part of your campaign!

N3   Never resort to violence against your opponent!

N4a   Choose that personal action or attitude which most probably reduces the tendency towards violence of all parties in a struggle!

N4b   Never act as a mere functionary, a representative of an institution or an underling, but always as an autonomous, *fully responsible* person!

Third-level hypotheses:

H4   You can give a struggle a constructive character only if you conceive of it and carry it out as a struggle *in favour of living beings* and certain values, thus eventually fighting antagonisms, *not* antagonists.

H5   It increases your understanding of the conflict, of the participants, and of your own motivation, to live together with the participants, especially with those for whom you primarily fight. The most adequate form for living together is that of jointly doing constructive work.

H6   If you live together with those for whom you primarily struggle and do constructive work with them, this will create a natural basis for trust and confidence in you.

H7   All human (and non-human?) beings have long-term interests in common.

H8   Cooperation on common goals reduces the chance that the actions and attitudes of the participants in the conflict will become violent.

H9   You invite violence from your opponent by humiliating or provoking him.

H10 Thorough understanding of the relevant facts and factors increases the chance of a nonviolent realisation of the goals of your campaign.

H11a Incompleteness and distortion in your description of your case and the plans for your struggle reduce the chance of a nonviolent realisation of your goals.

H11b Secrecy reduces the chance of a nonviolent realisation of your goals.

H12 You are less likely to take a violent attitude, the better you make clear to yourself what are the essential points in your cause and your struggle.

H13 Your opponent is less likely to use violent means the better he understands your conduct and your case.

H14 There is a strong disposition in every opponent such that wholehearted, intelligent, strong, and persistent appeal in favour of a good cause is able ultimately to convince him.

H15 Mistrust stems from misjudgement, especially of the disposition of your opponent to answer trust with trust, mistrust with mistrust.

H16 The tendency to misjudge and misunderstand your opponent and his case in an unfavourable direction increases his and your tendency to resort to violence.

H17 You win conclusively when you turn your opponent into a believer and supporter of your case.

Third-level norms:

N5 Fight antagonisms, not antagonists!

N6 Live together with those for whom you struggle and do constructive work with them!

N7 Formulate the essential interests which you and your opponent share and try to cooperate upon this basis!

N8 Do no humiliate or provoke your opponent!

N9 Acquire the best possible understanding of the factors relevant to the nonviolent realisation of your goals!

N10 Seek unbiased description in all matters!

N11 Refrain from secrecy!

N12 Announce your case as clearly as possible, distinguishing essentials from non-essentials!

N13 Seek personal contact with your opponent and be available to him. Bring conflicting groups into personal contact!

N14 Do not judge your opponent harder than yourself!

N15 Trust your opponent as you trust yourself!

N16 Turn your opponent into a believer in and supporter of your case, but do not use coercion!

There are also several points which should be kept in mind to encourage the success of actions within a movement and within the larger social sphere.

(1) Avoid proclamations like 'My movement is the most important', or 'Without first reaching the goals of my movement nothing can be done.'

(2) Resist the tendency to look for weaknesses in alternative movements other than your own which have similar practical goals in mind.

(3) The 'stupidity' or 'badness' of opponents is not to be an issue.

(4) In debate, avoid technical or academic language as much as possible. Every profession has the tendency to think that the serious discussion must proceed in its own technical jargon.

(5) Always keep in mind how the goals of your movement relate to the *ultimate* values and goals of others.

7   The rich and the poor countries: from exploitation to mutual aid

Pollution and resource problems make up a real part of the concerns of the ecological movement, but the way these problems are taken up in the industrial countries has not been satisfactory for several reasons, neither in short- nor in long-term perspectives. Firstly a priority has been given to them without attacking deeper links of the causal chains: the systems of production and consumption, the technologies, the lack of global and local solidarity, the lifestyle anomalies. One can perhaps go as far as to say that pollution and resource discussions have pushed away all the deeper aspects. The shallow movement has dominated the deep.

Industrial countries can control outflow of garbage and pollutants in a way that is economically impossible for developing countries to follow. Industrial countries can reduce the requirements in turn for political benevolence from the side of the developing countries, for example press them to open their countries for certain hard technologies and immense industrial undertakings which can ignore the environmental laws of the rich industrial countries.

It seems powerful multinational corporations still lead the current development. Government's and people's opinions permit them to exploit the poor lands' cheaper resources and raw materials and labour on the grounds of a long-lasting relationship of exploitation where the developing countries are the losers. Their capacities for fighting environmental degradation are different from ours. We are not all in the same boat, but in several different boats, all of them charting a course for catastrophe.

This is a real problem today: for people knowledgeable in the field of ecology to decide to what degree they will let themselves become involved only in the shallow approach, as experts or advisers in currently available positions. Most jobs that stand open for them as advisors require that they keep silent in public about their deeper sentiments (Naess, 1986a, 1987b). Employers choose the questions, mostly shallow. Advisers are asked to compare projects A and B leaving out C which goes deeper. Potential employers choose the questions which the ecologically learned are paid to answer. Ecologists can freely choose more essential questions but certain opinions remain dangerous to their careers if they are published under their names.

Experts within most institutions still are forced by constraint to take up the shallow approach. Yet more and more within the elite in developing countries are asking for assistance in carrying out ecological policies. They seek to use publications like the *World Conservation Strategy* (1980) and here is the hope for the future, if strong enough institutions can enforce such policies. Its implementation would herald a transition from exploitation to mutual aid.

8   Critiques of the *Limits to Growth* approach

The reception received by the text *Limits to Growth* sponsored by the Club of Rome was politically very significant. It made an impact on certain powerful sections of society which until then did not see any limits to human exploitation of the planet. The quantitative and sophisticated approach made the report readable within circles of experts who never would read the more romantic literature of the deep-ecology movement. What I find interesting to note is the politically unsatisfactory reaction to the report within the deep ecology movement itself. The issue is not without importance because every new report which is quantitatively tinged with statistics, computer-generated printouts, and in general what is called sophisticated technology tends to be received negatively within the movement. This is something which weakens the impact of the movement in the long run: in discussions with opponents with some technical background, reference to such reports are likely to have more impact than reference to any other kind of literature.

Among the negative comments which in my view are rather weak I should like to mention the following.

(1) The investigation was financed by big industry. That could only happen because the conclusions are in favour of the unecological policies of those industries.

Historically that is incorrect. The industry supported the research without being so clear on what sort of result would be obtained. In the actual case, the results pointed towards a change that would adversely affect current ways of production and choice of products within those industries.

(2) *Limits to Growth* supported the maxim that we are all in the same boat. The class differences, national and international, were ignored. Thus it serves the overclass among the nations and within nations. People are in different boats.

But the investigation only set out to treat global quantities. It did not serve only the 'overclass' in doing that. Later works in the field of global modelling modified the overly simple procedures of *Limits to Growth*. This is well outlined in Donella Meadows' history of the first decade of global modelling, *Groping in the Dark* (1984).

(3) The investigation does not show the exploitation of the poor by the rich. Johan Galtung reacted as follows.

> When the evils are placed at the foot of the weak they are not resisted, not even pointed out, because the weak are too weak to do so . . . [as] their life is a struggle to obtain very primary, essential goods. No cry of WOLF printed out by a computer in the very centre of the Centre part of the world can change these priorities . . . . What is almost incredible is that it has not struck the authors that over-population, over-pollution, and over-depletion are just those three conditions under which perhaps

the majority of the population of the world are already living, and have been living for a long time. (Galtung, 1973)

These arguments are mentioned because again and again investigations made within the framework of the establishment are met by similar criticisms which are then published in such a way that makes the investigation less read among people neutral towards the deep ecological movement. Being more or less neutral they can be swayed one way or the other. We need more readers within such circles. The best thing to do so far as I can see is to get as many people as possible to read these things and think critically upon them. One cannot rely entirely on literature written by explicit members of the movement. One must also consider literature by people who take a more establishment line. Different methods of communication and different types of rhetoric will reach different kinds of people, and that is essential if the movement is to be anything but a small partisan faction.

Looking back over the last fifteen years, I think it is justifiable to conclude that the work of the Club of Rome has had a positive impact on policies concerning the environment. Even in the most optimistic technological circles there is now acknowledgement of the limits to growth. From surveys done in several countries it would seem that in Germany and in the UK this thought is now the opinion of the majority and that only in the US do the majority still tend to believe there is no limit to growth (Milbrath, 1984).

9   Are green political parties desirable?

Fundamental within the deep ecology movement is the insight that its goals cannot be reached without a deep change of present industrial societies. This means the goals cannot be reached without change in politics. One of the debates which will go on and has been going on for fifteen years at least is the following: should we work within existing parties or should we try to create a special party?

One may immediately answer that conditions in the various countries are so different that no general outlook can be maintained. The next thing to say is that we should distinguish between green parties which are created with the aim of achieving the status of a well-established party, and those created with more of an aim of making a temporary political impact within the special milieu of the politicians, but not presupposing anything about having a long political lifetime themselves (Porritt, 1984). The last alternative is an alternative somewhat between party creation in a usual sense and working within the existing parties. In short: (1) change existing parties in a green direction; (2) establish a new party; (3) change existing parties through the creation of an intermittent new party. Of course such reasoning is most appropriate in countries which work within a framework of a handful of competing parties, not the bipolar division of such as the United States.

Following the first line of thought, one tries to change current politics by establishing 'fifth columns' in existing political parties, pressing for change in the deep ecological dimension. In Scandinavia for many years this first solution has been favoured and as recently as 1985 a proposal for a green party in Norway was abandoned after much discussion among once-eager proponents.

If there is a big, clearly recognised, and established issue of an ecological kind in a country, for instance the question of nuclear energy plants for energy purposes, then there is a possibility of creating a party with that as a central theme. There is the possibility of attracting the attention of all people in the country. But if there is no such central controversy on which the green party could focus then it is difficult to create enough interest among the populace for a new party. And how successful can a single-issue party be in the long run?

A difference here exists between Sweden and Norway because in Sweden there is a tremendous debate concerning nuclear power whereas in Norway, with its great hydropower potential, there is no central political controversy with a marked green aspect.

In Germany there has been success with introducing a green party with central aims relevant to the total population and the results so far seem to confirm the conclusion that green political parties may have substantial impact (Capra and Spretnak, 1984). But it would also confirm possibility (3) – namely that even if the Green party explodes into competing small groups and even if those who are against taking part in established politics gain headway the era of the green party will have had a lasting impact. It was certainly a good idea.

A negative aspect of a green party is that if it only gets three or four per cent of the vote then the population gets a wrong picture of the real importance of a green point of view and the number of people who are really in favour of the principles behind green politics. It may be better not to have a party than to have one that clearly cannot reach even 10 per cent of the population.

As regards the third possibility I think that this is a way that in any case must be continued even if a party is created. There is always a need to have fifth columns in the other parties again and again taking up green points of view without needing to mention them as green, but merely as responsible positions within the established frameworks. An important plus here is that the traditional parties are then not going to gather against the green party: they do not feel the necessity to do so if they are quietly able to *absorb some of the green positions* without being threatened. They have no new party to hunt out and kill.

In politics tactics are important. Even if this goes against the grain in many deep ecology people, it is important at least that they do not turn against those few supporters who are tactically minded. If we work within existing parties, we must use a terminology that encourages the voters to listen. For instance, it is not good to write and talk as if one is against industry in general. Our point of view should be that we should support 'industry', and then point out that 'industry' has historically been something very different from what is going on at the moment – *big* industry.

Similarly, we should not have general slogans against technology or belittle its importance. The diversity of human cultures through history shows a tremendous diversity of technologies, and without this diversity we would not have had deep cultural diversity. This could also be said the other way round, but certainly in any culture so far the way people make and use things and the way priority is given to certain techniques over others has largely coloured the culture in general. It is here of course important to remember that *advanced* technology is to be seen as those techniques which advance the basic goals of a culture, not any equipment that is itself the more complicated or difficult (see chapter 4).

Furthermore, derogatory talk about big cities and city lifestyles may be counterproductive. For centuries human population is likely to be colossal (if there are no major nuclear wars) and big concentrations within small areas are necessary to minimise devastating effects upon other kinds of life than the human, and upon the landscapes of the planet in general. More effort is needed to improve life quality in the areas of concentration, not more effort to spread the population all over the globe.

Unfortunately, there has been a lot of easy criticism of politicians among supporters of deep ecology. It is 'easy' in the sense that they are critical of the rhetoric of politicians even when this rhetoric seems to be necessary within the current system. Politicians who have been courageous enough to take up fairly radical green positions on controversial issues must be hailed by supporters of the movement. They cannot be expected to continue being courageous if those who should be grateful only give criticism, reprimand, indifference, or silence.

Does the population get the politicians it deserves? To ensure this, one should from time to time send politicians letters of acclaim and support when one thinks they have done well. Fan mail as well as hate mail is needed.

A person active in politics should try to make it clear to the public that they as a private person may entertain some views which are politically unrealisable within election terms, but which nevertheless are important for their personal political motivation. The impact of continued population growth on conditions of life and on the ecosphere in general is intolerable and still increasing geometrically. Even if it is *politically* suicidal to plan changes of this dimension as part of a political platform, it is irresponsibility on the part of the politically active not to admit that they as private persons entertain these green views. If these views are hidden, the many people who do not play an active part in politics, but entertain radical green views, feel even more powerless than they are. They get the feeling that taking part in the struggle for power is incompatible with having green views.

10   The deep ecological movement and the big political issues

(a)   The basic ideological choices

Which are the political traditions or ideologies or systems most likely to colour green politics – using the customary vague and ambiguous terms? Let me immediately admit that I feel uncomfortable when having to use those terms.

(1) Reform or revolution? I envisage a change of revolutionary depth and size by means of many smaller steps in a radically new direction. Does this essentially place me among the political reformists? Scarcely. *The direction is revolutionary, the steps are reformatory.*

I can only say that I do not think that something resembling the revolutions we read about in history textbooks, or which we may wish would take place in South America, would be of help in the industrial countries.

(2) Capitalism or socialism? While there may be said to be economic policies conveniently called capitalistic, there is hardly any capitalistic political ideology. Socialism has one, but is it sufficiently concerned with nature instead of its own bureaucracy?

(3) Any relation to communism and anarchism? Roughly speaking, supporters of the deep ecology movement seem to move more in the direction of nonviolent anarchism than towards communism. Contemporary nonviolent anarchists are clearly close to the green direction of the

political triangle. But with the enormous and exponentially increasing human population pressure and war or warlike conditions in many places, it seems inevitable to maintain some *fairly* strong central political institutions. Recommendations such as that contained in the *World Conservation Strategy* (1980) are steps in the right direction, but there are no authorities strong enough to implement them. Experience suggests that the higher the level of local self-determination the stronger the central authority must be in order to override local sabotage of fundamental green policies. Or is this too pessimistic? Anyhow, the green utopias, such as those of Sigmund Kvaløy, Johan Galtung, Erik Dammann (The Future in Our Hands), Edward Goldsmith (the Blueprint for Survival), Ernest Callenbach (Ecotopia), much as the *panchayat* utopia of Gandhi, are not focusing on how to combine life in green communities with concern for safeguarding it from forces of disruption and violence which are likely to continue for some time on this planet.

(b)   Socialism and ecosophy

The most forceful and systematic critique of capitalism is found in socialist literature. This makes it natural for supporters of the deep ecology movement to use socialist criticisms of capitalism in their own work, and, looking at the slogans of green parties it is immediately clear that many of these slogans are also socialistic or at least compatible with some sort of socialism. As examples: no excessive aggressive individualism. Appropriation. Community, production for use, low income differentials, local production for local needs, participative involvement, solidarity.

On the other hand, it is also clear that some socialist slogans still heard are not compatible: maximise production, centralisation, high energy, high consumption, materialism.

Historically there has been a move from traditional socialist positions to ecological positions among many people. Many of the most self-relying teamwork-oriented direct action people have a background in socialism (learned or experienced). It is still clear that some of the most valuable workers for ecological goals come from the socialist camps.

One of the basic similarities between socialist attitudes and ecological attitudes in politics is stress on social justice and stress on social costs of technology. The basic question raised in ecologically oriented socialism is: what are the social consequences of a definite environmental policy? What is the social cost of products which are polluting the environment and how should the social costs somehow be integrated with market costs?

On the other hand, there is a usage of the terms 'people' and 'society' which is dangerous in ecopolitics if it is said that society or community should have control of the means of production. The application of these terms is such that it is not the society or the community itself that gets control but certain politicians or central administrative units deciding on behalf of the community. (Using the term 'community' in these contexts makes the slogans of socialism much more valuable.)

The utopias of green societies point towards a kind of direct democracy with local control of the means of production as the best way of achieving the goals.

Because of the ambiguities of the terms it is perhaps a bit paradoxical to say that the rather backward ecological position in Eastern Europe is irrelevant to the socialist–capitalist question. On many points, these states are not looked on as being truly socialistic. There was an attempt, but it failed. Supporters of the deep ecological movement may however find some confirmation of their anti-bureaucratic attitudes by looking at Eastern Europe. But, at least in the Soviet Union, the problems ecological movements have to face are not so different from our own. Boris Komarov (1980) writes on the official hearings on the future of Lake Baikal:

> At one such meeting one old academician began to scream at us: 'But why are we going on so about this Baikal? Pollute it if we have to. Now we have nuclear energy, and if later we have to, we can easily make a big pit and fill it with water, and that's that. We'll make Baikal again.' This nonsense resounded under the vaults of the Academy of Sciences, yet the vaults of our Temple of Science did not crumble. No one even chased out this senile academician. The meeting went on and the attacks on us continued. I repeat, this was a time of real arm twisting . . . (p 8–9)

11   Bureaucracy

This leads us to the basic question of bureaucracy. In capitalist countries mixed or pure, there is a distinction between private initiative and public initiative where public initiative involves channelling through the bureaucracy. In ecopolitically sane societies we shall retain the term 'initiative' as a greatly positive term, but it will be personal initiative rather than private initiative, and a maximisation of personal initiative will be one of the norms. This means a fight against bureaucratic dimensions which is just as hard as in capitalistic societies. Socialism here seems to be in a weak position because when it is said that the people should rule, very often it implies that the government should take up a great many questions which in green utopias will be decided by each person, family, or small community. One of the salient aspects of socialist critique in Europe is that at present there are too many meetings and too many decisions made *for* the people, not by them.

Then to the term 'regulation' which is such a minus in capitalism – from the literature on green utopias one gets the impression that its supporters are not afraid of regulations. This points again to the importance of personal initiative: regulations can only be minimised through an *internalisation of norms* (see chapter 4).

The main point here is that we need a change in mentality such that many of the regulations will be unnecessary. But there will nevertheless be a danger of proliferation of regulations in a green society: witness what makes regulations increase in our own society: we have so many minute regulations for each little situation or problem, instead of broader regulations that cover more situations in a holistic and integrated way. Few regulations in our current system could stand to be internalised as norms. We need those with a greater depth of intention, and a more basic quality.

Theoreticians like Nils Christie look upon the question historically and show how the tight communities of the last century solved the problem of regulations. They solved the problem by simple daily interaction within the small community. Children learnt not only in school or from their parents but from everyone in the community. In such a way they also learnt the skills they would need for the rest of their lives. If there was too much drinking, immediately members of the community would make it unpleasant for transgressors within the community. But also if there were too little drinking there might be some pressure. Here there was little police activity and very little violence within the community. There was a pressure towards conformity, 'structural violence', which cannot be tolerated in the green society. It reduces both personal initiative and self-determination. According to Christie we must find a way in between the bounds of tradition and the complete chaos we have today in big cities.

How are we going to do this? The answer 'through green education' is not very convincing because, if you mean formal education, we know that is not such a powerful agent of change any more. If we mean informal, not much has been done (Pepper, 1984, pp. 215ff).

A term that is useful here is 'naturalist', in its original, deep romantic sense (Sessions and Devall, 1985, pp. 79ff). We engage not teachers as we know them today but instead people who have internalised the deep ecological norms, even if a small minority, and make them more central in the day-to-day dealings of communities. It is here that such naturalists, by their very example, can get people aware of things that they never thought of before, and they will thus help with internalising of norms in the larger populace.

In short, there is clearly both in capitalist and socialist politics things which can be modified and used in sane ecopolitics but essentially green politics will be something deeply different.

12   The deep ecological movement and the peace movement

In the early 70s close cooperation between supporters of deep ecology and activists in the peace movement was out of reach. Rather suddenly this situation is totally changed. Nuclear war would be an ecological catastrophe. The planet does not deserve such treatment. No life forms except one are vitally interested in different political ideologies or big power rivalries. The present level of armaments with its exponential growth is a heavy burden ecologically. One factor often overlooked is the mishandling, even torture, of millions of animals in experiments involving nuclear radiation. These animals live and die in a nuclear war today. (This reasoning may sound ridiculous at present in the face of the human horrors of the nuclear world, but in ten years such thinking will, I suspect, be commonplace.)

Some of us, like myself, favour unilateral disarmament and establishment of unheroic nonviolent defence (Naess 1986c). But politically it is completely unrealistic in northern NATO nations to work for getting out of NATO. This is not necessary, however. The basic documents of NATO establish it as a defence organisation with no clauses against nonviolent defence. More realistic politically is a gradual introduction of anti-nuclear and pro-nonviolent proposals within NATO.

Politically it has been important to clarify that the highly successful anti-nuclear campaign (as part of the peace movement) is a definite, limited campaign. Supporters of a more radical disarmament, or of non-nuclear politics of various kinds, should not try to force the campaign to widen or change its identity. One may take part in several campaigns, but the frequent attempts to change the anti-nuclear campaign so as to cover other goals are politically dangerous, leading to ruinous struggles among campaigners.

13   Green political programmes from day to day

We need not agree upon any definite utopia, but should thrash out limited programmes of political priorities within the framework of present political conflicts. Our questions are of the form 'What would be a *greener* line in politics at the moment within issue *x* and how could it be realised?' rather than of the form 'What would be the deep green line of politics within issue *x*?' Green is dynamic and comparative, never absolute or idealistic.

The term 'political voluntarism' is a term that may be helpful in this connection – as something to be wary of. It is a term characterising political activity in which you think that you can rapidly force a deep change of society by sheer will power through direct action. It was used, for instance, by Marxist criticisms of students engaged in the so-called student revolutions of the late 1960s. Some Marxists said that universities are peripheral institutions: 'Power inside universities does not count. The *will* to change society by means of student power is nonsensical. You must have a much broader and more realistic basis of activity.' In this sense, political voluntarism is a kind of romantic delusion.

Back to the problem of combining basic ideals of ecopolitics and day-to-day political fights for very limited green gains! An example may make the complicated situation clearer.

An energy problem exists in Norway and Sweden, but it is primarily the problem of how to reduce the fantastic *waste* of energy. It is a problem of how to limit the use of energy essentially to vital needs. From the green point of view the present level of yearly consumption is more than sufficient for any needs. Nevertheless some supporters of green policies take part, and should take part, in discussions concerning which sources of increased energy supply have the *least* detrimental consequences socially and for life conditions in general. The situation is rather awkward: the greens are led to promote decisions they detest. As long as we constantly make clear that any increase of energy production is unnecessary and detrimental, the participation in the debate on how to increase it with the least detrimental effect is justified and important. At the moment policies of stabilisation or decrease of energy production should be vigorously propagated, but politically they are dead or hibernating. Proposals for such policies have no chance of being adopted at the moment, and existing parties avoid them. Presently politically powerful plans call for exponential increase of energy production until 2020, retaining the wasteful production to the aluminum industry. A green party, however, would have to adopt stabilisation or decrease as a programme even if this immediately would limit the number of votes.

'Everything hangs together.' This is still a good slogan. One consequence of the interrelatedness is that we all have the capacity to do something of relevance within a framework of our own interests and inclinations. *The ecopolitical frontier is immensely long* but we can only work effectively at one place at at time. It is more than long, it is multidimensional, and the pull of the pole of greenness can be felt in all our political positions and actions.

14   Concluding remarks

(1) The green utopias draw pictures of societies and ways of life expressing how people in the deep ecological movement would like to see the future. The pictures, if fairly detailed, include political institutions. In thinking about future life conditions on the planet, questions of political structure are unavoidable.

(2) Different from sketching utopias, but not entirely independent of them, we find environmental thinking focusing on how to move in the direction of the utopias.

(3) For the shallow or reform ecological movement, the central political questions are significantly different from those of the deep movement. For the former the task is essentially one of 'social engineering', modifying human behaviour through laws and regulations posed by ministries and departments of the environment – for the short-term well-being of humans.

(4) The deep ecological movement sees the present unecological politics as necessary consequences primarily of social and economic priorities, the ways of production and consumption, and only significant changes of this will make the goals of the movement realisable. This implies deep changes of political priorities, and possibly new green parties.

(5) In the early 70s ecopolitical thinking hammered out a great number of concrete goals marking steps on the way to a green society. Looking back fifteen years later, most of these goals are still considered to be well-chosen and important. But no established party anywhere grabbed the chance to incorporate the goals into its platform. The strength of the movement to realise these goals is scarcely less than it was in the past decade, but the inertia of the old material growth policies is holding back the change.

(6) It seems that life conditions will have to worsen considerably before the formulated goals are adapted by any major political parties.

(7) 'There is no point of no return.' This holds for the prospect of stopping the accelerating devastation of life conditions on the planet. It does not hold for a large number of devastations like that of the rain-forests. But it does hold for an immense diversity and richness of life forms and landscapes. Green political activism is one of the assets we must count on.

7

Ecosophy T: unity and diversity of life

In the face of increasing environmental problems, the solutions proposed during the late 60s and early 70s revealed two trends, one in which it was presumed that a piecemeal approach within the established economic, social, and technological framework is adequate, another which called for critical examination of the man–nature relation and basic changes which would affect every aspect of human life. The latter trend, that of the deep ecological movement, involves *both* concrete decisions in environmental conflicts and abstract guidelines of philosophical character. It is not a mere philosophy of man–nature.

In the previous chapters a large number of problem areas have been touched upon, primarily the technological, economic, and political. Ultimate foundations have also been considered, particularly the contrast between atomistic and gestalt thinking. It remains to go into a number of philosophical issues, and also to touch upon the religious background of man–nature thinking in the West. The treatment will have to be more personal in the sense of leading into particular aspects of my ecosophy, Ecosophy T. But it is not the aim to point to my own particular view in special detail. Much has been already said without explicitly connecting it to the Ecosophy T logical structure. The main goal, as announced in chapter 2, is to emphasise the responsibility of any integrated person to work out his or her reaction to contemporary environmental problems *on the basis of a total view*.

The chapter falls into three parts. The first will elaborate the notion of Self-realisation through identification, thus connecting the individual's unfolding to that of the whole planet. The second part brings in, rather schematically, some antecedents to ecosophy from Western religion and the history of ideas. The third and final part of the chapter will present a brief systematic exposition of the more logically basic norms in Ecosophy T.

1   **The universal right to self-unfolding and the**
      correlative intrinsic value of every life form

(a)   Ecosophy ties together all life and all nature

'To have a home', 'to belong', 'to live' and many other similar expressions suggest fundamental milieu factors involved in the shaping of an individual's sense of self and self-respect. The identity of the individual, 'that I am something', is developed through interaction with a broad manifold, organic and inorganic. There is no completely isolatable I, no isolatable social unit.

To distance oneself from nature and the 'natural' is to distance oneself from a part of that which the 'I' is built up of. Its 'identity', 'what the individual I is', and thereby sense of self and self-respect, are broken down. Some milieu factors, e.g. mother, father, family, one's first companions, play a central role in the development of an I, but so do home and the surroundings of home.

Ecological and psychological research furnish overwhelming evidence of the connection our unfolding self has with an unsurveyable variety and richness of natural phenomena, predominantly with the life in the ecosphere, but also with non-organic nature. The tiny infant gradually distinguishes its mother from the rest of its surroundings, and it concentrates positive feelings around the relations, the context, with her. The 'grown-up child', the naturalist, extends this positive feeling to all of nature through the insight that everything is interconnected.

This vaguely outlined development can naturally be destroyed by severe tragedy – such as loss of mother and later repeated losses and self-denials. Self-realisation receives a blow which can contribute to a hostile attitude towards a great deal, even to everything: a destructive urge addressed to the whole world and existence as such. There are many examples of this, but the essential point is that such development is not a necessary progression. Favourable conditions for Self-realisation extend the radiation of good feelings to more and more nature.

In this chapter a basic positive attitude to nature is articulated in philosophical form. It is not done to win compliance, but to offer some of the many who are at home in such a philosophy new opportunities to express it in words. This is necessary so that society and politics will give consideration to the kind of lifestyle which is a natural consequence of such a philosophy.

(b)   'The unfolding of potentialities is a right'

That one order is just and another is unjust is an old thought, and it has never been restricted in application only to humanity. One exercises justice or injustice to plants and animals as well. In the newer so-called tradition of the 'rights of nature', we find these thoughts expressed philosophically. Through countless ages, they have been expressed religiously and mystically. Plants and animals also have a right to unfolding and self-realisation. They have the *right to live*.

What is the *right* to live? A definition is often arbitrary, and it leaves out the mythic component. A good definition, by definition, lacks a mythic function. But sentences with mythic function are still required today. The scientific and philosophical turns of phrase can easily come to overlook important sources of meaningfulness and general appeal. 'All living creatures are fundamentally one' is a good example of a sentence which has a mythic function, but which may also be precised in the direction of a testable hypothesis or norm. While it has cognitive usage, it is also associated at the same time with the more or less mythic conception of a just or injust order in the world. In the beginning of the 60s, Rachel Carson incited opposition to the poisoning of nature, using both scientific and 'mythic' forms of expression. She felt that mankind did not have *the right* to devastate nature and found it unjustifiable that we, mere 'drops in the stream of life', should permit ourselves to do whatever we please with 'the work of God'.

We are not outside the rest of nature and therefore cannot do with it as we please without changing ourselves. We must begin to see what we do to ourselves when we say 'only change external nature'. We are a part of the ecosphere just as intimately as we are a part of our own society. But the expression 'drops in the stream of life' may be misleading if it implies that individuality of the drops is lost in the stream. Here is a difficult ridge to walk: To the left we have the ocean of organic and mystic views, to the right the abyss of atomic individualism.

(c)   *Life as a vast historical process*
The geological history of our globe tells of tremendous changes: the uplifting of mountain chains, the unceasing work of erosion, the slow movements of the continents. Among these enormous processes in time and space, one is nearest to us: *the unfolding of life*. Human beings who wish to attain a maximum perspective in the comprehension of their cosmic condition can scarcely refrain from a proud feeling of genuine participation in something immensely greater than their individual and social career. Palaeontology reveals the various phases in the development: the extension of the boundaries for where life can thrive, the establishment of ever more potentialities for life in the inorganic environment, the development of a nervous system culminating in the brain of the mammals.

The entire study leaves the impression that the development of life on earth is *an integrated process*, despite the steadily increasing diversity and complexity. The nature and limitation of this unity can be debated. Still, this is something basic. 'Life is fundamentally one.'

Homo sapiens is singularly well equipped to comprehend this unity in the light of human extreme lack of biological specialization. Our hand is just as 'primitive', i.e. unspecialised, as that of the lizard, and much more primitive than horse hooves or eagle claws. The *cortex cerebri* is the decisive factor. It takes over more and more instinctual activities, and allows us to approach the unspecialised state of a clump of protoplasm. Our lack of a definite biological place to call home allows us to feel at home everywhere. We can sympathise with *all* the more specialised life forms. The educational value of palaeontology in its fullness is not yet appreciated, but will in the future be seen as greater than mere attention to evolution and some spectacular dinosaurs.

The traditional way of expressing what is common to all species of life, and more generally to all forms of life, is to point to a basic striving, that of self-preservation. This term is misleading, however, in so far as it does not account for the dynamics of expansion and modification. There is a tendency to realise *every* possibility for development, to explore all possibilities of change within the framework of the species and even to transgress its limits. Palaeontology tells of the 'conquest' of, or 'expansion' from sea to, land and air, and the development of mutual aid.

In view of the defensive passivity suggested by the term self-preservation, I favour Self-realisation or Self-unfolding. Historically I trace the conception back to Spinoza's *perseverare in suo esse*, to persevere in one's own (way of) being, not mere keeping alive. Ecosophy T concentrates especially upon the aspect of general unfolding *in suo esse*. For life in general it implies the 'creative evolution' (Bergson), the steady extension of the biosphere, from the comfortable lukewarm, shallow seas to arctic oceans and steaming hot-water springs. The emergence of human ecological consciousness is a philosophically important idea: a life form has developed on Earth which is capable of understanding and appreciating its relations with all other life forms and to the Earth as a whole.

(d)   The universal right to live and blossom
         The right of all the forms to live is a universal right which cannot be quantified. No single species of living being has more of this particular right to live and unfold than any other species. Perhaps it is *not* the best way of expressing this to say that there is a right – the *equal* right for all life forms – to unfold its specific capacities. 'Equality' suggests a sort of quantification that is misleading.

From the point of view of analytical philosophy the term 'right', like many other terms used in daily life – 'fact', 'verification' ('shown to be the case'), 'duty', 'value in itself' – is rather suspicious. Does it have any meaning that can be clarified? Is it just a question of coercive power when somebody says that we have no right to do so and so? I do not think so. As I use the term I do not pretend that it has a clearly formulatable meaning, but that it is the best expression I have so far found of an intuition which I am unable to reject in all seriousness. But I completely accept that some environmental philosophers avoid the term and advise others to do the same.

When we attempt to live out our relationships with other living beings in accordance with such *a principle of equal rights* of all fellow beings, difficult questions naturally arise. (This always happens when a normative idea in the central reaches of a norm system is practised.) It suggests a guideline for our behaviour, but it does not tell anything about behaviour. Additional norms and hypotheses are, for instance, necessary as premises in order to derive a norm that killing violates the right. It is not some kind of unconditional *isolatable* norm to treat everything the same way. It is only a fragment of a total view. Our apprehension of the actual conditions under which we live our own lives – that is, certain 'hypotheses' high up in the systematised total view – make it crystal clear that we have to injure and kill, in other words actively hinder the self-unfolding of other living beings. Equal right to unfold potentials as a principle is not a practical norm about equal conduct towards all life forms. It suggests a guideline limiting killing, and more generally limiting obstruction of the unfolding of potentialities in others.

Many contend that living beings can be ranked according to their *relative intrinsic value*. The claims of rankable value are usually based upon one or more of the following contentions.

(1) If a being has an eternal soul, this being is of greater intrinsic value than one which has a time-limited or no soul.

(2) If a being can reason, it has greater value than one which does not have reason or is unreasonable.

(3) If a being is conscious of itself and of its possibilities to choose, it is of greater value than one which lacks such consciousness.

(4) If a being is a higher animal in an evolutionary sense, it is of greater value than those which are farther down on the evolutionary scale.

None of these standpoints, so far as I can see, have been substantially justified. They may appear to be reasonable at first glance, but they fade after reflection and confrontation with the basic intuitions of the unity of life and the right to live and blossom.

The contention that one life form has a higher value than another sometimes leads to the argument that the more valuable being has the right to kill and injure the less valuable. A different approach is to specify under which circumstances it is justifiable to hunt or kill other living beings. We might agree upon rules such as will imply different behaviour towards different kinds of living beings without negating that there is a value inherent in living beings which is *the same value* for all. But it is against my intuition of unity to say 'I can kill you because I am more valuable' but not against the intuition to say 'I will kill you because I am hungry'. In the latter case, there would be an implicit regret: 'Sorry, I am now going to kill you because I am hungry.' In short, I find obviously right, but often difficult to justify, different sorts of behaviour with different sorts of living beings. But this does not imply that we classify some as intrinsically more valuable than others.

Modern ecology has emphasised a high degree of *symbiosis* as a common feature in mature ecosystems, an interdependence for the benefit of all. It has thereby provided *a cognitive basis for a sense of belonging* which was not possible earlier. Family belonging, the tie of kinship, has a material basis in perceived togetherness and cooperation. Through the extension of our understanding of the ecological context, it will ultimately be possible to develop a sense of belonging with a more expansive perspective: *ecospheric belonging*.

'The task is to find a form of togetherness with nature which is to our own greatest benefit. Any other definition is hypocritical.' If such a statement is accepted, 'our own benefit' must then mean 'that which serves the great Self', not merely the individual ego or human societies. If a lesser self is implied, the sentences are misleading. One can desire well-being for an animal or a plant just as naturally as one can for a person. For some dog owners, their dog's well-being is more important to them than that of their neighbour. The identification is stronger, and empathy is greater. One can, without hypocrisy, *desire something which is for the benefit of other living beings* – and one normally obtains great, rich satisfaction from it.

The technical development together with our insight into mutual, symbiotic relationships makes it possible for human beings to allow *cooperation and togetherness* to colour our work days and leisure life much more than before. Unfortunately this is at the moment primarily a theoretical possibility. The coming decades will probably see certain dichotomies between human societies play themselves out (e.g. the North–South conflict), as well as between mankind and other living beings (the destruction of habitats of other species).

Let us examine a rather provoking thought experiment. *Homo sapiens* may be capable, in suitable circumstances, and upon the basis of a wide perspective, of *recommending its own withdrawal* as the dominant living being on earth. By such an act humans would confirm (just as we do in many other actions) that mankind is not bound to the values 'useful for human beings' or 'suitable to human self-preservation' when 'utility' and 'self' are taken in a *narrow* sense. If the terms are understood very broadly, we are bound to our Self, but then as the circle is bound to π (3.14159 . . .). To the great Self of mankind, it may be useful to transfer some power over others to a more sensible and sensitive species.

It is realistic to ask how we would behave faced with living beings from distant planets which look like *Homo sapiens*, so that identification would be easy. Would we as human beings subject ourselves freely to the political will of an alien species which had more or less the same characteristics as us, but which lacked our tendency to torture, torment and exploit one another? The decision would perhaps take a few centuries, but I believe it would be positive. We would abdicate, if we were sure of them.

This thought experiment makes assumptions which cannot be said to be probable. Members of *Homo sapiens* are not genetically or in any other way *bound* to torture, torment and exploit one another for all eternity. The possibility that future research will indicate such a dismal conclusion about human nature can presumably be characterised as extremely unlikely. But the thought experiment intimates that human drive for Self-realisation requires us to give way for the more perfect. Human beings would lose something of their own essential nature if they refrained from abdication.

(e)   *The uniqueness of humankind should not*
            be underestimated

Palaeontology teaches us about the overwhelming richness and diversity of life forms. There have perhaps been 100 million species which now are extinct. But among these and the present living ones, *Homo sapiens* is in many ways unique. Unique biologically through its brain, unique physically through its hundreds of main, and bewildering manifold of lesser, but not less original cultures.

Such statements are important to make from time to time because environmentalism often, and deep ecology always, underlines what we have in common with other life forms and how intimate our relations are and ought to be with life forms and the ecosphere more generally.

Why, it is sometimes asked, should not the unique capacities be used to 'conquer the world' and complete the job of creating one great human habitat of all the habitable parts of the Earth? Why should a creature *limit* its Self-realisation by letting other life forms retain their habitats – if they are not obviously useful?

Such questions seem, however, to be characteristic of only a fraction of human cultures. Perhaps they reveal, not a concern for specific human Self-realisation, but its neglect.

A biology which clearly states the biological peculiarities of human beings, as well as the differences, e.g. between human and animal communication, is fully compatible with an ecosophy of identification and equal right. A specific feature of human make-up is that human beings consciously perceive the urge other living beings have for self-realisation, and that we must therefore assume *a kind of responsibility for our conduct towards others*.

Ethology, the general study of behaviour of living beings, suggests that the violence found within modern industrial societies is more malignant and self-destructive than that found in almost any other mammalian society. The methods other mammals use to avoid and reduce violence appear to be more effective and less brutal than our own. These animal societies are worthy of study and in some *limited* respects worthy of being used as models for human behaviour. This does not imply a lower evaluation of mankind and our future possibilities.

Modern ecologists almost unanimously emphasise the importance of togetherness and cooperation in the plant and animal world. The ecologists emphasise the restrained forms and conduct displayed in conflicts, and the importance of the utilisation of dissimilar 'niches' in existence, that is the avoidance of direct collision.

We regard some of the abilities of animals with admiration and astonishment. For instance, the ability of salmon to cross untold reaches of ocean, find a given river mouth, and brave the many rapids to reach their spawning grounds. There is no reason to think of the human ability to discover this about salmon as anything less awesome. My concern here is the human capability of identification, the human joy in the identification with the salmon on its way to its spawning grounds, and the sorrow felt upon the thoughtless reduction of the access to such important places.

The principle of biospheric egalitarianism defined in terms of equal right, has sometimes been misunderstood as meaning that human needs should never have priority over non-human needs. But this is never intended. In practice, we have for instance greater obligation to that which is nearer to us. This implies duties which sometimes involve killing or injuring non-humans. (Naess, 1984a.) But it is a serious matter when animals are submitted to painful experiments in order to test the chemicals used, for example, in food colourings. Human beings are closer to us than animals, but there is no unsatisfied vital human need driving the food cosmetic industry. The norm about the precedence related is only one norm. Responsible decisions closely require one to consider the entire norm system. The dimensions of *peripheral* needs of humans must be compared with *vital* needs of other species, if there is a conflict.

'You shall not inflict unnecessary suffering upon other living beings!' This norm offers an important guideline here. The necessity must be legitimised in a statement of objectives plus a statement which explains why the objective cannot be achieved without the infliction of suffering. There is no necessity of meeting demands on a market.

On the surface, paradoxical tendencies seem to be afoot. On the one hand, we find thoughtless mistreatment and domination, on the other hand a clear front against 'unnecessary suffering'. In Oslo, if a rat is discovered trapped in an inaccessible ventilator, it is clearly cause to warn the SPCA to come and end its suffering – by putting it out of its misery. This tradition of concern has proceeded side by side with extermination campaigns which use unnecessarily painful means. In the long run, increased awareness of such inconsistencies will (I hope) result in merciful means or, better, in making extermination unnecessary, and the joys of symbiosis more widespread.

The uniqueness of *Homo sapiens*, its special capacities among millions of kinds of other living beings, has been used as a premise for domination and mistreatment. Ecosophy uses it as a premise for a universal care that other species can neither understand nor afford.

2   Identification, oneness, wholeness, and Self-realisation

(a)   *Identification and alienation;*
         ideas of oneness and wholeness

In the heading of this section four terms are brought together. Perhaps four contrasting terms should also be kept in mind: alienation, plurality, fragmentarity, and Self-abnegation. The interrelations of these terms may perhaps contribute to the clarification of ecosophy. Let an example introduce the issue.

In a glass veranda with one wall open away from the sun a bunch of children are playing with an insect spray. Insects are trapped flying against the wall pointing towards the sun. Spraying makes them dramatically fall to the floor. Amusing? A grown-up appears, picks up an insect, looks at it with care, and utters dreamingly: 'perhaps those animals might, like you, prefer to live rather than to die?' The point is grasped, the children for a moment see and experience spontaneously and immediately the insects as themselves, not only as something different but in an important sense like themselves. An instance of momentary identification! Perhaps it has no effect in the long run, or perhaps one of the children slightly changes an attitude toward small fellow creatures.

Before the intervention the children saw the movements of half-dead insects but presumably did not react. From the point of view of ecosophy they were alienated in a particular sense of the word, namely being indifferent to something that with normal upbringing would have caused empathy based on identification. Indifference, rather than feelings of strangeness, apartness, aloofness, is of prime importance in the situation.

So much about insects. But what about identification with mountains? The more usual terms are here 'personalising', 'animism', 'anthropomorphism'. For thousands of years, and in various cultures, mountains have been venerated for their equanimity, greatness, aloofness, and majesty. The process of identification is the prerequisite for feeling the *lack* of greatness, equanimity in one's empirical self. One 'sees oneself in the other', but it is not the empirical self, but the self one would aspire to have. Given adverse conditions a mountain will stand for threat and terror, an adversary to be overcome. The so-called conquest of mountains relieves the threat.

The term 'identification' is used in many ways and the way it is used in the story may be rare and difficult to make clear except through many instances, positive and negative.

The relationship between identification and the narrower process of *solidarity* is such that every deep and lasting state of solidarity presupposes wide identification. The essential sense of common interests is comprehended spontaneously *and is internalised*. This leads to the *dependency of A's Self-realisation upon B's*. When B seeks just treatment A supports the claim. A assumes a common stance upon the basis of an identification with B. A *may* also assume a common stance upon the basis of abstract ideas of moral justice, combined with a minimum of identification, but under hard and long-lasting trials the resulting solidarity cannot be expected to hold. The same applies to *loyalty*. When solidarity and loyalty are solidly anchored in identification, they are not experienced as moral demands; they come of themselves.

Continental European critique of western industrial society stresses the alienation caused by a kind of technology that reduces everything to mere objects of manipulation. *Verdinglichung!* Not only animals are thus treated, workers tend to be mere factors – mostly causing trouble – in the production process. Big finance tends to enhance this trend. What is produced and how it is produced is irrelevant, what counts is profitable sale. Comparing the alienation process in various cultures one might often find technologies involving cruelty and vast indifference to suffering. What is expected today is that societies are rich enough to afford the gradual elimination of alienation.

From the identification process stems unity, and since the unity is of a gestalt character, the wholeness is attained. Very abstract and vague! But it offers a framework for a total view, or better, a central perspective.

The above seems to point in the direction of philosophical mysticism, but the fourth term, Self-realisation, breaks in and reinstates the central position of the individual – even if the capital S is used to express something beyond narrow selves. The widening and deepening of the individual selves *somehow* never makes them into one 'mass'. Or into an organism in which every cell is programmed so as to let the organism function as one single, integrated being. How to work out this in a fairly precise way I do not know. It is a meagre consolation that I do not find that others have been able to do this in their contemplation of the pair unity–plurality. 'In unity diversity!', yes, but how? As a vague postulate it has a specific function within a total view, however imperfectly.

(b)   Identification and Self-realisation

Death of individuals and extinction of species are indispensable parts of evolution. So is the killing of one individual or species by another, even if non-organic environmental causes predominate. But evolution also shows the rise of mutual aid, and mature human beings cannot but work toward a state of affairs a little more like what their phantasy suggests could come in the very long run.

The maxim 'live and let live' suggests a class-free society in the entire ecosphere, a democracy in which we can speak about justice, not only with regard to human beings, but also for animals, plants and landscapes. This presumes a great emphasis upon the interconnectedness of everything and that our *egos* are fragments – not isolatable parts. We, as egos, have an extremely limited power and position within the whole, but it is sufficient for the unfolding of our potential, something vastly more comprehensive than the potential of our egos. So we are more than our egos, and are not fragments, hardly small and powerless. By identifying with greater wholes, we partake in the creation and maintenance of this whole. *We thereby share in its greatness.* New dimensions of satisfaction are revealed. The egos develop into selves of greater and greater dimension, proportional to the extent and depth of our processes of identification.

The conceptually simplest and historically speaking most ancient access to such an ecosophy is perhaps the one which analyses *dissimilar conceptions* of the 'self'. The first years of life, the self is not much broader than the ego – the narrow selfish centre which serves to satisfy the simplest biological needs. It is then best to eat the whole cake *alone*. About the age of seven, and until puberty, a socialisation takes place which extends the self appreciably: the self comes to comprise one's family and closest friends.

The intensity of identification with other life depends upon milieu, culture and economic conditions. The ecosophical outlook is developed through an identification so deep that one's *own self* is no longer adequately delimited by the personal ego or the organism. One experiences oneself to be a genuine part of all life. Each living being is understood as a goal in itself, *in principle* on an equal footing with one's own ego. It also entails a transition from I–it attitudes to I–thou attitudes – to use Buber's terminology.

This does not imply that one acts, wishes to act, or consistently *can* act in harmony with the principle of equality. The statements about biospheric equality must be merely taken as guidelines. Even under conditions of intense identification, killing occurs. The Indians in California, with their animistic mythology, were an example of equality in principle, combined with realistic admissions of their own vital needs. When hunger arrives, brother rabbit winds up in the pot. 'A brother *is* a citizen, but oh, so temptingly nutritious!' – This exclamation is too easy: the complicated rituals which surround the hunt in many cultures illustrate how closely people feel bound to other beings, and how natural it is to feel that *when we harm others, we also harm ourselves*. Non-instrumental acts develop into instrumental.

Immanuel Kant's maxim 'You shall never use another person only as a means' is expanded in Ecosophy T to 'You shall never use any living being only as a means'.

A lack of identification leads to indifference. Distant objects or events which do not seem to concern us are at best relegated to the indifferent background.

The pesticide azodrin reduced the number of certain 'obnoxious' insects to almost zero, which was the intention, but in addition it exterminated the natural enemies of the pest. The result after some time was more unwanted insects than ever. Such accidents have motivated a new slogan: you must know what will occur upon intervention in nature. If you don't know the consequences, don't intervene. But is this realistic? No more than a small fraction of the consequences can ever be known. Our ignorance now and in the near future about the consequences of intervention is appreciably greater than was initially assumed. Our indifference to the environment of life has meant that it is ordinarily experienced merely as a grey background. With identification, all this changes.

Suppose we spread a chemical substance upon a piece of land and take up a single gram of earth. What is happening in this tiny piece of our 'grey background' and what would happen in the event of our intervention? An investigation of just such a small clump of earth revealed that an astounding number of small organisms lived there: among other things 30,000 protozoa, 50,000 algae, 400,000 fungi and 2,500,000,000 bacteria (Ehrlich, 1970, p. 180). The fertility of the Earth depends on an unsurveyable, intricate interaction – a crazily complex symbiotic network which embraces all these small living beings.

The greater our comprehension of our togetherness with other beings, the greater the identification, and the greater care we will take. The road is also opened thereby for delight in the well-being of others and sorrow when harm befalls them. We seek what is best for ourselves, but through the extension of the self, our 'own' best is also that of others. The own/not-own distinction survives only in grammar, not in feeling.

Philosophically, the concepts ego, self, and Self (the deep, comprehensive and ecological self) are braided into dissimilar systems which originally were closely associated to the world religions. Because of the reduced influence of these religions in our industrial societies, the philosophies of identification have become almost inaccessible. The hotbed for many kinds of spontaneous religious experience is no longer a cultural gift of the cradle.

It is noteworthy that a 'democracy of life forms' is or was characteristic of some primal societies. Their conception of the human situation is more realistic than that offered in our techno-natural scientific education. While we derobe nature as such of all sensory diversity, and assert that it is really colourless, animism moves in the opposite direction.

While warning against an 'unconscious' plunge into the technocratic society of the future, one of our foremost scientists has remarked: 'We own nature together with our fellows'. But the ideology of ownership of nature has no place in an ecosophy. The Norwegian people or the

Norwegian state does not own Norway. The resources of the world are not only resources for human beings. Legally, we can 'own' a forest, but if we destroy the living conditions for life in the forest, we are transgressing the norm of equality.

This egalitarian attitude is manifested when the hunter has a long discussion with the spirit of the bear, and explains apologetically that the larder is bare and that he must now kill the bear to nourish his family. In return, the hunter can remind the bear's spirit that both he and his family will die one day, and turn to dust, and so to vegetation, sustenance for the descendents of the bear. In other words, this is a *realistic* egalitarian attitude, an acknowledgement of the cycles of life and their interconnection in nature.

Wildlife and forest management, and other professions in intimate contact with nature, change people's attitudes. It is only through work, play, and understanding that a deep and enduring identification can develop, an identification deep enough to colour the overall life conditions and ideology of a society.

The egalitarian attitude is not restricted to pre-industrial societies. 'Nature mysticism', as it is often called, is a genuine aspect of Western culture. To identify with all life does not imply an abandonment of our cultural heritage. Moral exhortation, punishment of ecocriminals, economic sanctions, and other negative tools have their place, but the education towards greater and wider identification though widening the Self is a thoroughly positive way.

(c)   *'That which is not of value to any human being*
        is of no value at all'
        Some people who partake positively in important environmental decisions report that they are inhibited by the thought that somehow *any* valuation whatsoever is a human valuation and therefore must be a value *for* humans. They feel that there are philosophical reasons for downplaying or eliminating reference to nature as such, the planet as such, wilderness as such. To avoid irrationality, one must stick to homocentric utilitarian positions: one must point to usefulness *for* humans.

Philosophical reflection convinces us that only humans formulate value statements on this planet. Value statements, like theories of gravitation, are formulated by humans in human language, not by mosquitoes in mosquito language. We may speak of gravitation for us and its absence whether we are in a gravitational field or not. Newton's laws were made by Newton, but stones fall without him.

Our conclusion is quite simple: the mere fact that *humans* say 'this is valuable', does not imply that 'this is beneficial for humans'. It is misleading terminology to maintain that values humanly conceived as valuable are such *for human beings*.

The subjective stance implied by 'good means good for mankind', if applied consistently, easily leads to solipsistic egotism: 'good is *good for me*'. If I give anything, it is because I get satisfaction from it. If I am altruistic, it is solely because I am better off when others are better off. Few have any conception of the entire human population, or of what is good for such a mass of people. Good 'for myself, my family and friends' is perhaps more clearly meaningful for most of us. But we correctly refuse to admit that we, by '*x* is good', mean '*x* is good for myself, my family and friends'.

Common sense can be a guide here. We acknowledge our mixed motives, and realise that our evaluations are more or less egocentric, that we have our own benefit more or less in mind and seldom give priority to others before ourselves. The demarcation lines cannot be drawn, and there are great individual and collective differences. Often, however, we will completely agree in practice. Let us say that we are planning a trip together. Some places will be visited because it is to A's advantage, while we others *see no value in it*, other places may be chosen by B, etc. At the same time, we are, as friends, aware that *each* of us thinks it is valuable that we visit a place *someone* thinks valuable to visit. This brings in evaluations of relevance on the meta-plane.

These propositions suggest that to ascribe value to animals, plants, landscapes, and wilderness areas independently of their relation to human utility or benefit is a philosophically legitimate procedure. To relate all value to mankind is a form of anthropocentrism which is not philosophically tenable.

Human nature may be such that with increased maturity a *human* need increases to protect the richness and diversity of life for *its own sake*. Consequently, what is useless in a narrow way may be useful in a wider sense, namely satisfying a human need. The protection of nature for *its own sake* would be a good example of this.

(d)   Friluftsliv: exuberance in nature

Contrary to expectation, urbanised life has not killed human fascination with free nature, but only made the access more difficult and promoted mass tourism. There is fortunately a way of life in free nature that is highly efficient in stimulating the sense of oneness, wholeness and in deepening identification.

The words 'outdoor recreation' are often used for the activities more and more people in the industrial societies are engaging in during their leisure time. But in Norwegian, there is a clearer, more value-laden word that refers to the type of outdoor recreation that seeks to come to nature on its own terms: to *touch the Earth lightly*. Literally, 'friluftsliv' means 'free air life', but it has been translated as 'open air life' and 'nature life' (see Reed and Rothenberg (1987)). In the following, we retain the original term to indicate a positive kind of state of mind and body in nature, one that brings us closer to some of the many aspects of identification and Self-realisation with nature that we have lost.

The satisfaction of the need for outdoor life and the need for machine-oriented technical unfolding cannot take place *simultaneously*. At present, the socio-economic forces in the industrial countries are lobbying in favour of priority for the capital-intensive apparatus: the apparatus-poor life is a hindrance to 'progress'. We should see true *friluftsliv* as a route towards paradigm change.

Friluftsliv plays a more and more important role as the dark shadows of the urban lifestyle of the industrial states have become more evident. The polar explorer and Norwegian national hero, Fritjof Nansen, remarked that *'friluftsliv* is a partial continuation of an aspect of an earlier form of life'. Human beings, until quite recently, have been hunters and gatherers, that is, lived and worked in nature. Much less than one per cent of our history has been devoted to the attempt to live a life characterised by machines and crowded quarters. As recently as the beginning of this century, many prominent futurists, including H. G. Wells, believed that 'progress' would succeed, and that human beings would be completely happy in their new radical form of life.

At the same time, *friluftsliv* caught on: more or less playful kinds of short excursions in nature. These excursions do not serve to procure food, nor do they fit any other characterisation as work. Outdoor life has assumed forms which resemble the physical activities in the hunter and gatherer cultures: on water – swimming, diving, rowing, paddling, sailing, fishing, in fields and forests – hiking, camping, skiing, riding, hunting; in mountainous terrain – glacial walks, climbing, cross-country skiing, mountain climbing on skis, fishing, hunting. Where do the competition sports fit in? Nils Faarlund (1973) says:

> Competition as a value represents a form of self-realisation which is reserved for the select. The competition-motivated lifestyle presupposes 'losers'. Self-realisation for the elite presupposes that the others are denied self-realisation. Competition as a value is thus excluding and elitist. Outdoor life in the sense of exuberant living in nature presupposes on the other hand the self-realisation of others to

achieve one's own (i.e.: a presentation of self which does not separate the individual from nature).

An important element is the necessity of effort. Without effort, no quality, and without quality, reduced enjoyment. Enjoyment of the quality in one's personal life conduct is an autotelic experiencing of value, or inner motivation. Competitive motivation is external motivation and thus a weaker mode of motivation.

With the near future in mind, it is important to stake out guidelines for ethically and ecologically responsible *friluftsliv*. These can be formulated as follows.

(1) Respect for all life. Respect for landscape. The elimination of pleasure hunting necessarily follows, except for 'photographic hunting'. Hunting must be restricted to ecosophically justifiable wildlife management. Traceless passage through the wilderness: one leaves no tell-tale 'droppings' in the landscape. No more cairn construction, and no expansion of backwoods urbanisation (highways, motels, etc.) of the natural areas.

(2) Outdoor education in the signs of identification. Children's (and adults') longing and capacity for identification with life and landscape is encouraged. Conventional goal direction: to get there, to be skilful, to be better than others, to get things done, to describe in words, to have and use new and fancy equipment – is discouraged. The ability to experience deep, rich and varied interaction in and with nature is developed.

(3) Minimal strain upon the natural combined with maximal self-reliance. This is a great challenge today. Greater knowledge about the use of local plants and other locally available material allows one quite often to live in nature with local resources. But acquaintance with nature's carrying capacity is simultaneously required. This limits the number of people who can be almost self-sufficient within a given landscape.

(4) Natural lifestyle. All-sided forms of togetherness with as much dwelling upon goals as possible, as little as possible upon that which is *solely* a means. The greatest possible elimination of technique and apparatus from the outside.

(5) Time for adjustment: those who come from urban life ordinarily have a certain appreciation for peace, stillness, and other aspects which contrast sharply with the stressful lifestyle of the city. After a few days, or a week, a certain *underestimation* usually sets in: the lack of radio, television, cinemas, etc. It takes time for the new milieu to work *in depth*. It is quite normal that several weeks must pass before the *sensitivity* for nature is so developed that it fills the mind. If a great deal of technique and apparatus are placed between oneself and nature, nature cannot possibly be reached.

The foregoing five points are meant to be guidelines. In the eyes of the growth economy, these points are poison. One cannot count on any immediate government efforts to protect the existing basis for ethically and ecologically responsible *fritluftsliv*. Recently, though, the Norwegian Ministry of the Environment (*Miljøverndepartmentet*) has gone quite far in limiting the notion of *friluftsliv* to what is compatible with these five points. In the growth economy at large, goals and intrinsic values are forgotten in favour of tourism and profitable capital investments.

Extremely powerful forces are attempting to replace *friluftsliv* with mechanised, competitive, and environmentally destructive intrusions into nature. These forces can only be countered through a long contest upon many fronts.

When rampant urbanisation began to cripple human life in the rich industrial states, the establishment of national parks and other large free areas was advocated. Nonetheless, the need for elbow room and activity under the open sky has been shown to be much more than a luxury need of the elite. Among many people it has developed into a vital need.

The easily accessible free areas have proven to be insufficient, and quickly assumed an urban façade – lineups, littering, the devastation of vegetation, fatal curtailment of freedom of movement, luxury residences and luxurious living rather than simple *life*.

In the 1980s, many parks in the USA are so overloaded with people (often Europeans in caravans!) that extremely strict regulations have been introduced. A typical stepwise trend can be traced: forbidden to camp in certain areas – forbidden to camp except in designated areas – camping forbidden; forbidden to prepare food except in cement grilles – forbidden to prepare food outdoors; forbidden to move in steep terrain (erosion) – forbidden to walk off the paths – forbidden to stray from the asphalt – only short sojourns allowed – ticket required every day – 'Entrance forbidden: trespassers will be prosecuted'.

Instead of entering a realm of freedom, one feels that one is in some kind of museum ruled by angry owners.

In a country where *friluftsliv* is accepted as a vital need, such restrictions would be considered an outrage.

Cooperation between the representatives of industry and competitive sports has created an *outfitting pressure*: new so-called improvements appear and are marketed continuously, and norms about equipment replacement are impressed upon and accepted by large sections of the population. A refinement which *can* be important in top competition, but is frivolous in *friluftsliv*, is nonetheless sold to the well-to-do and more lethargic groups of the public who are susceptible to sales pushes. As equipment to outdoor generalists is much less expensive than specialised equipment, people are encouraged to specialise. Furthermore, it is more profitable to sell things which require large capital outlays.

After a gigantic outpour of resources and technique, the barriers are overcome – the happy consumer stretches out on the simple bunk in the log cabin, listens to the birds singing, opens a creaky wooden door to watch the lively salmon jumping in the swirling waters. People swallow the equipment hook, line, and sinker, and lengthen their working day and increase stress in the city to be able to afford the 'latest'. Worn out, and with only a little time to spare, they dash off to the outdoor areas, for a short respite before rushing back to the cities. Still starved, they keep right on biting!

Friluftsliv is a rather concrete theme, but it cannot be separated from metaphysics. So the jump back to philosophy is not unduly long. Understanding of anything in nature begins with direct experience, but this soon stimulates reflection.

3 Cruelty in nature; the tragedy and the comedy of life

We may 'praise nature' using unconditional superlatives in our poetry and rhetoric, but not in our philosophy or our politics. The phenomena of social Darwinism, fascism, and national socialism contained an unrestricted 'cult of life' with special emphasis on exploitation and brutal competition. These political trends made use of untenable descriptions of life, but we should as ecosophers avoid making people believe we say 'yes!' to everything in nature.

The process of identification leads us to see much cruelty in nature. But it does not necessarily lead to conceiving any animal to be cruel. A behaviour may be deplored without applying negative ethical standards to the actor.

In the 'oneness and diversity' philosophy which Ecosophy T presents, independent treatment of four different fields of phenomena is required:

(1) Identification with living beings individually (distributively) and within limited life situations;

(2) Identification with living beings collectively or in their essence ('life itself', ecosystems, species);

(3) Ethical judgement (by different scales) of the individual beings in specific situations;

(4) Ethical judgement of life collectively or in its essence.

Contemporary inspiration from naturalism essentially leads to identification with *all life, distributively*. Abhorrence and rejection are scarce, and arise, for example, at the sight of or treatment of the cruel conditions caused by overpopulation. Presumably these reactions often have an ethical component. But they do not imply an ethically negative judgement of animal life as a whole.

A more adequate treatment of this topic would require a discussion of various ethical standpoints and their relevance for an appraisal of nature. The literary historian Joseph W. Meeker (1972) has combined his expertise with experience in ecology. Is the conception of the human relationship with nature found in literary comedies more true and useful in the environmental crisis than that found in the tragedy? He suggests that it is.

The heroes in Greek and other tragedies generally struggle with tremendous forces and their heroism ultimately destroys them. Their suffering is as great as their passions – soaring love, burning hate, glowing patriotism. The ideals are sky-high, but nature doesn't measure up. Storms kill heroes as much as villains. The hero succumbs to metaphysical desperation: natural forces are not on his side – as they should be.

In the comedy, sky-high ideals and the resulting extravagant sufferings are jokingly depicted as some kind of madness or as ungenuine. Like animals, humans have their small weaknesses, enjoy life more or less as it is, have simple pleasures, moderate virtues, moderate level of aspiration, and a sense of humour. The unheroic fumble and stumble their way through existence without pretentions. The 'heroes' of the comedy survive in a fairly decent manner while those of the tragedy succumb, leaving a trail of sorrow and despair in their wake.

Meeker could also have referred to the Faustian character, longing and longing, grasping to get hold of something ephemeral, always hurrying to something else because 'happiness is where you are not'.

The tragic view of man, Meeker suggests, leads to cultural and biological catastrophe, and it is time to look for alternatives which might encourage better the survival of our own and other species.

Comus, the demigod whose name may have been the origin of the word 'comedy', was preoccupied with fertility, harmonic family life, and social togetherness. He left matters of great intellectual importance to Apollo, and gigantic passions to Dionysus.

Meeker believes that biological evolution shows more of the elasticity of the comedy than the weight of 'monolithic passion'. Mature ecosystems are arranged in a relatively stable equilibrium between a host of various species of living beings.

Mankind during the last nine thousand years has conducted itself like a *pioneer invading species*. These species are individualistic, aggressive, and hustling. They attempt to exterminate or suppress other species. They discover new ways to live under unfavourable external conditions – admirable! – but they are ultimately self-destructive. They are replaced by other species which are better suited to restabilise and mature the ecosystem. If mankind is to avoid being replaced then the struggle *against* nature must cease. Some kind of 'back to nature' attitude must be nurtured. This does not imply that lifestyle and society will become too simple in relation to our great intellectual capacity. On the contrary, the relationships in a mature ecosystem are more composite than any mankind has mastered. With increasing understanding, increasing sensitivity towards internal relations, humans can live with moderate material means and reach a fabulous richness of ends.

Ecosophy T has certain of Meeker's comedy characteristics: equality, joy, unfolding in small communities. But also a little of the tragedy: ideals (guidelines) for nonviolence are suggested which are impossible to attain if they are understood strictly and absolutely. Furthermore, it actively stresses inspiration for working to better social conditions. The more relaxed comic mode with its penchant for personal adaptation seems to abandon the less resourceful to the mercy of the elements. The comic mode may be the mode of the future, but hard political contests stand between us and that goal. Our time is not one for total relaxation!

Human conduct still today as a pioneer invading species present a catastrophic cultural lag. It is a conduct systematically counteracting the process of identification with its fruit of compassion and living light on Earth.

4   A historical perspective I: the Bible

Why haven't we in the Western countries managed to reach high levels of identification? Because it is not primarily a *technical* problem? Because our submission to technology as such requires alienation from the object of our manipulation? It is difficult to furnish a complete answer.

The Bible has influenced and still influences our view of our place within the ecosystems. This is true for Christians, and for non-Christians.

The Bible has already been studied from an ecological viewpoint. Radically different attitudes appear. This must be expected when the history of the origin of the Bible is taken into consideration. I will restrict myself here to a few notes on positive passages.

Many places in the Bible indicate that God has given human beings some kind of privileged position in relation to the rest of the creation, but the question 'what kind of privileges?' necessitates an examination of specific statements within special sections.

According to Genesis, chapter 1, verse 28, it seems that God intends man to subdue the earth and fill it with his offspring. We are allotted dominion but far from a *free hand* do do whatever we like. The Authorised Version reads, '. . . replenish the earth, and subdue it: and have dominion over the fish of the sea . . .'. This verse, in *isolation*, can be used to cultivate an arrogant and inconsiderable attitude towards the entire Creation.

According to Genesis 9:3, God *gives* 'all things' to Noah. But Noah's ship must have been quite crowded and uncomfortable for him, and he may have looked with great annoyance at the many completely useless creatures, perhaps mumbling, 'if I had dominion I know what I would do!' His dominion seems to include those things Noah and his descendants require to *lead a healthy and God-fearing life.* In other words *practically nothing* in comparison with the average Western material standard of living. The passage *can* be interpreted to mean that God bequeathes the earth as some kind of personal property, but a more reasonable interpretation is that God places everything at Noah's disposal with the strict stipulation that it be used in accordance with the commandments of God. Noah receives rights of disposition, not property rights. Rather extensive dominion of the same sort is intimated in the Book of Psalms, 8:5 and 8:6. 'For thou has made him a little lower than the angels, . . . thou hast put all things under his feet.'

But there are also more egalitarian tendencies in the Books of Moses. Great whales, and every living creature, and winged fowl are to be fruitful, and multiply, and fill the seas and earth (Genesis I: 21, 22). God scarcely had the whaling business in mind! It seems to be presumed that human beings are to fill the Earth, but not by squeezing out other creatures He created. It would be difficult even for Norwegians to justify our whale and seal catch with Genesis 1:22. God blesses all equally: *each thing is blessed separately and referred to as good.* 'And God saw that this was good.' A strong value judgement was made even before He created Adam. The individual parts of the creation seem to be afforded intrinsic value. Nothing of that which is created has value only as *means.* Nothing is created only for the sake of human beings alone or solely for any other earthly being. A principal point in 'egalitarianism in the biosphere' is thereby won: every living being is equal to all others *to the extent* that it has intrinsic value.

Other places in the Old Testament also deny our autotelic uniqueness, e.g. Psalm 104:18: 'The high hills are a refuge for the wild goats; and the rocks for the conies.' It does seem to be implied that human beings are to gain from the conies (alpine rabbits). The high hills and rocks were placed at the disposal of the conies in the same way that He allowed human beings use what we need for a healthy and God-fearing life.

The human function as guardian or keeper is much more important for ecosophical interpretations. 'And the Lord God took Man, and put him into the garden of Eden to dress it and keep it.' (Genesis 2:15). The garden was small and presumably not a threat to the habitats of other living beings.

In this and other passages, it appears that human beings must answer for their activities on Earth. In certain situations, mankind must *moderate* the effects of wild animals upon other beings, extermination, seeing to it that a certain order and harmony reign. That which God has created is not to be exterminated, not even snakes in the Garden.

Mankind is accountable to God, in the light of our uniquely responsible position; regent, caliph, deputy, guardian, administrator, steward, and servant are some of the terms used in the Bible and the Koran.

Unhappily, the role of guardian with its duties and responsibilities cannot be said to be systematically outlined anywhere in the Bible. In the New Testament it is natural to refer to the parable of the faithful and unfaithful servants. 'A certain man planted a vineyard, and set a hedge about it, and dug a place and went into a far country' (Mark 12:1). The husbandmen did not give the owner any wine. Things did not go well for them. 'The kingdom of God shall be taken from you and given to a nation bringing forth the fruit thereof' (Matthew 21:43).

Many have used this parable in support of the attitude that mankind must be accountable for how he behaves ecologically. There is a great deal of evidence which corroborates the importance this interpretation has had throughout the ages.

The Earth does *not* belong to mankind, according to Paul: 'For the Earth is the Lord's, and the fullness thereof.' (I Corinthians 10:26). Everything which God has created is good (I Timothy 4:4). There is, all in all, less mention of external nature in the New Testament. The world has soon to end. The spiritual salvation of mankind is more central than in the Old Testament. There was no time to lose by nature conservation as James Watt among others let us understand.

But back to the Old Testament . . .

Everything which is created by God is good and more wisely arranged than anything mankind can create, and more diverse. Therefore, nature bears witness to God, *not only in its diversity*, but also in the ecosystem where the food chains lead to lower conditions:

> The young lions roar after their prey, and seek their meat from God. (Psalm 104:21)
>
> O Lord, how manifold are thy works! in wisdom hast thou made them all: the Earth is full of thy riches. (Psalm 104:24)
>
> So is this great and wide sea, wherein are things creeping innumerable, both small and great beasts. Psalm 104:25)
>
> . . . the LORD shall rejoice in his works. He looketh on the Earth, and it trembleth: he toucheth the hills, and they smoke. (Psalm 104:31,32)

In this ecologically famous psalm, mankind is not glorified. An unsurveyable diversity of animals and processes geological of not the slightest utility to mankind are praised on an equal footing with everything else.

The Lord is also encouraged to rejoice in earthquakes and volcanic eruptions. These events are meant to be good and beautiful, but not especially for human beings.

The Lord rejoices in His Creation, says the Bible. And so did mankind. But sometimes too much! Enjoying the Creation, but forgetting the Creator. This is one of the sources of Christian *contemptus mundi*, contempt for the world. Sinners 'who changed the truth of God into a lie, and worshipped and served the creatures more than the Creator . . .' (Romans 1:25), even though 'the invisible things of Him from the creation of the world are clearly seen, being understood by the things that are made, even his eternal power and Godhead . . .' (Romans 1:20). It is tempting to draw the ecosophically desirable conclusion that 'Paul attributes the sin of man to his failure to see in nature the works of God'. This is C. J. Glacken's conclusion in his exceptional eco-historical work, *Traces on the Rhodian Shore* (1967), p. 161. However, Paul seems to say that human beings presumably see God in the Creation, but that they transgress his commandments nonetheless. Paul emphasises the manifestation of God in the Creation, that is, nature, because this very manifestation renders human misdeeds sinful. They have no excuse. They know their God, and see him in Creation, but they conduct themselves godlessly and unjustly nonetheless.

Praise of creation without praise of God is thus a form of heathenism. So is the identification of God with creation. To refute the latter, the wonder of God has been *contrasted* with that of nature, a mere reflection. Preoccupation with nature has therefore been regarded as pernicious.

Another source of *contemptus mundi* builds upon Genesis 3:17: 'And unto Adam he said, Because thous hast hearkened unto the voice of thy wife, and hast eaten of the tree, of which I commanded thee, saying, thou shalt not eat of it: cursed is the ground for thy sake . . .', Genesis 3:18 begins 'Thorns also and thistles shall it bring forth to thee . . .'. Some have concluded that less hospitable things like thistles were created after the fall of man from divine grace. After the fall of man, nature was *reduced in quality*. This poor quality then justifies contempt.

It is difficult to decide how influential such nuances of interpretation have been. The foregoing quotations have only intimated how much ecosophically relevant material there is in the Biblical Scriptures. Throughout the ages, the Bible has been referred to as a support for vastly different and mutually inconsistent positions. In recent years, some very representative interpretations have emphasised the human responsibility to God for how to deal with the wonders of nature. The preceding has essentially tried to undermine the impression that our role has been uniformly interpreted down through the ages, and that this interpretation has only expressed arrogance, utilitarian thinking, and blind dogmatic faith. A person's opinion about the ecological movement cannot be derived from the fact that he or she 'believes in the Bible'.

The wisdom of God is ridiculed if He is said to have engaged so ignorant and so ignoble a creature as *Homo sapiens* to administer or guard the vastness of nature, of which we understand so little. Nature is not a vegetable patch!

The arrogance of stewardship consists in the idea of superiority which underlies the thought that we exist to watch over nature like a highly respected middleman between the Creator and the Creation. We know too little about what happens in nature to take up the task.

The most important weakness of the expression is probably that, when it comes to the administration of nature, simple, so-called factual conditions reveal our extremely limited ability to plan for its development – even if evolution, continental drift, and other vast primary processes on our Earth are not included in the attempt.

The administrator idea is less unreasonable if it is confined merely to domestic animals and agricultural land. The word 'nature' is then less comprehensive than an ecosophic perspective demands. Our responsibility today is not that of the guardian, but that of the thief and manipulator. We must face this responsibility. The notion of our ignorance about consequences implies a norm about limitation and careful control of our intervention. Moderated, and more closely associated with Christian humility, the administrator idea may contribute to a strengthening of awareness of ecological responsibility. *The religious background for such an awareness is an irreplaceable plus.* But he who stops wreaking havoc does not thereby become an administrator.

Christian theologians who have studied mankind's critical ecological situation tend to embrace the ecological movement, and they find full support in the Bible. Christian theology is by no means homogeneous and it should not be dealt with as such. To attempt to do so is perhaps characteristic of an attitude which *abhors diversity*, when differences are deeper than they can fully command. The differences in Christian theology frustrate those who deplore variety.

As an example of a fragment of a Christian ecosophy, let us consider some ideas put forth by E. F. Schumacher in a very short article entitled *The Age of Plenty: A Christian View* (1974). We shall call his view 'Ecosophy S' for the purpose of comparison of terminology.

Schumacher announces that he will in the article 'take an overall view' which 'can be obtained only from a considerable height'. In the terminology of Ecosophy T, ' a considerable depth'. Facts are not enough: they need to be evaluated, that is to say fitted into a value system, to be of use. In my terminology: hypotheses need to be joined with norms in order for decisions to be derived. I would rather emphasise 'Only from the height of an overall view can we obtain a meaningful value system.'

Corresponding to the top norm and hypotheses of Ecosophy T, Schumacher suggests the use of what Ignatius of Loyola called 'The Foundation':

> Man was created to praise, reverence, and serve God our Lord, and by this means to save his soul;
> And the other things on the face of the earth were created for Man's sake, and in order to aid him in the prosecution of the end for which he was created.
> Whence it follows
> That man ought to make use of them just so far as they help him to attain his end,
> And that he ought to withdraw himself from them just so far as they hinder him.

From the point of view of a normative system we might start with a norm 'Man ought to do what he was created to do!' using two supporting hypotheses from the first four lines of the quotation: from these three ultimate premises we derive the two norms expressed by the last four lines.

'The logic of this Foundation is unshakable; it is in fact the kind of logic we invariably try to apply in our everyday affairs, whether it be business, science, engineering, or politics,' writes Schumacher, using the term 'logic' in a much more everyday manner than that favoured by authors of symbolic logic textbooks.

'Anybody who is prepared to accept the two premises cannot possibly refuse to accept the conclusion.' One might make this statement more credible by rather unconventionally interpreting the term 'God' in the first sentence as a kind of normative sentence 'God!', that is, making automatically any sentence about what God has created us to do into a combination of a norm and a hypothesis.

Schumacher mentions two norms representing a third level of derivation within his system. The two last sentences of the quotation from Loyola imply 'that where people do not have enough to attain their ends, they should have more, and where they have more than enough they should "withdraw" from that which is excessive'.

Loyola reflects the dominant view of his time when saying that 'other things on the face of the earth were created for Man's sake . . .'. It is difficult to harmonise this with the basic views within the deep ecology movement. For Schumacher it does not seem difficult. He cites the greatest Catholic thinker of the Middle Ages:

> The smallest mosquito, as St. Thomas Aquinas said, is more wonderful than anything man has produced and will ever produce. So man must never lose his sense of the marvellousness of the world around and inside him – a world which he has not made and which, assuredly, has not made itself. Such an attitude engenders a spirit of nonviolence, which is a form or aspect of wisdom.

Schumacher scarcely means that mosquitoes are more wonderful for man to make use of than anything man himself has made. He seems somehow to refer to the wonderfulness of God's creations as such, and if he does he acknowledges the intrinsic value of all living beings.

Schumacher makes use of vague and ambiguous key terms in order to indicate rough guidelines for policy. This is akin to the T_0 formulations which I make use of. It is too late to interview Schumacher in order to clarify how he stands in relation to the near-common points of the deep ecology movement. But we may safely assert that a Christian 'Ecosophy S' might be elaborated on the basis of his influential writings.

5   A historical perspective II: from Plotinus to Descartes

In later antiquity, trends arose which directed human attention 'upwards' and to the 'pure' spirit. Spirit was contrasted with body: '. . . whilst we are at home in the body, we are absent from the Lord' (Paul in II Corinthians 5:6). Inner reflection was encouraged to the detriment of the so-called external human being, society, and milieu. The body, things, the material world – all were considered to be hindrances to the life of the spirit.

The Christian sects made up only a small part of those who led this transformation throughout the entirety of the Hellenistic-Roman world. The tendency is described by classics scholar H. P. L'Orange (1953):

> Human beings must overcome the perceptual and conceptual chaos into which our senses have tricked us, and seek a higher reality. This can be achieved by collecting the soul in an inner life, in a concept- and idea-oriented contemplation of 'things'. The essence of 'things' lies in the ideas. Even Plotinus, in the third century AD, sees in the sensible reality of nature a beautiful reflection of the ideas. But the things of nature gradually lost this reflection. One withdrew from the external world, from the 'beautiful body' and collected oneself with the inner life through renewed probing.

This one-sidedness involved a depreciation of physical reality in its entirety. Or, ecosophically: one aspect of existence was isolated from the others and named 'physical reality'.

A search for supernatural being can easily become an endeavour hostile to man and environment. True enough, it can lead to splendid art. And a violent striving upwards need not, in theory, imply depreciation of physical reality in its entirety, but it seems to have done that. L'Orange contends that this characteristic can be traced in all forms of art, in all forms of philosophy, and in all forms of social thought in the West:

> Classical art is therefore an expression of an equilibrium, a reconciled relationship between mankind and the world. It is this happy equilibrium between inner and outer which is lost in later antiquity. Human beings denied themselves the immediate, sensual loyalty to the external world, and withdrew to isolated positions in their inner lives. This is the tower from which the art of later antiquity and the early Middle Ages looked down upon reality.

Thus Petrarch suffered from a bad conscience when he admired nature: 'I was stunned . . . angry with myself that I still admired earthly things. I ought to have learned, long ago, even from pagan philosophers, that nothing is admirable besides the mind: compared to its greatness nothing is great.' (Seneca Epistle 8.5, Petrarch (1966))

What a poignant example of glorification of mankind *to the detriment of something else*! 'If *x* is glorious and *y* is different from *x, y* cannot be glorious!' But is not a Both-and solution presumably possible? (See chapter 2.)

The role of inner reflection is obvious as the quote continues:

> . . . I was completely satisfied with what I had seen of the mountain and turned my inner eye towards myself . . . How often, do you think, did I turn back and look up toward the summit of the moutain today while I was walking down? It seemed to rise hardly higher than a cubit compared to the height of human contemplation, were the latter not plunged into the squalor of earthly mud and filth.

From the point of view of Ecosophy T Petrarch exemplifies the regression from a wide self to a narrow. He cuts off his previous identifications and reifies the distinction inner–outer, alienating himself from the mountain.

The distinction between 'in the Self' and 'out in nature' makes it quite difficult to describe our relationship to nature. When this distinction is successfully transcended, another concept of nature and another conception of 'self' will arise – the concept that is the fundamental intuition behind Ecosophy T.

This glorification of human beings at the expense of nature becomes ecosophically relevant when it is manifest in value priorities. To the extent that it serves to depreciate, or blind us to, on-human realms, it has an obviously negative ecological effect.

Towards the end of the Middle Ages, the power wielded over individual minds by the established religion declined. This is widely acknowledged to have been partially due to the de-mystification of reality brought about by science, technique, and the rise of capitalist economies. We relaxed our striving upwards, *but without a return to a relatively harmonious attitude to nature.* Our depreciation of the 'physical' reality continued, now in the form of exploitation. *Nature came to be interpreted as both slave and raw material.* Like the slaves, nature could revolt, and the expression 'struggle *against* nature' has been in continuous use since then. Hostility to 'physical' reality had been transferred to nature in general.

Europeans have retained the idea that our association with nature is external and narrowly utilitarian. Therefore, it seems hypocritical to pretend that we could be considerate to animals or plants if this did not directly or indirectly reward the Master of Creation, after the demise of the God of the Middle Ages. The undercurrent of identification persisted throughout the Renaissance and more recent times, while the mechanical, alienating image of nature was simultaneously founded in league with 'practical' exploitation. All the ingredients were on hand for the ideological about-face made by René Descartes. He claimed, in his *Discourse on Method*,

> . . . the speculative philosophy taught in the Schools can be replaced by a practical philosophy . . . knowing the power and the effects of fire, water, air, the stars, the heavens . . . we might thereby make ourselves, as it were, masters and possessors of nature.

6   Our self-respect is not solely due to our own significance: the Milky Way also stimulates respect

Is the individual deprived of anything if it is accepted that (1) he or she does not represent a preferred position in the universe, and (2) there are other perspectives which are just as valuable as human perspectives?

Aristotle was willing to acknowledge the existence of total perspectives other than those of human beings:

> For it would be strange to regard politics or practical wisdom as the highest kind of knowledge, when man is not the best thing in the universe. Surely, if 'healthy' and 'good' mean one thing for men and another for fishes, whereas 'white' and 'straight' always mean the same, 'wise' must mean the same for everyone, but 'practically wise' will be

different. For each particular being ascribes practical wisdom in matters relating to itself to that thing which observes its interests well, and it will entrust itself to that thing. That is the reason why people attribute practical wisdom even to some animals – to all those which display a capacity for forethought in matters relating to their own life.

Nicomachean Ethics 1141, 20–6

Is the principle of the 'infinite value' of each individual and his or her unique and irreplaceable nature more plausible within the tiny cosmos of the New Testament, in which mankind forms the centre and the time perspective is short, than within the immense ecosphere of ecology? My negative reply rests upon the idea that 'life is fundamentally one'.

An important and essential matter for all individuals is one's personal conduct. Each individual has responsibility, each has something to preserve, something to develop. To counter apathy and low self-esteem, moral philosophers have occasionally made the mistake of placing humankind in a unique position in respects incompatible with an open attitude to the rest of nature. In relation to other living beings on our planet, *Homo sapiens* is unique: it is valid to call ourselves unique *on Earth*. But what is our situation in the Milky Way?

If we estimate the number of stars in the Milky Way system to be one hundred thousand million (there are probably more), and we assume that one one-millionth of them have planets with good, enduring conditions for life, this would mean one hundred thousand planets with life. If beings with cognitive organs of greater capacity than our brain have evolved on half of these planets, we are faced with 50,000 species of life who occupy an analogous position to our relation with the other animals on our planet. A long evolutionary line can be drawn, with *Homo sapiens* in the middle, a mediocrity (if we retain our ordinary competitive thought) . . . Ladybird . . . *Rattus norvegicus* . . . *Homo sapiens* . . . *x* . . . *y* . . .

Some may object that good preconditions for life *may* be even more infrequent. OK. Let us make the assumption that they occur on the average in only one solar system in even a hundred thousand million. We are perhaps alone in the Milky Way. But at a conservative estimate, there are a hundred thousand million star universes of the Milky Way type within the range of our largest telescopes. If half of these have life below our brain capacity, and half with greater capacity, fifty thousand million species of life have come farther in the development of the brain than we have. But why be so preoccupied with competition?

We do not become less when seen in a Milky Way perspective as long as we have a certain sense for *participation in something great*. Our participation does not seem to be less important than that of anything else.

For all we know, life may have a great future in which we are participating and changing. As far as the cosmic possibilities are concerned, we can, without contradicting any 'hard facts', embrace theories such as those about the evolution of a consciousness which encompasses the entire universe. Personally, I can make do with less, but it would be arbitrary to set a theoretical limit to the development and power of conscious entities in the cosmos.

Notes on life in the universe are ecopolitically relevant, for they have expanded and presumably still can expand the perspectives of many people. Without a certain expansion in perspective, an ecologically responsible politics is impossible.

7   Nonviolence and the philosophy of oneness

The following does not pretend to represent more than one line of thought, one which combines a fundamental metaphysical or religious viewpoint with a pattern for dealing with the many conflicts which energetic support for ecologically responsible policy necessarily entails.

The strong tone of nonviolence found in Ecosophy T may be disliked by some. There is nonetheless one aspect of nonviolence which I believe to be required of all those who are ecologically engaged. Experience from recent years indicates that ecological viewpoints gain headway through nonviolent political communication which mobilises the grass roots. But this implies great emphasis upon the norm 'deal with issues, not with persons' and a certain openness towards the ecopolitical viewpoints of the opposition. Briefly, their statements must not be submitted to distorted interpretations, nor should the formulations issued by one's own faction be uncritically assimilated.

The importance of the acceptance of nonviolent conflict theory as a central part of an ecosophy must be seen in the light of our global situation. Within the next 20–30 years, a multitude of collective resolutions ought to be made, yet there seems to be little evidence that this will be done. Assuming that they are made, they will have to be backed by power and authority. To sabotage them must be considered a serious break in interhuman loyalty. Faced with these contests, I believe that all established decision-making institutions, as well as direct action, have to be used in the protection of nature. The more seriously these latter approaches diverge from the established decision-making processes, the more important it is that they maintain a high standard not only with respect to ecological knowledge, but also with respect to conflict behaviour. The more radical the direct action, the more people will be hurt unintentionally. A certain humility naturally develops. The principles of vigorous nonviolence must be stressed even more.

The ways of nonviolence and the philosophies of wholeness and oneness have been closely associated historically. Gandhi gathered strength and inspiration from the *Bhagavad Gita*. It contains several central statements which can be considered to be the common denominator for large sections of Indian philosophy. Most notable is chapter 6 verse 29: 'He whose self is harmonised by yoga seeth the Self abiding in all beings and all beings in the Self.' Rabindranath Tagore adds: 'he is nevermore hidden'. The philosopher Shankara comments on this: 'When humanity understands that all creatures feel the same joy and pain as ourselves, we will harm no creature.' The association with nonviolence is immediate.

But pain rather than joy furnishes the most urgent experience of oneness. This is expressed clearly in the opening words of Peter Wessel Zapffe's 'The Last Messiah' (see Reed and Rothenberg (1987)):

> One night, irretrievable ages ago, Man awoke and *saw himself* . . . when the animals came to their waterholes, where he awaited them as was his custom, he no longer felt the urge to pounce, but a great psalm on the brotherhood of suffering amidst all which lives.

According to philosophies of oneness, *the path goes first inwards only to lead out again to everything*. The path of action (*karmamārga*) leads an action-yogi (*karmayogi*) into contact with all creatures, whether or not they can feel pain. This is the path followed by Gandhi.

The great Western emphasis upon the subjugation of nature goes against this insight of unity. This tendency is manifest even among the able leaders of global health programs of this century. Karl Evang said:

> We *Homo sapiens* live in a hostile nature which consists of bacteria and viruses. . . . Nature is still our principal enemy. Nature would, if we unleashed her, destroy us in no time at all. *Culture* stands between man and nature, and it provides organisation to protect us.

One could perhaps say that the *culture* which encircles us like a buffer between man and nature will 'destroy us in no time at all' if it is allowed to ride freely in the industrialised countries. The world's health organisations are perhaps in need of an ideology influenced to a greater extent by the health evidenced in nature.

Community with the animals in the extremer forms of the philosophy of oneness rests upon deep identification manifesting itself through the experience of equal worth, equal rights. It is not authoritarian like the cryptic Brother Wolf who humbly obeyed Francis of Assisi, repented, and thereafter led a better life. Gandhi did not imagine wolves or lions who became 'kind' and did no wrong. The ecological viewpoint presupposes acceptance of the fact that big fish eat small, but not necessarily that large men throttle small.

'The philosophy of oneness' is a name which can be misleading: it can give the impression that one who honestly and fairly accepts such a philosophy has thereby succeeded and behaved consistently and unproblematically in a certain way and maintained a certain frame of mind towards our fellow creatures. In that case, the 'philosophy of oneness' would be the name of a total system with obvious consequences in every kind of situation – otherwise one would be abdicating one's freedom as a person. But history is full of examples in which abstract fundamentals and an impressive number of admirable derived norms have been accepted, while they have not been reflected in practice; the path of derivation through norms and hypotheses is *too* long to be mastered and our ability to act spontaneously is *too* great!

The theoretical starting points of the philosophy of the one and the many cannot replace the concrete time- and situation-determined deliberations which must be made in a choice of appropriate political action. An egalitarian norm is not misleading, but only a guideline, if one wishes to consider political decisions in the widest possible perspective. This can and must be done without a review of philosophy before each choice and action. The ecopolitical situation is such that one must elicit support from experts of many professions, while on the other hand efforts must be made to assimilate their insights into a whole which not only is inter*disciplinary*, but also comprises the articulation of profound basic attitudes.

In the terminology of Ecosophy T the capital S in 'Self-realisation' carries a heavy burden. It insinuates a philosophy of oneness as does chapter 6, verse 29 of the *Gita*. But of course the difference in content is vast, Ecosophy T as a total view belonging to a vastly different cultural tradition. The S insinuates that if the widening and deepening of the self goes on *ad infinitum* the selves will realise themselves by *realising the same*, whatever this is. Because the infinite level of Self-realisation only makes sense metaphysically, the capital S should be used sparingly. At any level of realisation of potentials, the individual egos remain separate. They do not dissolve like individual drops in the ocean. Our care continues ultimately to concern the individuals, not any collectivity. But the individual is not, and will not be isolatable, whatever exists has a gestalt character.

Speaking about human individuals, it is in our competitive society unavoidable to ask: Who have in historical times been pre-eminent in approaching Self-realisation? There can be no good answer, because in

written history such pre-eminence does not count: there must be regis-
tered influence on a great scale. And the extraordinary level must be
manifest, which is perhaps never the case. What about Gandhi? After all,
he was under close, in part very critical, scrutiny for half a century. Yes,
a genius of nonviolence, but also a fierce fighter, a cunning politician.
Talking about pre-eminence in approaching Self-realisation I suspect
more anonymous persons have reached higher. The manner of posing the
question may however reveal a rather provincial western way of thinking.

8   The systematisation of the logically ultimate norms and hypotheses of Ecosophy T

(a)   The idea of models of logical relations

The complete formulation of an ecosophy is out of the question:
the complexity and flexibility of such a living structure make that impossible, perhaps even meaningless. There may also be logical reasons for the
impossibility of the formulating of a total view: it would be like a gestalt
without a background, an absurdity. One may, however, simulate such a
system. One may make a model of parts of it, isolating certain patterns
and aspects of it for close scrutiny, implicitly pretending that the rest
somehow exists in the realm of pure thought.

In what follows I shall work out such a model as a conclusion to this
book. It expresses the vision of an ecosophy in the form of a pyramid or
tree.

The direction from top to bottom, from theory to praxis, is one of
logical, not genetic or historical, derivation. It is not a ranking order. It
does not indicate value priorities. At the top levels there are a small
number of general and abstract formulations, at the bottom singular and
concrete ones, adapted to special situations, communities, time intervals,
and actions.

The direction from the bottom up offers the genetic and historical
derivation – including all the motivations and impulses resulting in
formulations of norms and hypotheses.

What is modelled is a moving, ever-changing phenomenon: norms and
hypotheses being derived more or less logically, applied in praxis, and the
outcome motivating changes. The tree can be arranged to form a triangle
or parallelogram with a wide horizontal base line and a narrow top line.
The difference in breadth expresses the fact that from the abstract and
general norms and hypotheses indefinitely many more specialised norms
and hypotheses follow giving rise to indefinitely many decisions in
concrete situations.

If we decide to reject a low-level norm, this implies that we will have to modify some hypotheses or norms at higher levels. The whole upper pyramid gets to be shaky. However, a rejection tends, in practice, to cause only slight modification, or simply the adoption of a somewhat different precisation of a higher norm or hypothesis *formulation*.

A sentence like 'Seek Self-realisation!' will within social science tend to be interpreted as a sentence in the imperative mood, and from a social point of view it is pertinent to ask: who are the 'senders' and who are the 'receivers'? Not necessarily so in T_0-expositions of models of normative systems. The question of how to understand the function of a one-word sentence like 'Self-realisation!' is a large and deep one which I am not going to attack. Let it suffice to say that there are examples of the use of the exclamation mark with a sender, but no definite receiver. When terrible things happen, like the collapsing of a bridge, or the loss of one's keys down a drain, we may meaningfully say 'No!', but at least some of us have in such cases no definite receiver group in mind. The function of the sentence is clear enough without. An archetype of this function appears in the Bible when God says 'Let there be light!' To ask who are the intended receivers of the exclamation is in this case rather intriguing if we suppose there is not yet anything created. But to ask the question is itself questionable.

In short I find it to be my duty to point out that there are questions concerning the function of norm-sentences in the exposition at hand which one should acknowledge but not necessarily engage in 'solving'.

What follows is only one particular exposition of Ecosophy T. Other versions may be cognitively equivalent, expressing the same concrete content in a different abstract structure.

(b)   *Formulation of the most basic norms and hypotheses*

   N1: Self-realisation!

   H1: The higher the Self-realisation attained by anyone, the broader and deeper the identification with others.

   H2: The higher the level of Self-realisation attained by anyone, the more its further increase depends upon the Self-realisation of others.

   H3: Complete Self-realisation of anyone depends on that of all.

   N2: Self-realisation for all living beings!

Comments:

The four formulations N1, H1, H2, and H3 make up the first level of the survey. N1 and H1 are ultimates in the sense of not being derivable from the others within the chosen version of the logical systematisation of Ecosophy T. H2, H3 and N2 are supposed to be logically derivable from the ultimates. Formal rigour would of course require us to add some premises which would be of greater interest to the logician than to the ecosopher. (For instance: if A identifies with B, and both are beings such that it is a meaningful to talk about their higher Self-realisation levels, complete Self-realisation of A requires complete Self-realisation of B. Our consolation: the formal logical derivation of the theorems of the first part of Spinoza's *Ethics* seems to require about 160 additional premises – but with them at hand consistency is achieved.)

All norm- and hypothesis-formulations are T_0-formulations, that is, at the most primitive level from the point of view of preciseness.

The decrease of egocentricity is inevitably linked to an increase of identification and care for others. Which 'others'? One good answer is to draw circles of interest and care, corresponding to stages of development: family, clan, tribe, humanity. But obviously animals, especially the tamed or domestic, often enjoy interest, care, and respect (at times status of divinity) before humanity at large. The series of circles will differ in different cultures. In any case higher levels of realisation of potentials of the self favour the Self-realisation of others.

Considering the widening scope of identification as internally related to increased Self-realisation, this increase depends on the Self-realisation of others. This gives us H1. It implies that 'the others' do not lose their individuality. Here we stumble upon the old metaphysical set of problems of 'unity in diversity'. When the human being A identifies with B, and the wider self of A comes to comprise B, B is not supposed to reject the individuality of B. Thus, if B and A are persons, the self of A comprises that of B and vice versa.

The importance of H1 for the whole *conceptual* development of Ecosophy T stems from the way those who think it is a tenable hypothesis – those who feel at home with it – are apt to view nature and what is going on in nature. They see a lonely, desperately hungry wolf attacking an elk, wounding it mortally but being incapable of killing it. The elk dies after protracted, severe pains, while the wolf dies slowly of hunger. Impossible not to identify with and somehow feel the pains of both! But the nature of the conditions of life at least in our time are such that nothing can be done about the 'cruel' fate of both. The general situation elicits sorrow and the search for means to interfere with natural processes on behalf of any being in a state of panic and desperation, protracted pain, severe suppression or abject slavery. But this attitude implies that we deplore much that actually goes on in nature, that we deplore much that seems essential to life on Earth. In short, the assertion of H1 reflects an attitude opposed to any unconditional *Verherrlichung* of life, and therefore of nature in general.

For H3, a somewhat more precise formulation would be 'Complete Self-realisation of anyone depends on that of all beings which *in principle are capable of Self-realisation.*' For the sake of brevity in the survey these beings are in what follows called 'living beings'. We define 'living beings' in this way.

The fact that N2 is derivable from N1 through the aforementioned hypotheses does not automatically make it into a purely instrumental norm in Ecosophy T. It is only instrumental *in relation* to N1. A norm is purely instrumental only if its definition excludes it from being non-instrumental in any single relation. Example: it may pay in the long run to be honest, but this does not exclude the possibility that honesty can be a valid non-instrumental norm, independent of profits.

Saying unconditionally yes to N1 implies a yes to the question whether Self-realisation is something and something of value. Since there is nothing which could make Self-realisation a purely instrumental norm, the yes is announcing its intrinsic value. Saying yes to N2 implies the intrinsic valuation of all living beings. From these two norms, and norms derived from them (plus hypotheses) the proposed formulations of the platform of the deep ecological movement are derivable (see chapter 1, §5). In a common philosophical terminology, the platform is expressing an axiology whereas Ecosophy T expresses a deontology. The latter classification is suspicious, however, because the exclamation mark of N1 does not imply that what is expressed is a communication to somebody. N1 rather expresses an ontology than deontology. It is, however, not the aim of this chapter to go far into professional philosophy.

(c)   *Norms and hypotheses originating in ecology*
    H4: Diversity of life increases Self-realisation potentials.
    N3: Diversity of life!
    H5: Complexity of life increases Self-realisation potentials.
    N4: Complexity!
    H6: Life resources of the Earth are limited.
    H7: Symbiosis maximises Self-realisation potentials under conditions of limited resources.
    N5: Symbiosis!
Comments:

These seven formulations make up the second part of the survey. Whereas the first level is squarely metaphysical, the second level is biologically coloured, but still metaphysical because of the use of capital S in 'Self-realisation'. More precise formulations would refer to general ecology and conservation biology rather than human ecology.

H4 introduces the central term of 'Self-realisation *potential*'. In psychology and sociology there is much discussion of the potentials, potentialities, or possibilities which an individual, group, or institution has in life, including the life of nations. There is within ethics talk about talents and capacities and how to develop them. The term 'Self-realisation' is a kind of generalisation of this, except that, in using the capital letter S, certain norms are proclaimed which narrow down the range of what constitutes an increase of Self-realisation.

H4 has a metaphysical background. Life is viewed as a kind of vast whole. The variety of forms of life, with their different capacities, realise, that is, bring into actuality, something which adds to that whole. They realise the Self-realisation *potentials*. Each individual contains indefinitely many of these, not only one. An increase in qualitative diversity of life forms increases the possibility of potentials. From H4 and N1 therefore follows N3.

*(d)   The meaning of diversity, complexity, and symbiosis
         in the context of Self-realisation*

'Self-realisation!' with a capital S is a norm formulation inspired by the part of philosophy traditionally called metaphysics. The terms diversity, complexity, and symbiosis are all borrowed from ecology. There is a resulting kind of terminological tension between the first two levels of the survey, as well as a general tension between 'the one and the many'.

The conceptual bridge from Self-realisation to a positive evaluation of diversity, complexity, and symbiosis is furnished by a concept of Self-realisation potentials, and the idea that the overall Self-realisation in our world is increased by the realisation of such potentials. (The realisation is analogous to negative entropy.) No single being can completely realise the goal. The plural of potentials is crucial: it introduces plurality into unity. The intuition pushing us towards the 'Self' does not immediately acknowledge this.

A closely related idea is that of microcosm mirroring macrocosm, an idea especially potent during the Renaissance and now partly revived in hologram thinking. Each flower, each natural entity with the character of a whole (a gestalt) *somehow* mirrors or expresses the supreme whole. I say 'somehow' because I do not know of any good analysis of what is called mirroring here. The microcosm is not apart from the whole; the relation is not like that between a big elephant and a small mouse. Microcosm is essential for the existence of macrocosm. Spinoza was influenced by the idea when demanding an immanent God, not a God apart. The door is open for positive evaluation of an increase of the realisation of potentialities, that is, of the possibility that more potentialities will be realised. This is meant to imply *continued evolution at all levels*, including protozoans, landscapes, and human cultures.

The realisations should be *qualitatively different*. Numerical abundance as such does not count. One way of emphasising this distinction is to distinguish diversity from (mere) plurality. The term 'diversity' is well established in biology, mostly used in talking about diversity of species or of other qualitatively different living beings.

Further elaboration of the conception of diversity and the introduction of the concepts of complexity and symbiosis clearly require the support of hypotheses about the kind of universe we live in. Such support was, strictly speaking, necessary even when starting to talk about Self-realisation, but only now is explicit mention of such support clearly needed. The universe which we shall limit ourselves to mentioning is our planet, the Earth, which we may also call 'Gaia' to emphasise its status as a living being in the widest sense.

I make a lot of implicit assumptions about the life conditions of Earth, especially its limitations. Any total view requires that.

Diversity may be defined so as to be only a *necessary* condition of the growth of realising of Self-realisation potentialities. Then 'maximum diversity!' does not make sense, because many differences may not involve Self-realisation and may be inconsistent with symbiosis. Better to imply qualitative difference as mentioned above to introduce concepts of difference which distinguish it from mere plurality. The ambivalence of plurality stems from finiteness – not only of our planet as a whole. However, the adjective 'maximum' is added to some expressions of Ecosophy T when diversity is introduced. The intention is to proclaim that there is no inherent limit to the positive character of growth of diversity. It is not intended that an increase is good even if it reduces the conditions for realising other norms. If the adjective 'maximum' is to be retained, it must, at a more precise (T_1) level, be taken as an abbreviation for 'maximum, without hindering the realisation of other norms in the system'. The presence of a norm of 'symbiosis!' in the system should re-emphasise this – it knits the bond between complexity and diversity.

Now let us turn to complexity.

If we are permitted to vary three factors a,b,c in spatial horizontal arrangements, we can only realise six different patterns: abc, acb, bac, bca, cab, cba. If we add one more basic factor, d, the number of arrangements increases to 'four factorial', 24. This illustrates the *intimate relation between complexity and diversity*. When the number of elements increases linearly, the number of possible relationships increases factorially.

Let us then think that abc is a pattern of life, conceived as a kind of organismic or personal life. The pattern is characterised by three main functions or dimensions, a, b, c working together as a highly integrated system abc. Let the other five arrangements of a, b, and c symbolise five other systems with the same number of dimensions.

The principle of self-preservation now may be said to consist minimally in an internal mechanism such that the system defends itself against reduction to 2-, 1-, or zero-dimensional ones, and also against transitions to systems symbolised through the other five patterns, *and* tends positively to develop into systems with more dimensions, thus more diversity and more complexity.

Complexity as opposed to complication is in Ecosophy T a quality of organisms and their relation to their environment. It is characterised by intimate interrelations, deep interdependence of a manifold of factors or elements. After death a rhinoceros as a breathing entity is no more, but it remains a tremendously complicated part of nature inhabited and invaded by millions of other, less complex organisms. A human victim of African sleeping sickness manifests the intimate interrelations between a human individual and colonies of the flagellate *Trypanosoma gambiensis*. Each of the flagellates has an unfathomable complexity of structure, but we recognise the human being as a still higher order of complexity.

If complexity is defined in the biological direction of the opposite of simplicity, 'maximum complexity!' cannot support Self-realisation. Only if, as in the case of 'diversity!', some restraining clause is inserted, could maximising make sense.

Since the great time of the reptiles limbs much more complex than the human hand have developed. The simplicity of the human hand is from this point of view a combined victory of simplicity and effectiveness over complexity. There should be no cult of complexity.

In biological texts coloured by the conception of lower and higher animals, the term complexity nearly always is used in descriptions of *advantageous* cases of increases in complexity. 'Higher' functions are made possible through certain more complex differentiations of tissues. Eyes are developed from an earlier homogenous surface of skin. Less is said about unsuccessful increase of complexity, presumably because only species of great stability through millions of years have left fossils for us to study. I think it is most fruitful to use the term complexity as a rather general term covering also cases of no obvious advantage of any kind.

A simple biological example of increasing complexity of 'advanced' forms: the least complex type of sponge is similar to a sac. At one end there is an opening through which water and waste are thrown out. Through small openings in the walls water is drawn in. More complex forms have folded walls so that their surface is greater compared to the volume of the sac. This is thought to be an advance because it is a plus to have more surface cells compared to the number of other cells. A higher level of complexity is reached when special structures secure that waste is thrown out further away so that the sponge does not risk inhaling some of the waste again and again. On the whole zoologists are sure that increases of complexity have functions that could not be realised without those increases. There is no positive value to be attached to complexity as such, for instance walls of unequal thickness satisfying a certain rhythm, but of neither positive nor negative value for any discernible function of the organism.

In a diabolic world, evolution might have proceeded in many ways as in ours, except that parasitism might have made every being capable of conscious pain, suffering from birth to death. The increase of the amount and the intimacy of interrelations and interdependencies might, in the hypothetical world of diabolic parasitism, have resulted in a hellish level of intensity of suffering. Therefore complexity of organisms as such and complexity of interdependencies cannot in Ecosophy T be good in themselves.

From the point of view of biology, complexity comprises behaviour and gestalt processes whereby increasing complexity of consciously experienced wholes can be realised. But also here mere complexity as such cannot yield an increase of Self-realisation. The concept of symbiosis – life together – enters the framework. The existence of interdependencies in which all partners in a relationship are enriched furnishes a crucial idea in addition to diversity and complexity.

Proceeding from non-human to human ecology, the symbiosis idea may be illustrated in relation to various ways of realising a caste sytem. When Gandhi sometimes spoke positively about a caste system, he had an ideal system in mind. Parents were to instruct children and work together with them as they grew up. No schools. The useful occupation of each family would be interrelated with and interdependent with families specialising in other kinds of services in the total community. Interaction between castes of this kind was to be encouraged, not prohibited. The status of each in the sense of dignity, respect, material standard of living, should be the same – an egalitarianism among castes, an illustration of symbiosis between groups in a community. Gandhi detested the actual state of affairs in the existing caste system in India. It certainly violated the norm of symbiosis.

In any kind of community we know of, there have been conflict and strife, in varying degrees. The norms of Ecosophy T are guidelines, and if elaborated into a comprehensive system would have to include norms for conflict solution. (See chapter 6 on Gandhian norms.) It is unrealistic to foresee full termination of deep group conflicts or even to wish such termination. The conditions of life on Earth are such that increase of Self-realisation is dependent upon conflicts. What counts is the gradual increase of the status and application of nonviolence in group conflicts.

The *codification* of Ecosophy T is an action within the context of a conflict; it is my belief that many of the regrettable decisions in environmental conflicts in Norway and other places are made in a state of philosophical stupor. In that state people in power confuse narrow, superficial goals with fundamental broad goals derived from fundamental norms.

(e)   Derivation of the norms of the local community
The next ecosophical principles to be incorporated are those of self-sufficiency, decentralisation, and autonomy. These social principles are first to be linked to their biological counterparts.

The maximum success of Self-realisation is realised through a certain balance of interactions between organisms and environment. The stimuli are not to be too erratic and not too monotonous. The organs of control must not completely dominate influences from the outside nor get overwhelmed. The limited possibilities of control make it, on the whole, important to have a fairly high degree of control of the spatially (personal) near environment, or the environment in which the basic needs are satisfied. If a basic need is only met through a many-stage interaction with remote areas, there are likely to be more forms of erratic obstacles, more dangers of being cut out through processes of chance character.

Let this be illustrated with the life-space models of the kind gestalt psychologist Kurt Lewin made use of (figure 7.1).

Let A represent a living being in a two-dimensional space having four vital needs to satisfy. If the immediate environment furnishes, at least normally, satisfaction of the four needs, A can limit itself to try to control remote areas *only* if something unusual happens to the nearest. The quadruple a_1^1 to a_4^1 symbolises the four sources of need satisfaction.

If the sources are a_1^2, a_3^2, a_5^2, a_7^2 and separated from A by interposed, qualitatively different parts a_1^1 to a_4^1 of the environment, the organism is vitally and normally dependent upon control of these parts and also of a_2^2, a_4^2, a_6^2, a_8^2, the parts adjacent to the sources with another set of qualitatively different properties.

The illustration shows how the requirement of control increases with the remoteness of sources of satisfaction of needs – remoteness being measured in terms of distances in life space, not in kilometres. Making the supposition of limited means of control, the increase of remoteness correlates with increase of dangers, of inadequacy of powers of self-pre-servation and therefore with decrease of Self-realisation potentials. By the degree of local self-sufficiency and autonomy we shall understand the degree to which the living being has its sources of basic need satisfactions, or more generally sources of Self-realisation, nearby in the life space and, secondly, to what degree the organism has adequate control of this area to satisfy its needs.

The above model has been introduced with single living beings, espe-cially persons, as units of life. This is didactically sound as long as it has no scientific pretensions. The same model is useful if taking collectives – communities, neighbourhoods, societies, tribes – as units of life. But in that case we clearly need a model illustrating the relations within the collectives as well. Here we will not go into this.

By definition, single persons have less than maximum control over decisions of centralised authority, possibilities of control approach zero. The greater the manifold of persons and situations to be controlled, the greater the number of levels needed. Further, the greater the number of qualitatively different functions which are controlled, the more rapidly

Figure 7.1

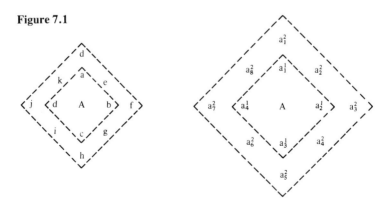

will the control by single persons tend towards zero. Centralisation is here intended to be defined through the above factors.

Using the reasoning suggested above, a set of hypotheses and norms are proposed for Ecosophy T:

H8:   Local self-sufficiency and cooperation favours increase of Self-realisation.

H9:   Local autonomy increases the chances of maintaining local self-sufficiency.

H10: Centralisation decreases local self-sufficiency and autonomy.

N6:   Local self-sufficiency and cooperation!

N7:   Local autonomy!

N8:   No centralisation!

Comments:

Doubt no. 1: Does not the realisation beyond a certain point of the three norms N6, N7, and N8 interpreted individualistically lead to strange conditions of life, in some ways similar to the famous terrifying 'state of nature' in the political philosophy of Thomas Hobbes? Doubt no. 2: Do the lessons of ecology really support the norms? Rejecting the individualistic interpretation, we are therefore confronted with the difficult task of making them more precise with the help of other justifications, taking into account a serious concern of both individuals and collectives.

(f)   Minimum conditions and justice:
       classes; exploitation

Human beings have needs. Any global policy of ecological harmony must distinguish the needs from mere wishes, that is to say from wishes that do not directly relate to a need.

Biological are those needs which must be unconditionally satisfied in order for an individual or species to survive. A minimum formula runs 'food, water, territory'. Then there are needs which are not necessary for all species. Clothing and some kind of shelter are necessary for most human groups, but not other species.

Further: we have needs necessary according to basic social organisations. We now approach needs which can only be separated from mere wishes on the basis of a system of values. Most societies are class societies in which the upper classes are said to need to live on a much higher material standard than the lowest, in order to avoid degradation (a major social calamity!). But are these wishes or needs?

The so-called basic needs, those necessary for survival are only made fixed magnitudes through verbal magic. And 'survival' is a term of little use if restricted to mere 'not dying'. Remember the final words of Chief

Seattle on the great change the White Man would bring to the land: 'the end of living and the beginning of survival'.

The transition from the discussion of such ethically basic norms to more political norms may be formulated in many ways. Here is one.

(1) The requirement of minimum conditions of Self-realisation should have priority before others.

(2) This requirement implies that of minimum satisfaction of biological, environmental, and social needs.

(3) Under present conditions many individuals and collectivities have unsatisfied biological, environmental and social needs, whereas others live in abundance.

(4) To the extent that it is objectively possible, resources now used for keeping some at a considerably higher level than the minimum should be relocated so as to maximally and permanently reduce the number of those living at or below the minimum level.

One can say that the derivation of basic norms in Ecosophy T splits in two different directions. The last level we have outlined presents the norms and hypotheses of the local community, a characteristic ideal of many utopian systems. Now we are ready to follow an argument towards politics to justify the norms and hypotheses against exploitation, as developed through debates with the Marxists in Norway in the early 1970s.

H11: Self-realisation requires realisation of all potentials.

H12: Exploitation reduces or eliminates potentials.

N9: No exploitation!

H13: Subjection reduces potentials.

N10: No subjection!

N11: All have equal rights to Self-realisation!

H14: Class societies deny equal rights to Self-realisation!

N12: No class societies!

H15: Self-determination favours Self-realisation.

N13: Self-determination!

Comments:

The above formulations are put forth mainly to show that the fundamental norms of Self-realisation do not collide with norms of increasing the reign of justice on Earth. On the contrary, the class differences inside societies and between nations are clearly differences in conditions of Self-realisation. Exploitation may be defined in terms of semi-permanent or permanent reducing of the possibilities of some groups in favour of others. Furthermore, calculations showing differences in the use of energy and other resources support an ecological approach in the fight against exploitation in class societies. The value of the model consists partly in the derivation of a general political attitude or posture without the use of certain terms such as 'communism', 'socialism', 'private enterprise', and 'democracy' which elicit more or less automatic positive or negative reactions.

(g)   The overview of Ecosophy T in diagram form

All these formulations (N1 to N13, H1 to H15) contain key terms from social, political, and life philosophy. They do no more than suggest how the systematisation of more precise norms and hypotheses could be related. Nothing more is pretended. Figure 7.2 illustrates in schematic form the logical derivations of these first four levels of Ecosophy T.

The slogan-like character of these formulations still deserves to be used in environmental debate, but there is today clear awareness of their limitations. In many cases local communities have fought sane ecological policies and invited disastrous development. And rather strong central authorities are required to implement the national and international policies recommended by the *World Conservation Strategy* (1980).

The above way of depicting logical derivations within an ecosophy has been greeted with an interest that is in part misplaced: what can be obtained by the normative systematisation of the illustrated kind is very modest, only a better survey of a few interconnections within a gigantic unsurveyable whole. After all, a total view, a philosophy centred around man–nature relations touches upon so many complex questions that the explicit formulations can only comprise a small part, especially when the formulations attain a decent level of preciseness and vague slogans are shunned.

A person using partial systematisations of Ecosophy T will normally find reasons (through increasing experience of life) to modify the formulations. The T_0-formulations can only act as guidelines, and modifications will normally consist of changing accepted precisations of these formulations. To find a formulation on the T_0 level false, mistaken, or invalid is a rather strange thing. It implies that one finds every plausible interpretation false, mistaken, or invalid.

Rejections in terms of falsehood or invalidity will occur on the levels of more precise formulations – formulations of which the set of plausible interpretations makes up a proper subset of the original formulation at the T_0 level.

The logical derivation diagram of a fragment of Ecosophy T cannot easily be broadened to accommodate a whole ontology. Field or gestalt

Figure 7.2

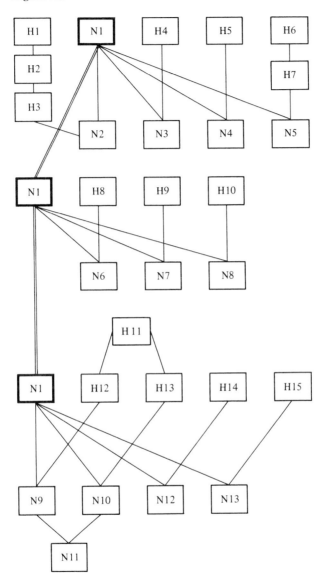

thinking goes against the status of the distinction man–environment as it is met in most environmental thinking. Here Ecosophy T joins contemporary non-cartesian philosophical trends. Looking towards the next century, the shock-waves of ecology will reach so far and penetrate so much that the flora of eco-terminology may seem redundant. The ecosophies will, I suppose, be absorbed in the general traditions of philosophy of nature (*Naturphilosophie*). In all this I may be wrong, but the signs of change through internalisation are already present.

9   The future of the deep ecological movement

The international, long-range ecological movement began roughly with Rachel Carson's *Silent Spring,* over twenty years ago. By 1975, many books had come out and been read by a large audience. The Norwegian edition of *Ecology, Community, and Lifestyle* had come out in five editions. There was great public concern for our environment. But let us examine what has happened over the past twelve years.

In 1975 there was a firm belief in many industrialised countries that a change in personal lifestyle might be necessary. It was on the whole quite clear what an ecologically responsible lifestyle would entail: anti-consumerism in general, with stress on low energy consumption, active support of 'self-made is well made', bicycling, collective transport, *friluftsliv*, family planning, participation in biodynamic agriculture, etc. But along a whole range of issues, defeats were many and depressing: more and more people were pressed into using private cars, the simplest and ecologically most irresponsible form of transportation. And arguments such as that stressing the small effect of low private use of energy compared to the effect of continued political support of energy-demanding industry undermined motivation. By 1980 it was not 'in' anymore to be 'ecologically minded'. Reading of ecology as a part of general education stopped practically completely. Worse: many people had the feeling that they nevertheless knew what it was all about, and did not want to hear any more distressing stories.

What will happen in the next twelve years in the realm of 'ecological' lifestyle? One positive factor is the increasing public awareness of the difference between standard of living and quality of life. A second factor: it is increasingly accepted that a large percentage of costly illnesses are caused by a harmful lifestyle. Many would disappear if we lived in an ecologically responsible manner.

Concluding that our individual lifestyle is important requires premises of a general ethical and social kind. Therefore speaking of an 'ecological lifestyle' is a tenet of the deep rather than the shallow ecological movement. Between 1975 and 1987 the deep ecological movement has gained formidably in strength, and the outlook is optimistic for further strengthening. But forces opposing the implementation of deep ecology policies have gained even more in strength, and the outlook here is also one of continuation.

One per cent increase in Gross National Product today inflicts far greater destruction of nature than one per cent 10 or 20 years ago because it is one per cent of a far larger product. And the old rough equivalency of GNP with 'Gross National Pollution' still holds. And the efforts to increase GNP create more formidable pressures against ecological policies every year.

So significant deterioration of ecological conditions may well colour the next years in spite of the deepening of ecological consciousness. The situation has to get worse before it gets better.

The general attitude among politicians has been that if a major type of interference in the ecosystem cannot be *proven* to be bad then it is justifiable to continue with business as usual. But the concern on acid rain has increased slowly and steadily over the past decade. The warnings of one government to another not to 'export' acid rain have been until recently rather polite. It is to be expected that the tone will be harsher and that the suffering involuntary 'importers', such as the Scandinavian countries, will do more to stop their own serious sources of pollution in order to give their complaints greater weight. The outlook is dark, however, especially in regard to the export of acid rain from Eastern Europe. From the point of view of the deep ecology movement, acid rain has had the positive effect of helping people understand more clearly that to conserve forests and fisheries one has to conserve worlds of micro-organisms, soils, and systems of life which most people never noticed or cared for before. Much broader ranges of identification and wonder have been opened!

Continued deterioration of life conditions may strengthen and deepen the urge to stop acid rain production to the extent that radical political measures will be taken against the offenders. Major changes in economic, political, and ideological structures may then at last begin to unfold.

Supporters of the deep ecological movement constitute a small minority, quite badly organised compared to established pressure groups. They are (sometimes for good reasons) reluctant to organise in large units. But there are lessons to be learned. Big demonstrations and other forms of large-scale, nonviolent direct action seem to work when what we try to communicate, and the way the action is done, come as a kind of surprise to the general public and cause people to stop and reflect for a moment – an increasingly difficult job, because of an increasing sense of repetition.

The years to come may see a greater emphasis on direct action directed to crucially important groups, such as politicians and heads of anti-ecological institutions. Other important groups to reach: teachers, experts, scientists, specialists in mass communication. Study of mass communication and cooperation with masters of that trade has been used to advantage by environmental groups such as Greenpeace.

The late 1970s saw cooperation between the peace movement and deep ecology. No calamity could be worse from the latter point of view than nuclear war. The arms race today supports the detrimental 'big is beautiful' trend and involves the misuse of millions of mammals in experiments with weapons, radioactivity and poisons.

Moving from the rich industrial portions of the world to the poorer majority, we find that the same type of destruction of natural systems which occurred hundreds of years ago in Europe and North America is now under way in the rest of the world, particularly Africa. But there is a major difference: in the former regions the process of destruction has been concomitant with a vast increase of wealth and standard of living, whereas in the latter this is far from the case. Thus, even the *potential* forces of wide- and long-range, responsible ecological policy are absent.

Aid from the rich is essential, but it can so easily be misused that extreme care and dedicated cooperation between institutions in both regions of the world must be at its foundation. It is important to note that the traditional cultural beliefs and practices of much of the world are favourable to the norms of the deep ecological movement.

The deep ecology demand for the establishment of large territories free from human development has recently gained in acceptance. It is now clear that the hundreds of millions of years of evolution of mammals and especially of large, territory-demanding animals will come to a halt if large areas of wilderness are not established and protected. Wild areas previously classified as 'voids' are now realised to be of vital importance and intrinsic value. This is an example of the kind of consciousness change that strengthens deep ecology. It must continue.

These guesses about the future of the deep ecological movement are inevitably influenced by hopes and fears. It is my hope that beings endowed with a brain like ours, developed through hundreds of millions of years in close interaction with all kinds of life will inevitably support a way of life not only narrowly favourable to this species, but favourable to the whole ecosphere in all its diversity and complexity. A uniquely endowed part of this ecosphere will not turn into its eternal enemy.

Bibliography

Alnaes, Finn (1969) *Gemini* Oslo: Gyldendal
Bahro, Rudolf (1986) *Building the Green Movement* London: Heretic Books
Barney, Gerald, ed. (1980) *Global 2000 Report to the President* Oxford: Pergamon Press
Bergson, Henri (1907) *L'évolution créatrice*, Paris: F. Alcan
Bohm, David (1980) *Wholeness and the Implicate Order* London: Routledge & Kegan Paul
Breivik, Gunnar, ed. (1978) *Friluftsliv: Fra Fritjof Nansen til våre dager* [*Friluftsliv*: from Fritjof Nansen to our time] Oslo: Universitetsforlaget
Bubolz, Margaret M. (1980) 'A human ecological approach to quality of life' *Social Indicators Research* 7 103–36
Callicott, J. Baird (1982) 'Hume's is – ought dichotomy and the relationship of ecology to Leopold's land ethic' *Environmental Ethics* 4 163–73
Capra, Fritjof (1982) *The Turning Point* New York: Simon & Schuster
Capra, Fritjof and Charlene Spretnak (1984) *Green Politics* New York: Simon & Schuster
Chamberlain, Kerry (1985) 'Value dimensions, cultural differences, and the prediction of perceived quality of life' *Social Indicators Research* 17 345–401
Dammann, Erik (1979) *The Future in Our Hands* Oxford: Pergamon Press
Darling, Frank Fraser (1965) *The Future Environment of America* Garden City, NY: Natural History Press
Devall, Bill and George Sessions (1985) *Deep Ecology: Living as if Nature Mattered* Salt Lake City: Peregrine Smith Books
Duncan, Otis Dudley (1975) 'Does money buy satisfaction?' *Social Indicators Research* 2 267–74
Dunlop, R. E. and K. D. van Liere (1984) 'Commitment to the dominant social paradigm and concern for environmental quality' *Social Science Quarterly* 1013–27
Ehrlich, Paul R. and Anne H. (1970) *Population, Resources, and Environment* San Francisco: W. H. Freeman
Elgin, Duane (1981) *Voluntary Simplicity* New York: Morrow
Evernden, Neil (1985) *The Natural Alien* University of Toronto Press
Faarlund, Nils (1983) 'Om verdigrunnlaget, friluftsliv og idrett' [On the setting of values in outdoor life and sport] manuscript
Farvar, M. Tagi and John Milton, eds. (1972) *The Careless Technology* Garden City, NY: Natural History Press

Fedorenko, Nikolai (1972) 'Optimal functioning of the Soviet economy' *Social Sciences* Moscow: USSR Academy of Sciences

Fox, Warwick (1986) *Approaching Deep Ecology: a Response to Richard Sylvan's Critique* Hobart: University of Tasmania, Centre for Environmental Studies

Galbraith, John Kenneth (1973) *Economics and the Public Purpose* Boston, Mass.: Houghton Mifflin

Galtung, Johan (1973) ' "The limits to growth" and class politics' *Journal of Peace Research* X/1–2

Galtung, Johan (1978) 'Alpha and beta structures in development alternatives' *Collected Papers of Johan Galtung* Oslo: International Peace Research Institute

Georgescu-Roegen, Nicholas (1971) *The Entropy Law and the Economic Process* Cambridge, Mass.: Harvard University Press

Gilpin, Michael E. and Michael E. Soulé (1986) 'Minimum viable populations: processes of species extinction' *Conservation Biology* Sunderland, Mass.: Sinauer Associates

Glacken, Clarence (1967) *Traces on the Rhodian Shore* Berkeley: University of California Press

Goldsmith, Edward, ed. (1972) *Blueprint for Survival* Harmondsworth, Middx: Penguin Books

Gullvåg, Ingemund (1983) 'Depth of Intention' *Inquiry* **26** 31–83

Gullvåg, Ingemund and Jon Wetlesen, eds. (1982) *In Sceptical Wonder: Inquiries into the Philosophy of Arne Naess on the Occasion of his 70th Birthday* Oslo: Universitetsforlaget

Hallen, Patsy (1986) *Making Peace with the Environment: Why Ecology Needs Feminism* School of Social Inquiry, Murdoch University, Western Australia

Henderson, Hazel (1981) *The Politics of the Solar Age: Alternatives to Economics* New York: Anchor Press

Hervik, Arild *et al.* (1986) 'Betalingsvillighet for vern av vassdrag' [Willingness to pay for conservation of watersheds] *Sosialøkonomen* **40** No. 1

Holte, Fritz (1975) *Sosialøkonomi* [Economics] Oslo: Universitetsforlaget

Jansson, Ann-Mari (1984) *Integration of Economy and Ecology*, Proceedings from Wallenberg Symposia

Klée, Paul (1961) *The Thinking Eye* London: Lund-Humphrey

Kohák, Erazim (1984) *The Embers and the Stars* University of Chicago Press

Komarov, Boris (1980) *The Destruction of Nature in the Soviet Union* White Plains, NY: M. E. Sharpe

Kropotkin, P. (1902) *Mutual Aid* London: Heinemann

Kvaløy, Sigmund (1974) 'Ecophilosophy and ecopolitics: thinking and acting in response to the threats of ecocatastrophe' *North American Review*

LaChapelle, Dolores (1978) *Earth Wisdom* Los Angeles: Guild of Tutors Press

L'Orange, H. P. (1953) 'Fra legeme til symbol' [From body to symbol] *Spektrum* No. 5, Oslo

Lorenz, Konrad (1959) 'Gestaltwahrehmung als Quelle wissenschaftlicher Erkenntnis' *Zeitschrift für experimentelle und angewandte Psychologie* **6** 118–65

Lovelock, James (1979) *Gaia: A New Look at Life on Earth* Oxford University Press

Marsh, George P. (1864) *Man and Nature* New York: Scribner & Sons

Meadows, Donella H. and Dennis L., Jørgen Randers and W. W. Behrens (1972) *The Limits to Growth* Boston, Mass.: MIT Press

Meadows, Donella H. (1982) *Groping in the Dark: the First Decade of Global Modelling* New York: Scribner & Sons

Meeker, Joseph W. (1972) *The Comedy of Survival: Studies in Literary Ecology* New York: Scribner & Sons

Milbrath, Lester (1984). *Environmentalists: Vanguard for a New Society* Albany: State University of New York Press

Miller, G. Tyler (1972) *Replenish the Earth: a Primer in Human Ecology* Belmont, Calif.: Wadsworth

Miller, G. Tyler (1975) *Living in the Environment* Belmont, Calif.: Wadsworth

Mishan, E. J. (1967) *The Cost of Economic Growth* New York: Praeger

Modell, Walther (1973) 'Drugs for the future' *Clinical Pharmacology and Therapeutics* **14**, No. 2

Müller-Markus, S. (1966) 'Niels Bohr in the darkness and light of Soviet philosophy' *Inquiry* **9**

Naess, Arne (1939) *Truth as Conceived by Those who are not Professional Philosophers* Oslo: Jacob Dybwad

Naess, Arne (1964) 'Reflections about total views' *Philosophy and Phenomenological Research* **25** 16–29

Naess, Arne (1966) *Communication and Argument* Oslo: Universitetsforlaget

Naess, Arne (1973) 'The shallow and the deep, long-range ecology movements' *Inquiry* **16** 95–100

Naess, Arne (1974) *Gandhi and Group Conflict* Oslo: Universitetsforlaget

Naess, Arne (1975) *Freedom, Emotion and Self-subsistence: the Structure of a Central Part of Spinoza's Ethics* Oslo: Universitetsforlaget

Naess, Arne (1984a) 'A defense of the deep ecology movement' *Environmental Ethics* **6** 265–70

Naess, Arne (1984b) 'Deep ecology and lifestyle' *The Paradox of Environmentalism*, ed. Neil Evernden, Toronto: York University, Faculty of Environmental Studies

Naess, Arne (1985a) 'The world of concrete contents' *Inquiry* **28** 417–28

Naess, Arne and George Sessions (1985b) 'Platform of deep ecology' Devall and Sessions (1985) 69–73

Naess, Arne (1985c) 'Identification as a source of deep ecological attitudes *Deep Ecology* ed. Michael Tobias, San Diego: Avant Books

Naess, Arne (1985d) 'Holdninger til mennesker, dyr, og planter' [Attitudes to people, animals, and plants] *Samtiden* **94** 68–76

Naess, Arne (1986a) 'Intrinsic value: will the defenders of nature please rise' *Conservation Biology* ed. Michael Soulé, Sunderland, Mass.: Sinauer Associates

Naess, Arne (1986b) 'Self-realization: an ecological approach to being in the world' Keith Memorial Lecture, Murdoch University, Western Australia.

Naess, Arne (1986c) 'Consequences of an absolute *no* to nuclear war' *Nuclear Weapons and the Future of Mankind* ed. Cohen, Avner and Lee, Totowa, NJ: Rowman and Allanheld

Naess, Arne (1987) 'The deep ecological movement: some philosophical aspects' *Philosophical Inquiry*

NIBR (1974) 'Forventninger til rekreasjonsmiljøet i Oslomarka' [Changes in the recreational environment of the Oslo Forest] *Arbeidsrapport 10*

O'Riordan, T. (1981) *Environmentalism* London: Pion

Passmore, John (1974) *Man's Responsibility for Nature* New York: Scribner & Sons

Pepper, David (1984) *The Roots of Modern Environmentalism* London: Croom Helm

Perminov, A. D. (1970) 'Tempel eller verksted' [Temple or workplace] *Ergo* 54

Petrarch (1966) 'The ascent of Mount Ventoux' in *Letters*, tr. Morris Bishop, Bloomington: Indiana University Press

Porritt, Jonathan (1984) *Seeing Green: the Politics of Ecology Explained* Oxford: Blackwell

Pratt, Dallas (1980) *Alternatives to Pain in Experiments on Animals*, Argus Archives

Reed, Peter and David Rothenberg, eds. (1987) *Wisdom and the Open Air: Selections from Norwegian Ecophilosophy* Oslo: Council for Environmental Studies

Rensch, Bernard (1971) *Biophilosophy* New York: Columbia University Press

Rolston, Holmes III (1985) 'Valuing wildlands' *Environmental Ethics* 7 23–48

Rothenberg, David (1987) 'A platform of deep ecology' *The Environmentalist* 7 No. 3, 185–90

Schrader-Frechette, K. S. (1985) *Science Policy, Ethics, and Economic Methodology* Dordrecht: Reidel Publishers

Schultz, Robert C. and J. D. Hughes, eds. (1981) *Ecological Consciousness* Lanham, Md: University Press of America

Schumacher, E. F. (1973) *Small is Beautiful – Economics as if People Mattered* New York: Harper Torchbooks

Schumacher, E. F. (1974) *The Age of Plenty: A Christian View* Edinburgh: Saint Andrew Press

Sessions, George (1981) 'Shallow and deep ecology. A review of the philosophical literature' Schultz and Hughes (1981)

Sessions, George (1987) 'Aldo Leopold and the deep ecology movement' *A Companion to a Sand County Almanac* ed. B. Callicott, Madison: University of Wisconsin Press

Simon, Julian, ed. (1984) *The Resourceful Earth* New York: Blackwell

Soulé, Michael E. (1985) 'What is conservation biology?' *BioScience* 35 No. 11 727–34.

Soulé, Michael E. (1986) 'Conservation biology and the real world' *Conservation Biology*, ed. Michael Soulé, Sunderland, Mass.: Sinauer Associates

Soulé, Michael E. (1987) *Viable Populations* Cambridge University Press

Spinoza, Baruch (1949) *Ethics* New York: Hafner

van Liere, Kent D. and Riley E. Dunlap (1980) 'The social bases of environmental concern' *Public Opinion Quarterly* 44 181–97.

Watson, Richard A. and Philip M. Smith (1970) *Focus/Midwest Magazine* 8 40–2

Watson, Richard (1985) 'Challenging the underlying dogmas of environmentalism' *Whole Earth Review* 5–13

Weiss, Paul (1971) 'The basic concept of hierarchical systems' *Hierarchically Organized Systems in Theory and Practice* New York: Hafner

Wenstrup, Fred (1985) *Arbeidsmøtet* Norwegian School of Management, No. 4

Whitehead, A. N. (1972) *Science and the Modern World* Cambridge University Press

Wilcox, Allen R. (1981) 'Basic needs, ethics, and quality of life' *Applied Systems and Cybernetics*, ed. G. E. Lasker, Oxford: Pergamon Press

Winner, Langdon (1977) *Autonomous Technology* Cambridge, Mass.: MIT Press

World Conservation Strategy (1980) Gland, Switzerland: International Union for the Conservation of Nature (IUCN)

Zapffe, Peter Wessel (1941) *Om det tragiske* [On the tragic], Oslo

Index